CARDINAL SUENENS

CARDINAL SUENENS

A Portrait

by

Elizabeth Hamilton

HODDER AND STOUGHTON
LONDON SYDNEY AUCKLAND TORONTO

Extracts from 'The Four Quartets' by T. S. Eliot are reproduced by permission of Faber and Faber Ltd.

Ad
SPIRITUM SANCTUM
Gaudium perenne
Spem aeternam
Lucem beatissimam

Acknowledgments

I WOULD LIKE to express my gratitude to His Eminence Cardinal Heenan, Archbishop of Westminster, for his kindness in sparing time to see me, and for the enlightening conversation that ensued.

I am particularly indebted to His Grace the Archbishop of Canterbury, Dr. Donald Coggan, for providing material for the description of Cardinal Suenens's visit to York in 1969, and for his valuable suggestions.

I want to record, too, my gratitude to the Most Reverend Thomas Roberts, S.J., for his colourful observations on the Second Vatican Council, and for sound advice tempered with humour.

I owe a special debt of gratitude to the Right Reverend Bishop B. C. Butler, O.S.B., who, during a phase when I feared I had taken on a task beyond my powers, restored my confidence and enabled the words to flow again.

I am also deeply grateful to the Right Reverend Alexander Carter, Bishop of Sault Sainte-Marie, Ontario, for allowing me to use his lively description of the Cardinal's visit to Canada in the spring of 1971.

It is not possible to enumerate the acts of kindness for which I am indebted to the Very Reverend Joseph Dessain, Canon Residentiary of Malines Cathedral. I appreciate perhaps most his integrity coupled with a sense of humour.

Again, I cannot thank adequately the Reverend Wilfried Brieven, Secretary to Cardinal Suenens. Whatever my problems, needs, or difficulties—and they have been many—he has not only never failed to help me, he has never shown a trace of impatience.

I want to express my abiding gratitude and my appreciation of the kindness shown me by Professor and Madame Luc Indestege, Dilbeek, Belgium.

I am particularly indebted to the Reverend Anselm Cooney, O.D.C., the Carmelite Priory, London W.8, who has consistently encouraged me and, as a Canon Lawyer, has taken pains to elucidate my sometimes confused thinking.

I am most grateful to the Reverend Michael Ivens, S.J., for enlightening me on the subject of Charismatic Renewal.

I am also appreciative of the very many kindnesses shown me by the Reverend Ronald Moffat, S.J., during the writing of this book.

I want to convey my gratitude for the generous help given me by the Venerable Bernard Pawley, Archdeacon of Canterbury, formerly an observer at the Second Vatican Council.

I am also most grateful to the Reverend Derek Allen for the hospitality he gave me at St. Stephen's House, Oxford, on the occasion of the Cardinal's visit to the city in October 1973, and to the Reverend Robert Halliburton, also at St. Stephens's House, for a most enjoyable conversation about Cardinal Suenens.

I am specially grateful to Mr. Ronald Browne of the Jesuit Library, Farm Street, London W.1 for his kindness and patience in helping me with my research for this book.

For the translations from the French on pages 58–61 and 76–78 I am deeply indebted to Miss Mary Scudamore.

I am also indebted to Miss Dorothy Fothergill who has helped me in ways too many to enumerate—most of all by her selfless, total availability.

I thank warmly Mr. Irvine Watson, Friend of York Minster, for his helpfulness—especially for his insistence, when I was beginning the book, that I should make the acquaintance of Canon Dessain.

Miss Priscilla Balkwill deserves a particular mention for the time and thought she has expended upon making the index.

I have not mentioned all who have helped me. An omission of a name is not, however, a mark of ingratitude. The explanation is a simple one. Even the most long-suffering publisher must set a limit to the number of pages an author may fill.

I will end, therefore, with one more name only, that of my literary agent, Miss Juliet O'Hea, of Curtis Brown Ltd., who in all circumstances, favourable and unfavourable, easy and difficult, has done everything in her power to further my writing.

ELIZABETH HAMILTON

Illustrations

ACKNOWLEDGMENTS:
[1] Foto Attualita Giordani, Rome
[2] *Paris-Match*
[3] Henri Willems, Mechelen
[4] *New Covenant Magazine*

'Cardinal Suenens, why are you a man of hope even in these critical times?'

'Because I believe that God is born anew each morning,
Because I believe that he is creating the world at this very moment.
He did not create it long ago in the past, then forget about it.
It is happening now: we must therefore be ready to expect the unexpected from God.
The ways of Providence are by nature surprising.
We are not prisoners of determinism nor of the sombre prognostications of sociologists.
God is here, near us, unforeseeable and loving.
I am a man of hope, not for human reasons nor from natural optimism, but because I believe the Holy Spirit is at work in the Church and in the world, even where his name remains unheard.
I am an optimist because I believe the Holy Spirit is the Spirit of Creation.
To those who welcome him he gives each day fresh freedom and a renewal of joy and hope.
The long history of the Church is filled with the wonders of the Holy Spirit.
Think only of the prophets and saints who, in times of darkness, have discovered a spring of grace and shed beams of light across our path.
I believe in the surprises of the Holy Spirit.
John XXIII came as a surprise,
        and the Council, too.
They were the last things we expected.
Who would dare to say that the love and imagination of God were exhausted?
To hope is a duty, not a luxury.
To hope is not to dream, but to turn dreams into reality.
Happy are those who have the courage to dream dreams, who are ready to pay the price so that their dreams take shape in the lives of men.'

Part 1

CHAPTER I

'Let the sparrows chatter!'

POPE JOHN XXIII

I FIRST SAW Cardinal Suenens, Archbishop of Malines-Brussels, Primate of Belgium, on a winter evening in 1970 when he was lecturing at the London School of Economics. I had known of him as an outstanding but controversial figure in the Second Vatican Council and in the post-Conciliar Church. I was familiar with a number of his books and other writings, and knew by heart a few lines he had written about the Holy Spirit. But of Léon-Joseph Suenens the man I knew next to nothing.

The face, illumined by a pool of lamplight, had, I thought, a rugged, almost primitive, quality, as though it had been hewn out of wood in a few bold strokes by the hand of an artist. It was, I decided, a Flemish face. Or, rather, I should explain, what I think of as a Flemish face—the kind, that is, I have seen in paintings by Flemish Masters: strong, intelligent, open; a little sombre perhaps, yet ready to light up; a face that could belong to a man of the world or to a mystic.

On Sunday, July 16th 1972, I visited the Cardinal at his residence in Malines.

If the Cardinal was associated in my mind with Flemish paintings, so was Malines. Indeed, for years the name had meant not so much a town as a cathedral, and not a cathedral built of stone, but unsubstantial, almost ethereal, glimpsed, in the background of a painting by Rubens, through a vista of trees across flat, peaceful pastureland. True, the town had vague associations with Margaret of Austria, grand-daughter of Charles the Bold: a woman of culture, who had encouraged scientists and artists and had been visited by Erasmus and St. Thomas More.

My recollections of Malines as I saw it that July morning are

15

impressionistic, for my mind was occupied less with the scene than with the purpose for which I had come—to discuss with the Cardinal the writing of this book. I recall, as I approached the city, a flat countryside, spread beneath a sky flecked with cloud; neat fields reaching to far horizons broken now by a church tower, now a farmstead, now a clump of deep-shadowed trees; in the foreground tall, reddish houses, Flemish in style, each standing alone, one wall blank and windowless, so that the building looked as though it had been sliced off from its neighbour; and, now and again, a factory, its blatant modernity striking a discordant note.

Then, all of a sudden, I was in Malines. I was aware of a great arched gateway with a round bastion; then the market place or Grote Markt, where, as though one style of architecture were struggling to outdo the other, early and late Gothic merge with Renaissance and rococo ornamentation. It was quiet, for the morning was still early. There must have been a fair in the town, I thought, for I noticed· a gaily coloured roundabout; plump, sleek ponies, ribbons tied to their harness; cages of bright, twittering birds.

Overriding all else, standing up from cobbled streets, was the cathedral, dedicated to St. Rombaut: no longer, as in the painting, unsubstantial, but solid, massive—at its western end a tower that is a masterpiece of solidity and grace, speaking at one and the same time of the temporal and the eternal, earth and heaven. A bell rang, its tone resonant yet sweet. Then another. And another. And another: the notes falling upon the quiet of the morning.

In the cathedral's cool interior I read, on the wall of the side chapel in which Cardinal Mercier is buried, the plaque dedicated on April 27th 1966 by Cardinal Suenens, in company with the Right Reverend Falkner Allison, Anglican Bishop of Winchester, to commemorate what came to be known as the Malines Conversations: informal gatherings held between 1921 and 1926, during which Roman Catholic theologians, presided over by Cardinal Mercier, entered into discussions with a corresponding group of Anglicans headed by Charles Lindley, 2nd Viscount Halifax.

The words on the plaque ran:

In thanksgiving for the life and example of
Désiré Joseph Mercier
for his service to the cause of Christian
unity and in commemoration of

Fernand Etienne Portal	Charles Lindley
pr de Mission	Viscount Halifax
Mgr Joseph Ernst van Roey	John Armitage Robinson
Hyppolite Hemmer	Walter Howard Frere C.R.
Mgr Pierre Batiffol	Charles Gore, Bishop
of the Roman Catholic Church	Benjamin Kidd of the
	Church of England

who took part with him in the
MALINES CONVERSATIONS.
1921, 1923, 1925, 1926.

I remembered how Cardinal Mercier, as he lay dying in Brussels in January 1926 (in the house in the rue des Cendres in which the Duchess of Richmond had given the Waterloo Ball) took from his finger his episcopal ring—an amethyst set in gold, depicting his patron saints, Désiré and Joseph, along with St. Rombaut, patron of Malines cathedral—and slipped it on to the finger of Lord Halifax. This ring today is in York Minster, embedded in the stem of a sixteenth-century silver-gilt Flemish chalice, given by Edward, later Earl of Halifax, to commemorate his father's efforts, and used on the feast of St. Peter as well as on the anniversaries of the deaths of Cardinal Mercier and Lord Halifax.

Little did either of these men know that some forty years later, on April 27th 1969, another Cardinal Archbishop of Malines, Léon-Joseph Suenens, who in his youth had been helped and inspired by Cardinal Mercier, would, in his turn, in York Minster, in the presence of descendants of Lord Halifax, dedicate, along with Dr. Donald Coggan, then Archbishop of York, a plaque given by the Archbishopric of Malines-Brussels.

Cardinal Suenens. How, I asked myself, as I came out of the cathedral, would he receive me? My encounters with prelates in high places had been few.

I recalled how, years before, at an audience given by Pius XI, I had noticed the scowl on the face of His Holiness as he came in. I had

17

felt almost sorry for him. Had something happened to put him out of humour? Or was it that in a moment of human weakness he revealed the boredom which a Pope might be forgiven for feeling from time to time when confronted with audience following upon audience? The incident came back to me later when looking at a picture showing the bored, scowling face of King Edward VIII as, a few months before his abdication, he received debutantes in the garden of Buckingham Palace.

I recalled how in Spain, when I was gathering material for a biography of St. Teresa, I had persisted, despite the disapproval of a cleric with pursed lips and downcast eyes, in being admitted to the presence of the Bishop of Avila, to obtain permission to enter the enclosure of the convents of the Incarnation and St. Joseph—and how, after I had duly knelt, kissed his ring and pleaded my cause in a garbled mixture of Spanish and Latin, the small white-haired figure, who seemed to be bowed beneath a weight of crimson, showered upon me, with an air of gracious detachment, permissions that went beyond anything I had asked.

Then there was the time—in England, since Vatican II—when, the only woman present, I had occasion to take my place at the lunch table with a bishop and four priests. The bishop was one of the 'old school'. When I came into the room he turned, looked at me, and, raising his bushy eyebrows, said: 'What? a woman?' To be fair, a shadow of a smile played on his lips.

I crossed the Grote Markt, passing the roundabout and the ponies. Then the Wollemarkt. Ahead was the Cardinal's residence. I say 'residence', not 'palace', because the word in use is either *Archevêché,* or, in Flemish, *Aartsbisdom.* It was an imposing building: white, flat-faced, with a large black door and, to one side, visible above a wall, the green of trees.

The door was opened by a dignified white-haired man in black. His name, I learnt later, is Petrus. For a period of over forty-six years he has served three Cardinal Archbishops of Malines—each with the same unswerving fidelity.

Then a young cleric, the Cardinal's secretary, stepped forward, his face smiling, and took me up a sweeping staircase into a sunlit room. At the far end, to the left, a door opened. I was aware of someone in a dark suit: tall, neat, and quick in his movements. It was the Cardinal. Again, I thought: 'He has a Flemish face'. But he looked younger than I remembered him in London. He was smiling. There was no ceremonial. His first words escaped me. Or, rather, they were lost in those that followed: 'Today's my birthday. The feast of Our Lady of Mount Carmel!'

There is something special about a birthday. When a person you hardly know tells you it is his or her birthday, it is as if a blind has been raised. The Cardinal's words had put me at ease. They set the tone of the meetings that were to take place from time to time between the writer of this book and the person about whom it is written. Neither a journalist nor an interviewer, I do not care greatly for putting questions: I prefer to listen—to let impressions make themselves felt gradually, facts to emerge without constraint. Yet, if this book were to be written with integrity, if it were to be about a human being not a cardboard figure, there were, I knew, questions which would have to be asked. Because the Cardinal has the art of creating a pleasant, relaxed atmosphere I would be able, I decided, to speak my thoughts aloud without saying to myself: 'Can I ask this?' 'Can I ask that?' 'Is this better said or left unsaid?' 'Will this be taken amiss?'

I speak out of my own experience at a first meeting. But I am one person out of many. In his own country and beyond I have heard many bear witness to the Cardinal's outgoing nature, his sympathy, his ability to enter into the mind of others—especially those in distress: a couple, perhaps, whose marriage is foundering; a bewildered adolescent; a disillusioned religious; a priest who has rejected the priesthood or the very foundations of belief.

There are others, however, who see the Cardinal in a different light. They say he is cold, withdrawn, unsympathetic, lacking the human touch. For the moment it suffices to say that, in my experience, many of those who criticise him adversely—I do not say all, and I do not speak of criticism expressed in temperate language, from which no public figure can expect to be immune—are either, in matters of religion, 'diehards' who see Pope John and the Second Vatican Council as an irreparable disaster, a betrayal of the Church; or, at the other extreme, they are self-styled 'progressives' who, under the pretext of implementing the Council, are determined to destroy rather than construct, demolish rather than build. It is not to be wondered at if, when exposed to a hostile milieu, the Cardinal does not appear at his best. Just as a plant responds to the sun, an animal to the tone of a voice or the touch of a hand, so, too, we humans are drawn out or, alternatively, driven back into ourselves in accordance with the atmosphere created by our fellow-men.

I have dwelt at some length on this first meeting because it seemed to me at the time—and has continued to do so in retrospect—that it highlighted two qualities in the Cardinal which have an important bearing on his role today in the Church.

The first is his openness. I felt I was in the presence of a human being. I was not confronted with a *persona* assumed as being appropriate to a high-ranking prelate. And yet there was no diminution on his part of the dignity proper to a prince of the Church, or, if this term is no longer acceptable in these 'democratic' days, a servant of Christ charged with an exceptional burden of responsibility.

The second quality is a sense of, and a sensibility to, the tradition of the Church, as instanced in his mention of Our Lady of Mount Carmel. In the Cardinal's thinking on the Incarnation, the Mother of Christ, seen in relation to the Holy Spirit, has a special place—nothing exaggerated, nothing sentimental, but based on theology, stemming from, indeed rooted and grounded in, the words of the Credo: *Et incarnatus est de Spiritu Sancto ex Maria Virgine.* 'And he was incarnate by the Holy Spirit of the Virgin Mary.'

Moreover, Our Lady of Mount Carmel is associated with a religious Order which in tradition, if not in history, reaches back to the prophet Elijah, thus calling to mind a truth to which the Cardinal reverts in his writings and which is emphasised in *Lumen Gentium,* the Conciliar document known as the *Dogmatic Constitution on the Church*—namely, that the roots of Christianity extend back not only to Christ and the Apostles but to the People of Israel: the Old Dispensation. The Cardinal, a man of our times, his eyes set on the future, believes nevertheless that the Church cannot be severed from its Hebraic past: a tree thrusting its branches into the sky can live and grow only if its roots remain embedded in the soil—boughs may need to be lopped, but the roots must not be disturbed.

We talked that morning in the Cardinal's study—a large, light room: the room in which, years before, the Malines Conversations had been held. I was aware, when I put some question to him, of the direct gaze of penetrating eyes that at first I thought were brown, but in fact are a deep blue. I noticed his long, thin hands with which from time to time, when driving home a point, he would gesticulate.

I had been told by a young Englishman, who interviewed the Cardinal for a newspaper, that His Eminence was a shy man, inclined to drop into silence, leaving his interviewer to take up the conversation. I, too, was aware of silences, but (though he is, I think, shy on occasion) I did not feel that morning that shyness was the reason for the silences. I came to the conclusion that he was silent only when taken unawares by a question and therefore unsure as to the exact answer—that, moreover, being himself a man of few words he assumed the questioner would understand.

Let me give an example. I asked the Cardinal if he would tell me his earliest memory. He did not reply but after a pause went on to something else. Not wishing to press the matter I said nothing. Later that day, without my reverting to the subject, he in fact told me what he believed was his first memory. Later still, again unsolicited, he told me another earlier memory, and then another. These may seem trivial incidents, but they contribute to my impression that he is a man of goodwill, anxious to co-operate, but not always aware (and in this he is not alone) of how another person will interpret what he does or does not do; says or does not say.

At midday that Sunday the Cardinal said Mass in his private chapel. On the way we passed through spacious high-ceilinged rooms, the sun pouring in the tall windows, the walls hung with portraits of earlier archbishops. In these great empty salons I saw the Cardinal, momentarily, in a different light. He had become all at once a solitary, indeed a lonely figure. How, I asked myself, could this be? How could this man, at home alike in the company of royalty and peasants, be lonely? And then I thought: it is the loneliness of those who are in high places—a price they must pay, a burden they must bear. But his is a special case: it is the particular loneliness of a man who—in putting before all else the truth, as he sees it—thus exposes himself (even among those whom he should be able to think of as friends) to disapproval, misunderstanding, misrepresentation.

These were my thoughts as we went through the vast, empty salons, pausing from time to time to look at a portrait.

The Mass is the same, whether it be celebrated in a Roman basilica, a Gothic cathedral, a reed-hut in the jungle, a school class-room; whether it be accompanied by all the splendour of the Roman or the Byzantine liturgy or stripped to essentials.

The Mass at Malines could scarcely have been more simple. There was the Cardinal, his chaplain, and myself. A single sturdy candle flickered on the small altar. Asters made a crimson and purple glow. At the point preceding the offertory, when it is customary for the celebrant to deliver a homily, the Cardinal, looking towards me, said: 'Let us ask the Holy Spirit to be with us today.' Perhaps these are not the exact words, but they amounted to this, and they were specially appropriate, for the Cardinal's coat-of-arms bears the motto: *In Spiritu Sancto*. I had known, before I came, that I wanted to write this book. But whether things would work out was another matter. His simple words gave me confidence. Yes, whatever the difficulties, I would write it *in Spiritu Sancto*.

But why am I writing this book? In the hope that the Cardinal's thinking may become more widely known; that his courageous, optimistic outlook, above all his confidence in the Holy Spirit at work in the Church of yesterday, today, and tomorrow, may lift men's hearts, dispel gloom, shed joy.

But are not his ideas set forth for all to read in his writings—in books, articles, and pastoral letters translated into many languages? This is indeed so.

But when the Cardinal writes, when he gives an interview or addresses an audience or congregation, he confines himself almost exclusively to ideas that he wishes to put forward; he says little or nothing about himself. There are, however, persons for whom ideas presented in isolation are not enough. To some, it is true, abstract thinking comes easily: they can absorb the ideas of an Aristotle or an Einstein without giving a thought to the man. But these are a minority. For most of us ideas, if they are to take root, if they are to make a lasting impact and appeal to the imagination, need to be related to the person from whom they emanate—for, since man is a whole, let us not underestimate the imagination, esteeming only the intellect.

The teaching of Socrates lives because Plato has brought alive the plump, snub-nosed philosopher—so that we can hear him talking as he sits, in the heat of the day, under a plane tree at the river's edge; or when, before he drinks the hemlock, he comforts his grieving friends, telling them his reasons for believing that the soul is immortal.

St. Augustine lives because he allows us to picture him in the garden, lying in the shade of a fig tree, when he is suddenly aware of a voice saying: *Tolle et lege*. 'Take and read.'

St. Teresa of Avila's dissertations on prayer would, for many, fall on deaf ears did we not know her—sanctity apart—as a lively, amusing, sensible, and unusually intelligent woman.

The theological ideas of Pastor Dietrich Bonhoeffer live not so much as a result of learned discourses, but thanks to letters written, when he was imprisoned by the Nazis, by a man who on Christmas day recalls with nostalgia the Christmases of childhood; who is cut to the heart when, looking out of the window of his cell, he sees that a bird's nest he has been watching day after day has been flung to the ground, the fledglings dead.

My purpose, then, is to set the ideas of the Cardinal in the context of Léon-Joseph Suenens the man. My book will be a personal one, built up from impressions—my own and those of others who have known him. This need not mean, I hope, that it is superficial. An impressionist painting may not be to everyone's taste, but, normally, it is not dismissed on the ground that it does not represent with photographic exactness every facet of a scene.

It is not my intention or wish to write a formal biography. The time is not ripe. Some day in the future a definitive life of the Cardinal will be written when it will be possible, in retrospect, to assess, weigh, view dispassionately, and see in perspective a man whom some have called 'a giant of Vatican II', others 'a sign of contradiction', others 'a false progressive'—a prelate whom the Archbishop of Canterbury, the Most Reverend Donald Coggan, sees as a humble, courageous man 'equipped with an incisive mind and possessed of a divine impatience with those things which seem to him to obscure the essentials and the glory of the Gospel'.

There are particular difficulties associated with writing about someone who is still living; especially a public figure. If the writer is sufficiently in sympathy to want to take on the task, there is a likelihood (though this does not necessarily follow) that the picture which finally emerges will be largely favourable. In that event—especially in the climate of today, when denigration is in vogue—the author may expect to be accused of bias or of trying to win approval in high places.

Furthermore, if the writer is a woman and the subject of the book a prelate of distinction, there are those—particularly, I regret to say, among clerics—who, conditioned to think of woman as a docile creature, easily manipulated, will dismiss what is said as lacking credibility, on the grounds that the author is a mere mouthpiece. Indeed, a wise archbishop, who wanted me to write this book, warned me that I would need 'the hide of a rhinoceros' to face the adverse critics. Having no such protective skin I can only accept these facts, put them out of mind, and, remembering Pope John's advice: 'Let the sparrows chatter,' write the truth as I see it.

But can a worthwhile book be written about a living person? A critic reviewing recently a study of a British statesman answered this question in the negative, going on to say that the book was a re-hash of what had appeared in newspapers. This brings up the matter of sources. In writing about a figure out of the past one is able—assuming there is the will and the energy—to draw upon documents, records, letters, journals, and in many cases previous works on the same subject. When, however, a book is about someone living, its authenticity does not depend solely on the industry and the talent of the writer. The author can and should read what has appeared in the press concerning the person in question; talk to those who have known him; become familiar with his writings.

Yet something further is needed.

If anything approaching a work of art as distinct from chronology is to come into being; if what Homer beautifully and mysteriously calls 'winged words' are to have any place in it, there must be co-operation between the writer and the person being written about. The latter (unless the writer is to be as restricted as a horse that is hobbled) must allow the quality within him which makes him a unique being, distinct from every other, reveal itself naturally, whether in words, actions, or attitudes. It is not a quantity of detail (to expect to be told every incident in a person's life would be an impertinence on the part of the writer) but the quality, the authenticity, of what is revealed that enables a writer to fashion a work that bears the stamp of truth. The writer, on the other hand, must learn to evaluate what is revealed, ponder on its inner meaning, penetrate beyond the spoken word, try to comprehend the motive for an action, select what throws light on a character, cast aside what is irrelevant.

The writer and the person who is the subject of the book have each a distinctive role, the one complementary to the other. As the Roman poet Horace has said in the *Ars Poetica*:

> *alterius sic*
> *Altera poscit opem res et coniurat amice.*
> 'Each asks the other's help, the two working together in harmony.'

When writing about someone living it is not possible to stand back with the same impartiality, the same detachment, the same objectivity, as when that person is no longer alive. And yet a book about a living person can have a truth that is all its own, provided it is written with integrity, the author refusing to yield, at the expense of truth, to the insidious temptation to flatter.

Moreover, what would many writers not give, when struggling to evoke someone long since dead, to be able to look upon the face of that person, watch his changing moods, listen to his words, hear his tone of voice? This, and much more, is the privilege of writing about a living person. 'Your task is impossible,' some pessimist will assure me. But what do we mean by 'impossible'? I like to think of words used by Cardinal Suenens in the context of unity between Christians: 'What is difficult can be done at once, what is impossible takes a little longer!'

CHAPTER 2

In my beginning is my end.

From *East Coker* by T. S. Eliot

LÉON-JOSEPH SUENENS, the only child of humble parentage, was born on July 16th 1904 at Ixelles, a suburb of Brussels, in a clinic run by the Sisters of Maternal Charity. 'The Sisters,' he says, 'clothed me in my first shirt.' He was baptised in the nearby church of Sainte-Croix by an uncle, the Abbé Edward Janssens, brother of Madame Suenens. The family name, Suenens, is said to be derived from Suen, a district in the province of Brabant, where the Cardinal's forebears established themselves as farmers in the eighteenth century. The farmhouse in which his grandfather Peter Suenens lived is at Lennik-St. Martin, some two hours' walk from Brussels.

The father of the Cardinal—who came as a young man to Brussels, married, and opened a *brasserie*—died when Léon was not yet four years old. A photograph shows a sturdy, determined-looking boy, wearing buttoned boots, seated on the knee of his dark-haired, dark-eyed father.

Did he love his father? A passion for truth, at every level, deterred His Eminence from replying to my question with an unqualified affirmative. 'I don't remember him well,' he answered, 'but if I'd *really* known him I'm sure I'd have loved him.'

The Cardinal's earliest memory is associated with a pilgrimage to Scherpenheuvel (in French Montaigu). He cannot have been much more than three years old, for his father was still living. During Mass when his parents went to receive Holy Communion, he was left behind in his place. Presently Madame Suenens, as she knelt at the altar rail, was aware that her little boy was at her side. Then, as the priest approached, she heard her son's voice saying: 'Me too, please.' Later that day the pilgrims were seated at a long table in a restaurant, having a meal. Léon, who had become restless, began to explore the world under the table. Finding a potato on the floor, and remembering how his mother used to say that a well-brought-up child does not 'eat like a pig,' he emerged and, potato in hand, proclaimed for all to hear: 'Mama, there's a pig at the table.' He was not going to allow himself to be ignored a second time in one day.

His next memory is concerned with his father's funeral. It is a dim, imprecise memory, but sombre, and powerful. All is darkness. His mother is wearing black. He is wearing black.

The impact made upon a child—in particular a sensitive child—by a death of a parent or close relation can hardly be exaggerated. Indeed, it is ineradicable. Upon some the effect is an abiding sense of insecurity—accompanied in certain instances by a melancholia—a tendency, too, to withdraw from participation in society. But this need not be so. The effect on Charles de Foucauld of the loss of both parents within months of each other, before he was six years old, was to make him, throughout his life, compassionate and protective to all in affliction and distress. To others death presents a challenge. The psychologist Dr. Alfred Adler—who was himself the victim of much illness in childhood and whose brother, when Adler was three years old, died in the bed next to his—decided early in life to become a doctor and thus combat death, the enemy.

The young Léon Suenens also saw death in terms of challenge. His response took the form of a determination to preach the Gospel—thus to bring happiness to men both in this world and in the world to come. Eternity preoccupied him as it had preoccupied St. Teresa of Avila and her brother Rodrigo who, as children, used to chant *Para siempre, siempre, siempre!* 'For ever, for ever, for ever.'

Looking up at the stars, looking into the vast expanse of the heavens, Léon thought about eternity.

But, lest the mention of eternity might suggest a form of escapism, there is no trace of this in Suenens either as a boy or in manhood. The thought and attitude of Suenens the man are, to a striking degree, the logical outcome of those of the boy. In neither case is life seen as a matter of alternatives. It is not a choice between man or God, earth or heaven, time or eternity. The perspective is man and God, earth and heaven, time and eternity. To be conscious of eternity is to be conscious of time; to think of the transcendent is to think of the transient; to be aware of life everlasting is to be aware, to a heightened degree, of a life in which, by the very reason of its shortness, each moment is the more precious. Indeed the Cardinal is quoted as saying that he thinks of himself as living on borrowed time—this giving to his undertakings an added urgency.

So, then, the boy Léon determined to spread the Gospel; to become a priest. From 1911 to 1912 mother and son lived at the presbytery at Klein Willebroek with the uncle who had baptised him. Contrary to what one might perhaps conclude, this uncle had nothing to do with his nephew's decision to enter the priesthood. He was a harmless, good-natured man, a parish priest who, like many another, carried out his duties conscientiously, but he did not 'inspire' Léon.

Intelligent, active, enterprising, the young Suenens was not of the calibre to be satisfied merely to exercise the functions proper to the priesthood, accept as a right the respect and the privileges that go with it. He wanted something more. He was an idealist: a dreamer who was determined to turn his dreams into reality; to do something positive, something constructive and beneficial to others. I do not mean that the small boy would have expressed himself in these words, but this was the direction in which his aspirations tended. There are those who have to feel their way, grope in darkness, before they can discover their purpose in life. Others already in early childhood see ahead of them, with unclouded gaze, a goal from which no obstacle can deter them. Léon Suenens was one of these.

His determination to spread the Gospel, make known the 'Good News' to all mankind, forms a leitmotiv running through his life. This explains why, later, during the period when he was Auxiliary Bishop to Cardinal van Roey at Malines (1945 to 1961) he made a number of journeys to Dublin to study the Legion of Mary. This was why he wrote his book *L'Eglise en Etat de Mission* which was translated into numerous languages, including an English version under the title: *The Gospel to Every Creature*.

Further, this wish to spread the Gospel more widely and more effectively was the well-spring of the major role played by Cardinal Suenens in the Second Vatican Council and in the Synods of Bishops during the years that have followed the Council. Hence, too, his book, *Co-responsibility in the Church*; the interviews he has given to the press; journeys that have taken him far afield, causing those of his countrymen who admire him to speak with affection of their 'jet-style Archbishop'; his critics to jibe at a prelate who is 'at home everywhere except in his diocese'.

To preach the Gospel is to preach love, and a requisite of love is justice. Injustice, in whatever form, is abhorrent to the Cardinal, whether it be social injustice; racial injustice; the injustice shown to woman down the centuries in a male-dominated Church; the injustice whereby rich nations prosper while the Third World starves. It is not surprising to find that one of the men whom Cardinal Suenens most admires today is Dom Helder Camara, Archbishop of Olinda and Recife, a courageous and forthright champion of the underprivileged.

Already in childhood Léon Suenens was preoccupied with justice. A sense of justice—a desire to have something to which be believed that he, no less than others, was entitled, impelled him at three years old to make room for himself at the altar rail beside his mother.

A later incident, again taken from childhood, expresses the vehemence with which he resented injustice. It took place in December 1909 at a school he was attending, run by nuns.

It was customary for parents to give the nuns toys which at the end of the Christmas term were to be distributed, in accordance with the merits of the pupils, by a bearded scarlet-robed Santa Claus. Rich parents brought expensive toys, poor parents inexpensive ones.

Léon, besides being intelligent, had worked well. Indeed he had given no cause for complaint. He deserved a worthwhile reward, and he knew it. He watched as elaborate gifts were handed out to some of his fellow-pupils who had done little or nothing to merit them.

Then his own turn came. To his humiliation, he was given a small drum utterly inappropriate to a boy of his age or attainments. On his return home he flung it to the ground in a frenzy of rage and trampled it to pieces.

Little did Léon know that the drum he had received from Santa Claus was the contribution his mother had made to the nuns—a widow and poor, she had given of her best.

Jeanne Suenens was a sensitive, sensible, and well-balanced woman. She understood her son's distress—his sense of outraged justice. And so she told him the truth—explaining precisely how the situation had come about. From then on Léon disliked the idea of Santa Claus and his gifts: it was a custom, he felt, tainted with falsehood—and always, from childhood to this very day, for Léon Suenens truth comes before all else.

This passion for truth at every level is something very much his own. But truth, sincerity, and openness were characteristics inherent in his mother's personality.

She was also warm-hearted.

When I think of Jeanne Suenens, the Cardinal's mother, I recall a story told of an artist who, left as a small boy to look after a younger sister, took out his paintbox, made a portrait of his sister, but in doing so daubed paint on the walls and furniture. His mother, on her return, said not a word about the mess he had made. Instead, she flung her arms round her son, saying: 'Why, you've painted a portrait of your sister!' It is women of this calibre who make good mothers: women who know how to encourage their children, praise their efforts, minimise their mistakes.

Madame Suenens was such a woman. Her kind, smiling face looks out from a photograph (taken in a garden against a backcloth of shrubs) that stands today on her son's desk in the Archevêché at Malines. She devoted her life to the welfare of her son. Yet because, in doing so, she did not swamp or constrict him, or resort to emotional black-mail; because she respected him as an individual, a person existing in his own right, independent of herself—because this was so, there was no tension between the two. One day in adolescence, Léon told her that he was going to begin smoking. She might have complained that money was short and could be put to better use. She did not do so. Unperturbed she replied: 'So you can. But I don't think it a very good idea.' Because she had not tried to dissuade him, because she had made no attempt to exercise pressure, he no longer felt the wish to smoke. He had no need to assert himself, prove his independence.

The school, the Onze Lieve Vrouw College of Boom, which Léon had attended while living with his uncle, was unsuitable: the pupils were years older than he. Because she realised this, Mme. Suenens decided to make a home for herself and her son in Brussels. Leaving Léon at Klein Willebroek till all was settled, she arrived one day in the spring of 1912 at the railway station at Schaerbeek on the outskirts of the city, deter-mined to find three things: rooms where the two of them could live; a school which her son could attend; and a church. She found all three.

First the church of the Sainte Famille. Then, adjoining it, a school run by the Marist Fathers. And finally, three rooms on the fourth floor of a tall, terraced house: number 60, Square Riga. Facing the house, on the opposite side of the road, was an expanse of grass and trees, and beyond these the church and the school. Each day on his return from school Léon used to go out on to the grass and play hand-ball. From time to time he would glance up at a window on the fourth floor of number 60. Presently he would see that the curtain had been drawn. This was his mother's signal that the evening meal was ready, and he would go indoors.

One of the three rooms was his. After the meal was over he would

31

settle to his homework. Alert and studious, he worked not simply because it was necessary, but because he wanted to. The evenings passed for him quickly and quietly. So as not to disturb him, his mother had few visitors.

At the Marist school Léon took his primary grades. When he was eleven years of age he went for his secondary education to the Institut Sainte-Marie, in the Chaussée de Haecht, under the direction of diocesan priests. He was learning Latin now. Latin phrases find their way into French essays that cover page after page in a neat copybook hand, the headings sometimes in a carefully worked out Gothic script. No space was wasted. It was not a question of his being parsimonious or stingy. That is not his nature. One has only to look at a typescript of his today—the wide margins, the lavish spacing, the tastefully set-out paragraphs.

During his schooldays the problem was poverty. Exercise books cost money and money was hard to come by. Hence every inch of paper was precious. And there was the added problem of books required for his studies. He could not have anything like the number he needed.

And this has left a twofold mark. The Cardinal, scrupulous in returning books lent to him, is 'furious' (he says), when his own are borrowed and not returned. Indeed, the failure to return books he describes as a 'universal plague'.

Léon's schoolboy essays are remarkable for an easy flowing style, clarity of thought, logical argument, perceptivity, imagination, humour. Moreover his sense of history shines through, and his patriotism. So does a sensitivity to the world of nature; the changing seasons; light and shadow; sunshine and mist.

His teacher's comments scrawled in red ink across the pages both of his original work and his translations are for the most part complimentary and encouraging. *Bien. Très bien. Excellent.* An occasional adverse criticism takes a constructive, often humorous form. Attention, for example, is drawn to *une cascade de 'qui's'*! One has the impression of there being a rapport between teacher and pupil. This, clearly, was work that he enjoyed.

By the time Léon was fifteen he had become increasingly interested in politics—particularly political discussions and debates. Indeed, if he had not decided to enter the priesthood he would have liked to become a politician or a professor.

Literature absorbed him. In 1921 a lecture he delivered on Péguy, Psichari, and Claudel made a considerable impact. His interest roused, his imagination stirred, he could speak with a fire, a vehemence, and a logicality which sometimes took his hearers by surprise.

Nevertheless this tall, somewhat taciturn adolescent, despite his intellectual gifts, was diffident. Nor today does everyone who hears the Cardinal preaching, lecturing, or answering pressmen, or who watches him officiating in the cathedral at Brussels or Malines with all the ceremonial proper to his office, realise that—behind an exterior indicative of a man who is self-confident, at ease, in command of a situation—there is concealed a diffidence (his own word is *timidité*) which goes back to boyhood.

At school he was often lonely.

He was conscious of the fact that, whereas his companions belonged to the *bourgeoisie* and came mostly from well-off families, he was poor. Moreover, since his primary studies had been in Flemish, he had to adapt himself to an entirely French régime. It took him some two years of hard struggle to make up this lee-way, but at the end of the period he came first in his class and continued to do so until the completion of his secondary studies.

In adolescence he suffered consciously (and probably unconsciously) from the deprivation of not having a father's example, guidance, and companionship. He learnt from a neighbour how to shave. And one of his professors taught him to use a telephone: 'Just experiment with any numbers you like! You'll soon see what happens . . . And be ready for anything from the other end!'

An awareness of what is missing in their lives spurs on some fatherless boys to a growth in independence and a self-discipline more exacting than many a father would impose. Léon Suenens was one of these, and he continued in later years to exercise this discipline—as a seminarian, a priest, an archbishop, and a cardinal. But it was a discipline directed towards himself and to fulfilling the demands made upon him at various stages of his life. In his relations with others there is, even if it is not always immediately apparent, a genuine concern for their welfare—indeed, a tenderness of heart.

Léon's talent for writing was evident in adolescence.

In August 1918, shortly after his fourteenth birthday he spent nearly a month at Marienbourg in the Fagne district, to the south of Belgium.

Under the title *Mon Premier Voyage* he records in journal form, in lively, colourful prose, his day-to-day impressions.

War makes travelling difficult. When he and his mother board the train at the Gare du Luxembourg, Brussels, it is already overcrowded.

33

Passengers sigh and grumble in the heat and, later, when night comes down (no light is permitted in the compartment) they whistle *Sur les Ponts de Paris,* to while the time away, drumming their feet on the floor.

As the engine pounds along the track Léon stares through the window at 'woods black against a sky the colour of pewter', and then, as the train approaches Charleroi, 'factory chimneys and clusters of red and green signal-lights'.

Having missed a connection, mother and son spend the night on a bench in the station waiting-room: Léon, his head buried in the hood of his jacket; his mother, a handkerchief over her face to shield her eyes from the lamplight. Fitful sleep is broken by the shriek of whistles and the coming and going of travellers. 'The hands of the clock move slowly, all too slowly.' Then a woman with 'eyes like a lobster's and mutton-chop sleeves', distraught at finding her train has gone, elicits from Léon a burst of laughter.

The latter part of the journey, Léon records, is in a train comprising only an engine, a luggage-van, and one coach divided into two compartments. In the first there is a stove, coal-bricks, electrical contraptions, and a board supported on four legs as if to suggest a restaurant car. The second is upholstered in a tattered material that was once the colour of 'crushed strawberries'. Tunnel follows tunnel. Then open, undulating country bright with daisies, clover, and butter-cups; fields traversed by the gleaming, meandering waters of the Sambre; cows chewing the cud; sheep grazing; foals gambolling.

From time to time the landscape is broken by grey slate-roofed houses or dark pine-woods. Léon, as he looks out of the window, has the illusion that the scene, no less than the train, is in a state of motion, as the engine, emitting plumes of smoke, speeds on its way along a track bordered with maidenhair ferns, white stone-crop, bluish-brown boulders.

At Marienbourg he notes every detail: the ancient, fortified town named after Queen Marie of Austria; the church's white-washed interior pierced by bullet holes, its blue, flagged floor worn with age. Beyond the town, sun-drenched fields of rye and wheat, ripe for the harvest; clouds floating on mountain-tops; raindrops glittering on blades of grass, trembling on leaves of trees; a biplane, grounded in a meadow, looking like an 'immense fish with white fins'; wheel-tracks criss-crossing the dusty road to Nîmes.

A ruined fortress, its rampart choked with nettles and rank weeds, fires his imagination with thoughts of deeds of prowess in days gone by, when, one after another, the flags of France, Austria, and Holland had flown from its turret.

If dreams of the past inspire him, he is also practical. Soapwort, he notes, can take the place of soap. Just 'rub the leaves between the palms of your hands and you have a lather!' He explains, too, how to make church candles—pouring melted wax into a contraption 'resembling a waffle-iron'.

At a wedding, the bride, he notices, is all in white—'unusual at a country wedding'—and the bridegroom so embarrassed that he can only stare at the polished toes of his shoes; how, moreover, as the couple leave the church, the work-mates of the bridegroom (he is a maker of sabots) presents the bride with her husband's tools, along with a white ribbon with which to tie them, this signifying: 'With these tools work courageously for your daily bread, remembering that your wife shares your labours, hopes, and joys.'

On the feast of the Assumption, a great day at Marienbourg, everyone (including Socialists and Liberals who otherwise never set foot in church) takes part in the procession which winds its way over the countryside, 'rather as if one were to travel from Brussels to Paris by way of London'—scarlet cassocks and white dresses creating from a distance an illusion of 'poppies and daisies in a meadow', while the murmur of prayers floats upon the air 'like the humming of bees'.

In Léon's youthful imagination a steep hill assumes the proportions of a mountain.

He clambers up the slopes, hot and breathless, stumbling on uneven ground; forces a way through thickets and brambles; finds a track, only to lose it; shudders at the sight of a snake slithering a foot or so away—a 'grey creature with black markings on its head'; fights against momentary dizziness, determined, no matter what the cost, to reach the summit. And then, what joy, what exultation, as he stands, looking down on the countryside reaching away as far as eye can see, and hears, in the distance 'the boom of guns fired in defence of Belgium's freedom'.

A year later Léon wrote a novel entitled *A Sa Conquête*.

The neat, clear handwriting covers page after page of an exercise book—no, not an exercise book, but a cashbook, its red verticle lines forming columns in which to enter figures. Again, there is no waste of space, no margins—only an occasional gap to separate the end of one section from the beginning of the next.

The story, a romance set in Belgium during the First World War, runs on, effortlessly, as though it were unfolding itself without the aid of an author. Scarcely a phrase has been corrected; scarcely a word has been erased.

The mood of the countryside is evoked: petals opening to the breath of spring; a shaft of light playing upon a leafy branch; the mysterious darkness of a forest; the melancholy of a neglected garden; summer and winter; sunrise and sunset; mist and snow.

And over all hangs the shadow of the war.

The shadow touches the lives of the characters—not least, those of Monsieur Georges and Mademoiselle Marguerite. Georges suffers, but he is not alone in his suffering; he is supported, indeed saved from despair, by his friend Maurice who is as faithful to him as Achates to Aeneas, Horatio to Hamlet.

And what of Marguerite? A fifteen-year-old author—especially a boy who had no sisters and little contact with young persons—could not be expected to convey in any depth the thoughts and feelings of a girl in love. And Léon had the good sense not to try. Instead, he evokes, convincingly, Marguerite as Georges visualises her—the Marguerite who lives in the mind and heart of the young man whose purpose is to share his life with hers.

As he walks in the woods Georges is suddenly aware that a change has taken place within him: that he is no longer, as formerly, alone. He can dream a dream—not to escape reality but to help to bring reality into being. *Il sentit que quelquechose était changé en lui, qu'il n'était plus si seul . . . il commence à rêver. Comment actualiser son idéal.*

Elsewhere in the story are the words: *J'ai confiance dans l'avenir.* Again, they are put into the mouth of Georges. But they do more than speak for a character in fiction. They give expression to the thoughts and aspirations of the boy who created the character: and not his only, but those of the man he has become: Cardinal Suenens, Archbishop of Malines-Brussels, who today looks to the future in a spirit of courage, hope, and determination.

Someone endowed with this degree of determination can be said to be ambitious. The word—from the Latin *ambitio* which was applied to a Roman citizen using legitimate efforts to win support when seeking public office—has acquired less pleasing overtones. To call someone ambitous can imply that he is ruthlessly pursuing his own ends. It is a question, then, of the sense in which the word is used. It can be applied, without disparagement, to scientists, doctors, artists, saints: men and women whose objectives have been, in one sphere or another, to further the good of the human race. Those who call the Primate of Belgium ambitious in order to denigrate him, should ask themselves whether his motives are directed towards the benefit of others or towards personal aggrandisement. And in putting this question I suggest they bear in mind words spoken by a fellow Cardinal who, I think it is fair to say, is out of sympathy with both the thought and the personality of Cardinal Suenens. 'The Primate of Belgium,' this Cardinal said, 'is a man totally devoid of personal ambition.'

To be Belgian can be as complex as it is to be Irish. In both countries so many threads cross, so many influences are at work. History, politics, religion, origins, ancestry—all these factors and more are involved, and, stemming from these, problems posed by emotions and prejudices sometimes as bewildering to those who think of themselves as natives of either country as they are to an outsider. In both countries it is possible to feel, in the depths of one's being, that one belongs here and yet, on another level or in different company, to feel a stranger. This has the disadvantage of fostering a sense of insecurity. It has the advantage, however, of enabling one to adjust to circumstances, whether it be life in a strange city or on an island in mid-ocean. When I asked a young friend of the Cardinal in what place he thought His Eminence felt most at home he replied without hesitation: 'Oh, I think he's as much at home in an aeroplane as anywhere.'

To be Belgian can mean that you are Flemish. Or you can be a Walloon. Or you can be Flemish on one side of the family, Walloon on the other. Or you can be a native of Brussels, which is different again. For whereas, in the rest of Belgium, Flemish-speaking and French-speaking areas are, in general, distinct, Brussels is bilingual. But not even this is as simple as would appear: a young man born and bred in Brussels told me that sometimes he did not know what he was nor in which language to address a fellow-passenger in a tram or an assistant in a shop.

But Brussels, whatever else is true of it, is a unique city. Even today, when buildings of character and distinction are being in many instances demolished or crowded out by what is slap-dash and tasteless, this city with its tall houses, its wrought-iron balconies, its gardens, its tree-lined streets, its fast-disappearing cream-coloured trams, retains something of the sophistication and elegance of Paris. Moreover, steeped in the past, it is also pre-eminently a city of the present and the future. Above all, it is cosmopolitan, reaching out to others, gathering others to itself.

The Cardinal belongs to Brussels. He was born and brought up in Brussels and, until he reached the age of seventeen, educated there. His family was Flemish. He has traits that one associates with the Flemish—among them, a quiet, solid determination, when his mind is made up, to go his way, carry out his purpose; a realistic, down-to-earth approach to problems and to finding a solution. His spirituality is, again, down-to-earth, unsentimental: it has the robust quality which characterises the thought of the Blessed John van Ruysbroeck, the fourteenth-century Flemish mystic who for twenty-six years was a parish priest in Brussels before he retired (at the age of fifty) with two friends to the hermitage of Groenendaal in the forest of Soignies.

Another Flemish trait is the Cardinal's feeling for nature: nothing rapturous or ecstatic, but innate—based on a careful, prolonged observation. It is in the tradition of the Flemish Masters who in their paintings dwell with loving care upon an animal, a bird, a flower, a tree, a leaf; or the book-binders of Antwerp who found in nature the inspiration for their complex, delicate patterns. To come down to our own times, I think of the Cardinal as being at one with the world depicted in the bold, imaginative paintings and drawings of the Flemish artist Felix Timmermans.

It is fitting that there should hang on the wall, as you enter the Cardinal's residence at Brussels, a picture of his grandfather's home at Lennik-St. Martin, in which, painted by Karel De Bauw in the Brueghel tradition, a leaden sky, snow, and dark, naked trees form a setting for the homely, brownish-red farmhouse, with, in the background, cottages and the village church.

But I must not dwell on one facet of the Cardinal to the exclusion of another that is no less significant. For if his background is Flemish, France is supremely important to him—France as a country; French thought; French literature; the French language. He writes his books in French, if only because, from the outset, they will command a wider readership, a wider publicity—for his books, one and all, are written with the purpose of making specific ideas more widely known. Fluent in French, he occasionally at the Vatican Council, during an intervention, broke into French, knowing that French was intelligible to some of those present—especially bishops of the Eastern Churches—whereas Latin (the official language of the Western Church) was not.

Also it was in French that he delivered in Rome his eulogy in commemoration of Pope John.

Again, if the Cardinal is Flemish in his origins, he feels himself a citizen of the world—and French has for him a universality which enables him to make contacts on a world level; to think and plan on a world dimension. Furthermore, Cardinal Mercier, who was among those who had the greatest influences on his life, was steeped in the thought and culture of France.

The admixture of Flemish and French in Cardinal Suenens has advantages. Cardinal Mercier was a Walloon; his successor Cardinal van Roey was Flemish. The consecration, therefore, of Monsignor Suenens as Archbishop of Malines-Brussels in 1962 was welcomed because, as a native of Brussels, he was likely to be acceptable to Flemish and Walloons alike. But it is impossible to please everyone. In the eyes of some of the Walloons he is too Flemish. There are Flemish, on the other hand, who complain that he is too French. He accepts the situation with a characteristic sense of humour, doing his best—not always with success—to please both sectors.

In July 1921 the young Léon Suenens completed his studies (*humaniores*) at the Institut Sainte-Marie, Brussels. In his examinations he had come out first in his year.

This being so, he would in the normal course of events have been sent to the Leo XIII Seminary attached to the University of Louvain and founded by Cardinal Mercier.

The Director of Sainte-Marie had, however, 'slipped up'. Owing to an error on his part Léon's name had not been submitted for Cardinal Mercier's approval. As a consequence, whereas two of his fellow-students, whose scholastic attainments were inferior to his own, were accepted for Louvain, he himself was allotted to the seminary at Malines, which, unlike the Leo XIII Seminary, did not have university status.

At the time, this, for Léon, was a bitter blow. In retrospect, however, he was to see things differently. As it transpired, the Director's error proved to be a *felix culpa*.

CHAPTER 3

O Roma nobilis, orbis et domina
Cunctarum urbium excellentissima,
Roseo martyrum sanguine rubea,
Albis et virginum liliis candida,
Salutem dicimus tibi per omnia,
Te benedicimus—salve per saecula!

A ninth-century hymn in honour of
ST. PETER AND ST. PAUL

ONE DAY in the late summer of 1921 a tall, well-built young man, his eyes a clear blue, his complexion fresh, his hair *en brosse,* presented himself at the Archbishop's residence in Malines, at the invitation of Cardinal Mercier.

When eventually the Cardinal had learnt of the error which debarred Léon Suenens from entering the seminary at Louvain, it was too late to rectify this: the vacancies were already filled.

Cardinal Mercier, however, did more than make amends. Having heard from one of the young man's teachers that Léon was outstandingly gifted in the field of philosophy, he decided to send him to the Gregorian University at Rome. In view of this he wanted to see him in person.

Canon Francis Dessain, secretary to Cardinal Mercier, (uncle of Canon Joseph Dessain who today serves the present Cardinal with a like fidelity) wanted a pretext to talk to this student in whom Mercier was showing exceptional interest. He suggested, therefore, on Léon's arrival at the Archevêché, that, as the Cardinal was busy, he himself should assume the role of *interlocuteur*. The young Suenens declined the offer. Cardinal Mercier, he said, had invited him and it was only to the Cardinal that he would speak about his affairs: it was not at all the same thing to talk to his secretary.

Canon Dessain, himself something of a 'fighter' (he had 'captained' the National Football Team of Belgium) admired the young man's spirit. Indeed, from this brief clash of wills there emerged a warm and lasting friendship. Furthermore Canon Dessain had remarkable perceptivity. After Suenens had been ordained, Dessain predicted that this young priest would one day be a successor to Cardinal Mercier.

Léon was seventeen, Cardinal Mercier over seventy. Yet there was immediate rapport between the two, which led to a close relationship that lasted until the Cardinal's death in 1926. They corresponded regularly, and Suenens visited the Cardinal at Malines twice a year: in July and early in October—at the beginning, that is, and the end of the summer vacation. At the young man's request ('I don't know how I had the nerve to ask,' Cardinal Suenens says today) Cardinal Mercier became his spiritual director.

Further, when Cardinal Mercier came to Rome in 1922 for the election of the Pope (Pius XI), he brought with him a copy of his book *A mes Séminaristes* which he gave to the young Suenens, asking him to read it carefully. Also, when Léon, in a letter, asked the Cardinal to suggest a motto from which he might derive inspiration, he received the reply: 'Train yourself little by little to renounce all that is not God: let your motto be *"Dieu seul"*.'

Portraits of Désiré Joseph, Cardinal Mercier, show an imposing, commanding figure: exceptionally tall; elegant; with a broad forehead, intelligent eyes, finely moulded features; and an expression which in some paintings is stern, but more often gentle and serene.

By any standard he was a remarkable man. Ordained in 1874 and subsequently professor of philosophy at the major seminary in Malines, he was appointed at the age of thirty-one to the Chair of Thomastic Philosophy newly founded at the University of Louvain at the wish of Pope Leo XIII. The course was viewed in some quarters with misgivings, as having been foisted on the university by the Pope.

Mercier, however, was determined to present scholastic thought in a manner that would have relevance in modern times. Moreover he launched the periodical *La Revue Néo-Scolastique*. Further, during the summer vacation of 1882 he followed in Paris the lectures of the distinguished Dr. Charcot who was attracting international attention. To suit the role of student, Father Mercier grew a black beard, wore a frock-coat and, as a final touch, a diamond tie-pin.

On his return to Belgium he founded the Institut Supérieur de Philosophie, as well as the Leo XIII Seminary. His books were translated into many languages and used in progressive seminaries throughout the world. He was still President of the Institut when in 1906 he was consecrated Archbishop of Malines and soon afterwards made a Cardinal. During the First World War he was the inspiration and moral leader of the Belgian people, the *defensor civitatis,* the voice of conscience that spoke loudly and fearlessly to the oppressors of his country, thus commanding international fame and respect.

When the war ended, no person of importance came to Belgium without paying a visit to Malines. Expressions of homage reached the Cardinal from every part of the world. In New York he was made a 'citizen of honour', and at the universities of Princeton and Harvard honorary degrees were conferred on him.

But Cardinal Mercier's work for the Church of Christ was his first concern. In this he showed his breadth of vision. Over and above the years devoted to his seminarians at Malines; over and above his outstanding achievements in the field of philosophy at Louvain, there were his efforts in the Malines Conversations to establish common ground between Anglicans and the Church of Rome. His contact with Anglicans exposed him to some disfavour in Curial circles, but that was no new experience: already, while at Louvain, he was in trouble for delivering lectures in French instead of Latin. His vision is exemplified in the support he gave to the work of the Belgian missionary Father Vincent Lebbe, particularly to the latter's efforts to persuade Rome to allow the consecration (for the Church in China) of bishops chosen from among Chinese clergy. On the day Cardinal Mercier died Father Lebbe said of him: 'Mercier? Here was someone who had the courage to meddle in affairs that weren't his business.' '*Voilà quelqu'un qui osait s'occuper avec auctorité de choses qui ne le regardaient pas.*'

Years later Léon Suenens, when he became Cardinal Archbishop, was to play a role in several respects similar to that of Mercier.

Each, while remaining devoted first and foremost to his diocese and his country, showed, at the same time, a universal concern for the Church and for humanity. To each is applicable the saying: 'The world is my parish.'

The young Suenens revered Désiré Joseph Mercier as a public figure in Belgium and beyond. But he also had his own reasons for holding the Cardinal in affection and esteem. He admired him for his kindness and understanding, as well as for a spirituality permeated with a belief in the Holy Spirit at work both in the Church and in each individual. He appreciated words spoken by Cardinal Mercier

43

on the occasion of his jubilee celebrating his fifty years in the priesthood, when he revealed to his clergy the secret of his serenity.

'I am going to reveal to you,' he said, 'a secret of holiness and happiness. Every day, for five minutes, let your imagination be at rest; close your eyes to the things of the senses; close your ears to the sounds of the world; withdraw into the sanctuary of your soul which, through baptism, is the temple of the Holy Spirit. Then, speaking to the Holy Spirit, say: "Holy Spirit, soul of my soul, I adore you. Enlighten, guide, strengthen and console me. Tell me what I ought to do and command me to do it. I promise to be submissive in all you ask of me, to accept all you allow to happen to me. Only show me your will."

'If you do this,' the Cardinal continued, 'consolation will abound even in times of adversity.'

As Léon Suenens saw it at the time, and still sees it today, it was not coincidence or blind fate that brought Cardinal Mercier into his life: it was Providence, or, if you prefer, the Holy Spirit.

Indeed Mercier and Suenens resemble each other in the simplicity of their faith and in their trust in Providence. In the case of Cardinal Suenens this takes the form of an awareness of the super-natural functioning somehow, somewhere, moment by moment in the background of our lives. 'As well as having exceptional intellectual powers,' one of his diocesan priests said of him, 'he has the faith of a child.'

Neither in his student days at Rome nor at any period of his life has Léon Suenens undergone what can be called 'a crisis of faith'. He has not shared Charles de Foucauld's experience of 'despairing of truth . . . living as though the last spark of faith had been quenched.'

The Cardinal's attitude of mind is at the same time, to quote his own words, 'critical and serene'. Far from pretending that intellectual difficulties do not exist, he confronts them, but with a tranquillity that only supernatural faith can confer. He dwells on this in his book *La Question Scolaire* to which I shall revert.

The Cardinal's problems belong to another level: they concern, not the basic truths of the Christian revelation, but how the Church can most effectively present these truths in the world of today and tomorrow. But, someone will ask, can a man who himself, it appears, has not known doubt, understand our doubt-ridden world? What has he to say to those who feel their belief in God shaken to its foundations; who, echoing Kafka, ask: 'Suppose, after all, there is

44

no one there?' Or, again, what of those who, if they can accept the reality of God, think of the Church as an incumbrance without relevance to life as they experience it?

Seeing human beings, not *en masse* but as individuals, each differing from the other, the Cardinal does not hand out textbook answers. He is a theologian in his own right, but his answers, when he is confronted with a human problem, rarely take the form of a theological statement; they come, rather, from a man who has so absorbed the basic teaching of theology that he is able to convey supernatural and invisible realities as if he had actually seen them or at least experienced them at the deepest level of his being. As a young man in Brussels put it: 'The Cardinal has the power to make the dry bones live.'

When a man came to him in distress, with one question only: 'What, Your Eminence, does Christ mean to you in your own life?', the Cardinal, with no beating about the bush, told him precisely this—what Christ meant to him personally. What he actually said I do not know. But I know that his thinking—revealed in his spoken and his written words—carries radiance and joy, along with a conviction that a relationship of mutual love can be established, by grace of the Holy Spirit, between Christ, the Son of the Eternal Father, and each human being.

As to the Church, while it has an essential role in the scheme of man's salvation—in that Christ founded it and sustains it for this, his eternal purpose—it is also a human institution, existing in a world upon which original sin has cast its shadow. The Cardinal stresses this aspect of the Church in a supplement to his pastoral letter for Pentecost in 1972 in which, quoting Pope Paul, he writes: '*L'Eglise n'est pas elle-même sa propre fin. Elle est du Christ et pour le Christ, faite d'hommes, parmi les hommes.*'

The Cardinal's answer to a question put to him about his reaction, as a seminarist, to the Church as he experienced it in Rome is revealing: 'No, I wasn't disillusioned, for I had no illusions.' These are the words not of a cynic, but a realist. They bring to mind the lines written by the Elizabethan poet Fulke Greville:

> *The sensual insatiable vast womb*
> *Of thy seen Church, thy unseen Church disgraceth.*

The sixteenth-century poet and the Cardinal of today are alike in their ability to distinguish between the visible Church—marred from its beginnings (we have only to read the Acts of the Apostles) by the defects of man's fallen nature—and the invisible Church.

45

Already in boyhood Léon Suenens was able to make the distinction between the earthly Jerusalem and the Jerusalem that is on high—while grasping at the same time the truth that the celestial Church is already present in the pilgrim Church on earth—so that there are not two Churches but one. The flaws, visible in the Church, far from discouraging him, spur him on to work the harder to put right what is wrong: all of which is in line with his childhood vision of the priesthood as a calling which would enable him to work in a positive, constructive manner for the good and the happiness of mankind in this world and in the next.

For some days, when I was staying in Malines before Christmas 1972, I had in my possession notebooks kept by the Cardinal when he was a seminarian at Rome. Their pages were closely covered in his handwriting—still neat, but showing more 'character'—as had been those of his schoolboy exercises. I used to read them at odd moments—in the great empty cathedral, or in the Cardinal's residence when waiting to see him or when, as sometimes happened, our conversations were interrupted.

Someone had said to me of the Cardinal—in friendliness, not malice—that he was inclined to be 'too cerebral'. I was touched, therefore, to read, written so many years ago, a prayer that Christ, granting to him a deeper understanding of fellowship among men, would 'warm with the fire of his love' a soul 'too prone to abstract thinking': 'trop poussé vers l'abstraction intellectuelle'. There are many prayers in his notebooks: prayers for those dear to him; prayers that he may be worthy of his priesthood; prayers for courage; prayers to be spared illusions; prayers that in the service of others he may go as far as man can go—and further: 'Apprenez-nous à dépasser nos limites, à aller au delà'. And always, as in childhood, there is the awareness of time versus eternity. In an entry made on September 3rd 1927, the day before his ordination, he incorporates, in the sonorous Latin, the words from the Gospel of St. Matthew:

Caelum et terra transibunt
Verba autem mea non transibunt

I quote sparingly from these notebooks. Just as wild flowers picked in a glade or meadow are quick to wilt if taken from their habitat, so there are words which, wrenched out of context, lose their freshness and potency. Moreover something else held me back. As I read these pages in which the young Léon Suenens reveals his innermost thoughts and aspirations, I found myself from time to time closing the note-books, feeling overcome by a sense that I was in some way an intruder— as one might feel on overhearing, accidentally, words spoken in intimacy by friend to friend, lover to beloved.

I must not, however, leave the notebooks without mention of a passage in which he writes of the Tyrrhenian coast and the ruins of Ostia. He writes of the pale sunlight of May; a green sea, flecked with silver, breaking on the beach in a froth of foam—the curving wave singing 'a song learnt on the shores of Sardinia'; here and there, along the coast, a sailing ship, 'white as a gull'. A walk across fields takes him to the ancient town of Ostia, its pillars and statues, broken yet beautiful, standing up against the blue of the sky; the ruins of the forum; the temple of Mithras—its initiation circles, suns, and moons, intact—and the well that caught the blood of a bull offered in sacrifice. He recalls, too, butterflies 'blue as the pimpernels that grow among the mosaics'; heavy-headed poppies; and the song of a lark soaring into the silence.

Ostia awakes in him thoughts of history. Was it not by this port that corn had come to feed the Roman people; wealth from the east; gold from the ends of earth; generals returning in triumph? Was it not here, he reflects, that Augustine and Monica his mother—in this place, dear to them both—bade each other their dramatic farewell?

By inclination an intellectual, eager to use every opportunity of widening his culture, he made the most of his journeys to and from Rome. The course at the Gregorianum began in October and ended in July, when he returned to Brussels. Each of the many journeys he made during this period he planned in advance, choosing for each a different itinerary. This was in the tradition of the Belgian College, which meant that he knew where best to stay, where best to break his journey. And so he became familiar with many areas of Switzerland, Austria, and France.

At Rome the young Suenens took his studies seriously not simply because such was his cast of mind, but because the priesthood for which he was being prepared was always in the forefront of his thoughts.

In 1926, the year that preceded his ordination, he wrote to Canon Francis Dessain, Secretary to Cardinal Mercier:

'I am making the most of the time left to me here to prepare myself as best I can for the great things Providence expects from me in the future.'

47

Commenting on this letter, Canon Joseph Dessain writes:

'The phrase "great things" must of course be understood as referring to the priesthood *per se*. No question of personal ambition is involved. Any good that the Cardinal has done he attributes not to himself but to the Holy Spirit working through him.'

Léon Suenens was ordained priest on September 4th 1927, by Cardinal van Roey at Malines.

Instead however of being assigned to pastoral work in the diocese, he spent two more years at Rome, by which time he held a Doctorate in Philosophy and Theology and a Baccalaureat in Canon Law.

'How did you find the teaching at the Gregorianum?' I asked Cardinal Suenens.

'Very disappointing,' he replied.

'The philosophy,' he continued, 'was too scholastic, too abstract. It was unrelated to real life. And any serious confrontation with modern philosophy was avoided. As for theology, it was speculative and there was too much in the way of apologetics. It was not related to its Biblical foundations, and historical perspective was totally lacking.'

'Weren't you discouraged?'

'No. Outside the university I was in touch with some remarkable men—today we would call them "prophetic figures". They opened new vistas for me and helped me, despite all, to preserve a certain confidence in philosophy and theology. The person who influenced me most was Dom Lambert Beauduin of the Abbey of Mont César, Louvain, at that time professor of theology in St. Anselmo, Rome.'

Lambert Beauduin, born at Rosoux-lez-Waremme, Belgium, in August 1873, was ordained in 1897 and having belonged for a while to the *Aumoniers du Travail* (a society of priests founded to care for the workers) became a Benedictine in 1906 at Mont César, where he was initiated into the study of the liturgy by Dom Columba Marmion. He established liturgical weekends—in which both clergy and laity participated—and wrote a number of books on liturgical matters.

Appointed professor of theology at Rome, he became interested in the Eastern liturgies and was encouraged by Pope Pius XI to act as mediator between the Roman and the Eastern Churches. He founded, at Chèvetogne, a monastery to further ecumenical studies, which is now an important centre. He also launched the review *Irénikon*.

Moreover it was Dom Lambert who composed the famous

memorandum, read by Cardinal Mercier at the Malines Conversations, entitled: '*The Anglican Church United to Rome, but not Absorbed.*'

Subjected to adverse criticism for views which some regarded as 'bold', others as verging on heresy, Lambert Beauduin was in trouble at Rome in 1931. Yet despite this he remained a dominant influence in establishing better understanding between the Orthodox, Anglicans, and Roman Catholics. Cardinal Angelo Roncalli, when Patriarch of Venice, commended him for adopting 'the true method of working for the reunion of the Churches'. In 1958 Dom Lambert, two years before he died, had the satisfaction of learning that Angelo Roncalli, now Pope John XXIII, had announced his intention to hold an Ecumenical Council.

Father Vincent Lebbe was indeed a 'prophetic' figure.

Léon Suenens had heard him lecture on various occasions. But it was a private conversation between the two, lasting for seven hours, that made on Suenens a life-long impression. The vital missionary problem, Father Lebbe explained, is that the Church, if the Gospel is to be preached effectively, must be Chinese in China, Indian in India— it must not persist in being Latin and European regardless of the milieu in which it functions.

This *ouverture* as to the meaning of true Catholicity left on the young Suenens an indelible mark. Moreover he felt that Father Lebbe's views confirmed those of Dom Lambert Beauduin who had already awakened in him a sympathy and regard—one that was to remain with him through the years—for the Eastern and Anglican Christians.

Frederic Vincent Lebbe, born in Ghent in August 1877, was a small man, slight in build, his blue eyes sparkling with good humour. Devoting his life to spreading the Gospel in China, he identified himself, as far as lay in his power, with the Chinese people: speaking, writing, thinking, and dressing as they did. He went to great pains, too, on behalf of Chinese students who were sent to Europe (many of them were sponsored by Communist organisations)—travelling tirelessly in Belgium, France, and Switzerland in his efforts to find places for them in Catholic schools, colleges, and families.

Father Lebbe's niece, a Canoness of St. Augustine, recalls her uncle as 'a lovable, most inspiring man of God, oblivious of self, totally dedicated to his work, yet never wavering in his affection for his family'. His labours were rewarded when, after much mis-representation and many setbacks, he watched the consecration by

D

Pius XI at Rome of six Chinese bishops, after which he returned to China, founded a religious congregation, and died in 1940, aged sixty-two.

The Cardinal has always been a wide reader.

As a student, he read during the vacations a book a week—indeed he had read nearly every volume in the library of one of his professors. In a notebook, its pages yellowed by the passing of the years, he listed over six hundred books read between 1919 and 1938. And this was 'recreational' reading, in that it did not include the numerous volumes on theology and philosophy essential to his studies for the priesthood.

In reply to my question: 'What non-religious book impressed you most?' he answered: *Augustin ou le Maître est Là.*

As a consequence of the Cardinal's words I read Joseph Malègue's novel, and did so with mounting interest.

The story is long-drawn-out and there is over-much about illness. But it reveals extraordinary insight, extraordinary sensitivity.

With a poignancy reminiscent of Virgil's, *Sunt lacrimae rerum et mentem mortalia tangunt,* the writer evokes the human predicament at many levels; not least man's need to communicate with another, coupled with an inability to do so—the need, also, to penetrate, whatever the cost, to the truth that lies at the heart of all our longings and aspirations.

What interested me most, however, was a certain resemblance between the Augustin created by Joseph Malègue and the living Suenens. This has nothing to do with the lives, as such, of the two —indeed their lives could hardly be more different. No, the resemblance is in traits of personality: a passion for truth; intellectual brilliance; extreme sensitivity, a reserve, indeed a *timidité* (Malègue applies this word to Augustin, the Cardinal to himself) which can mask the real person, creating, sometimes, an impression of coldness, even *hauteur.*

When I asked about books which had influenced the Cardinal's thinking in the religious sphere, he singled out four:

Etudes de Théologie sur La Sainte Trinité by Thomas de Regnon S.J. in four volumes: 'In these,' the Cardinal said, 'I discovered the Greek Fathers. This I can never forget—it was a revelation!'

The Life of Cardinal Newman by Thureau Dangin: 'These three volumes,' he said, 'opened my eyes to the wealth of the Anglican tradition.'

Histoire du Sentiment Religieux by Henri Brémond: he read and read again Brémond's eleven volumes.

L'Abandon à la Divine Providence by Jean-Pierre de Caussade S.J., an eighteenth century masterpiece unique for the light it throws on the meaning of Providence.

The Cardinal's thinking on Providence, as on many other matters, takes a practical form.

To be aware of Providence is largely, as he sees it, a question of making a consistent effort to penetrate beyond appearances, beyond what St. John of the Cross calls *lo pintado,* 'the painted exterior'; to look past secondary causes: '*Il nous faut sans cesse faire effort pour dépasser les apparences, pour aller au delà des causes secondes.*' His attitude should be seen against the background of his childhood awareness of eternity; in the context, too, of the impact made upon him as a boy by the words of Christ: 'My peace I give to you'. What impressed him in Caussade was an assurance that in every circumstance of life it is possible for man to learn how to surrender himself, in peace of soul, to the guidance of the Holy Spirit.

Quoting Caussade, the Cardinal writes in his book *Vie Quotidienne, Vie Chrétienne:* 'All creatures live in the hand of God. The senses perceive only the activity of the creature. Faith sees the divine activity in all things—believes that Jesus Christ lives in all things, and is at work throughout the entire course of the centuries: faith believes that the briefest moment, the smallest atom, contains something of Christ's hidden life and mysterious activity. The activity of creatures is a veil which conceals the deep mysteries of God's action. Jesus Christ after his Resurrection took his disciples by surprise each time he appeared to them; he appeared to them in disguise, and, as soon as he had revealed himself, disappeared. This same Jesus, who is always living, always active, still takes by surprise those whose faith is as yet unable to penetrate to the heart of reality.'

While studying philosophy and theology in Rome, Léon Suenens became increasingly interested in the problems of the Church in relation to the world.

Towards the end of his time at the Gregorianum, that is between 1927 and 1929, he became the Rome correspondent for *La Métropole,* a Belgian paper with liberal views and a concern for economics, published at Antwerp. It contained a *Billet du Vatican,* written each week by Monsignor Fontenelle, French correspondent of *La Croix,* Paris, until the time of his death. Then Léon—by now ordained, but continuing his studies at Rome—was invited to take over. His contributions on Italian politics and religious problems show, indeed, a talent for journalism—but for him this was never more than a sideline.

Observant by nature, he made full use of this trait when gathering material for his column. And what he saw did not always please him. He was unfavourably impressed by the scheming and flattery in Vatican circles—the 'gravitation' around the Pope by those whose aim was to 'shine' in high places.

Yet, distasteful though this was, it left him remarkably unperturbed. Man, he told himself, is relative, God is absolute. And in thinking along these lines he experienced a sense of liberation: all things pass, save God alone. Although as yet there was no Pope John to fire Léon's imagination with thoughts of an *aggiornamento,* he was aware in his mind and heart of the need for change.

While he was a boy at school Léon Suenens was specially interested in history lessons. But lessons are only lessons. In Rome, history was spread before his eyes. The history of the Church was there in all its splendour, its glory, its shame—spanning the centuries, extending back beyond the Renaissance, beyond the Middle Ages, to the city of the catacombs, the city of those early saints and martyrs whose names shine like jewels in the Roman Canon of the Mass. The history of the Church merged into, or was set in the perspective of, classical Rome; the Empire reaching back to the Republic, the Republic to the kings, the kings to the city's foundation lost in a mist of tradition and mythology.

He came to know Rome, sometimes by deliberate study of the sights that met his eyes, sometimes effortlessly, but, in either case, in the way that is best—on foot. 'I knew every stone,' he said to me one day. Another day (tired perhaps by being plied with questions) he said: 'I just took Rome for granted.'

On reflection I realised that there is no discrepancy between the two answers. It is possible to know every plant in a garden, every peak on a mountain ridge, every stone in a cherished building, and yet (so complex is the human mechanism) in a mood of abstraction or preoccupation to see nothing. Even so, surroundings, I believe—whether we are aware of them or not—make their impact on the level of the subconscious. 'I slept,' the bride says in the *Song of Songs,* 'yet my heart was awake.'

And so, when I ask myself what influences contributed to making the Cardinal the person he is today, I do not think it over-fanciful to include such sights and sounds as the deep-shadowed colonnades of temples; the splash of fountains; flights of steps that climb, to drop again; cypress trees waving like dark plumes against an azure sky; shrill-voiced swallows darting in and out of Vesta's shrine; the teasing smile on the mask-like face of a terra-cotta Apollo; beyond the city, Mount Soracte crowned with snow; and, on distant hills, towns such as Virgil looked upon, poised on precipitous ridges, rivers slipping beneath their ancient walls:

Tot congesta manu praeruptis oppida saxis
Fluminaque antiquos subter labentia muros.

And there were the churches. Not only the great basilicas, but small, dark buildings in which the light of candles flickered on mosaics portraying a grave Byzantine Madonna; or a Christ with hand upraised to bless; or the Lamb of God with, ranged on either side, the Apostles depicted as sheep. Churches whose names make a litany: Santa Agnese fuori le Mura; Santa Cecilia in Trastevere; Santa Caterina della Rota; Santa Maria Sopra Minerva; Santa Maria Scala Caeli; Santa Croce in Gerusalemme; San Niccoló alle Calcari; San Giovanni a Porta Latina; San Lorenzo in Damaso; San Pietro in Vincoli.

Little did Léon Suenens know, when in the last of these churches he used to look at the Moses of Michelangelo, that the day was to come when, raised to the College of Cardinals by Pope John XXIII, he would stand where once Cardinal Mercier had stood, to receive, in what was the titular church of both these men, the obeisance of the General of the Canons of the Lateran who served this basilica.

My stay at Malines in December 1972 helped me to visualise the years Léon Suenens had spent at Rome as a young man.

It helped me to understand also something of what it means to be archbishop of one of the largest and most complex dioceses in the world.

The two-fold diocese of Malines-Brussels comprises some 2,300,000 inhabitants, including nearly 1,900 priests. It covers the province of Brabant and a small part of the territory belonging to the province of Anvers, which takes in the city of Malines.

It is divided into three parts: Flemish Brabant (900,000 inhabitants); Walloon Brabant (300,000); and Brussels, the bilingual capital, which has a population of more than a million.

On becoming Archbishop the Cardinal proceeded to decentralise and regionalise the diocese, entrusting each region to a Vicar-General (supported by a Vicariate-General), who in his turn has full authority in all that concerns his area.

One of the results of this division is that the diocesan newsletter or *Pastoralia* gives only a partial view of what is happening in the diocese. In fact each region has its own newsletter. Walloon Brabant has *Printemps;* Flemish Brabant, *Trefpunt;* Brussels, two: *En Direct* for Walloons; *Kerk in De Stad* for the Flemish.

Every Friday the Cardinal presides at an Episcopal Council (from 10.00 a.m. until 4.30 p.m.) which brings together the Vicars-General, their assistants, and others entrusted with positions of responsibility. He gives particular attention to the problems posed by the regions and the pastoral implications of these.

Often regions have quite different problems and conflicting viewpoints. The Cardinal has therefore appointed four priests' councils—one Flemish, one Walloon; and at Brussels one giving expression to French, the other to Flemish interests. There are also four pastoral councils. To keep things running smoothly is no easy matter.

The complexities in the diocese can make themselves felt on the national level. And here the Cardinal is again involved. Moreover the task of reconciling opposing views can be enough, he admits, 'to make your head split:' *'C'est un véritable casse-tête.'*

A cause of particular distress to the Cardinal was the crisis which erupted in the Catholic University of Louvain with the result that finally the University was split into two—the Flemings remaining on the original site, the French establishing themselves twenty miles away at Louvain la Neuve.

But this breach was preceded by religious and political strife.

The University, situated in Flemish territory, had been a single entity for five centuries and became bilingual in 1921. Hence the crisis. For when, under pressure of Flemish public opinion, the presence of the French became intolerable, the Bishops, Flemish and Walloon (together they were responsible for the administration of the University) were faced with an insoluble problem—the Walloons argued that the University must not be divided, the Flemish demanded the expulsion of the Walloons.

Refusing to take the initiative in dividing the University, the Bishops, in a public declaration made on May 13th 1966, expressed their support for the *status quo.* Among the Flemish this added fuel to the fire. There were demonstrations and violence. The Flemish

Bishops were accused of being traitors—not least the Cardinal, *le Grand Chancelier* of the undivided University.

The Government intervened with the proposal that the University be divided on the level of the students, but remain united on that of degrees and doctorates. The Walloon bishops would not accept this compromise, and the Government fell.

Some months later Parliament decided that the University be divided, and that the French should leave.

This painful episode created a *malaise* which died down little by little. Nevertheless it breaks out afresh when either the Flemish or the Walloons believe, rightly or wrongly, that they have suffered some injustice.

The Cardinal published a pastoral letter exhorting the faithful to come to a mutual understanding. But without success. At the present moment things have improved: the problems caused in Belgium by language differences are, it seems, somewhat less acute.

I have said that my stay at Malines enabled me to understand something of what it means to be Archbishop of Malines-Brussels. The operative word is 'something'. For though the greater part of the Cardinal's thought, time, and enterprise, is expended on his diocese, it is not possible to write of this except on a superficial level: it is a task for an historian of the future.

At the present time, there is no access to the weekly reports of what has taken place during the Friday Episcopal Councils. Moreover the brief press reports of the meetings held by the Belgian Bishops once a month can be misleading: papers printed for a French-speaking public do not relate what the Cardinal has done in Flemish regions, and *vice versa*.

Comparatively few persons have any idea of the time and thought expended day and night by the Cardinal and the bishops of Belgium in composing the statement issued by the hierarchy after the publication of Pope Paul's encyclical *Humanae Vitae*, when the Cardinal appointed a theological commission presided over by Monsignor Philips who had played an important role in the formulation of the Conciliar *Dogmatic Constitution on the Church*. Indeed the Belgian statement was the first official reaction to the encyclical. Similar in tone to those of the Canadian, French, and German bishops it shows a deep pastoral concern for the faithful, while stressing at the same time the Church's classical teaching on conscience.

Anything that has a bearing on *Humanae Vitae* has news value. But this does not apply to the innumerable routine happenings in a diocese, which for a journalist, have no 'new's value' as compared with ecumenical tours taking in, say, New York, Hollywood, San Francisco, the Arizona Desert, and Latin America.

It is not always remembered that the Cardinal when out of his diocese is serving his diocese. The deacons who fulfil an important role in the Malines-Brussels diocese would not be there but for the Cardinal's forceful intervention at Rome during Vatican 11, when he advocated the restoration of a permanent diaconate. Moreover Charismatic Renewal flourishes at Louvain only because the Cardinal introduced it from the United States.

I learnt, too, at Malines something of the day-to-day, hour-to-hour demands upon the Cardinal's time. Letters to dictate and sign. Telephone calls to make and receive. Visitors coming and going, clergy and laity—some belonging to his own diocese, others from distant parts of the world.

It may be a courtesy call. Or a journalist. Or a friend passing through Belgium. Or someone burdened with a seemingly insoluble problem. There is no knowing who will come or with what purpose.

One day a personage of some importance announced to His Eminence:

'My dog has swallowed a cat!'

'Monsieur', the Cardinal replied with fitting severity, 'I can't have that—not in my diocese!'

I was impressed by the amount of time the Cardinal spared me. And not just the amount but the quality. For he thinks quickly and clearly, and has a remarkable memory. When called away during a conversation he is able on his return to resume where we left off.

'Doesn't the Cardinal ever fly into a rage?' I asked one of his staff, thinking of the little boy who trampled his drum to pieces—thinking, too, of a prelate of world renown who, I am told, used on occasion to 'roar like a bull' and 'scatter his entourage in terror'.

'No, no,' came the reply, 'the Cardinal doesn't lose his temper. He *can* appear cold—but that's if he's ill-at-ease or absorbed in thought. As a rule he's remarkably serene.'

'He *can* appear cold.' There is truth in this. It may be no more than a tone of voice, a brusqueness of manner, or a countenance that has become suddenly unsmiling, mask-like.

There has been the occasional moment (I will not pretend otherwise) when I have felt as though I were cast into outer darkness!

In writing this I have in mind others who—being like myself sensitive (perhaps over sensitive) to atmosphere—might be led to suppose that the Cardinal is in fact cold, even haughty. This would be a pity. For any lack of warmth on his part is something very much on the surface, something as transient as a shadow cast by a passing cloud.

It took me a while to understand this.

But I recall how on a December afternoon, after one such experience, as I sat in St. Rombaut's cathedral trying to collect my thoughts, things began to fall into perspective.

What if at moments, I asked myself, the Cardinal is cold, even forbidding? Better that than if he were utterly predictable: a robot or a 'plaster saint'. And are we not all of us, for causes too many to enumerate, at the mercy, to some degree, of moods, emotions, circumstances?

Moreover if I had been told that he can 'appear cold' had I not also been told of his serenity? Indeed, the latter was an aspect of his personality that I had been aware of myself. It explains, I believe, his attitude towards—and his way of speaking to—those whom for want of a better word I must call, I suppose, his 'subordinates'. His voice is calm, clear, quiet, friendly. He is not at all the 'commanding officer' giving orders on the parade ground. No, I don't think he would like the word 'subordinates', for his approach is after the manner of Pablo Casals who said to his orchestra: 'You're not servants of mine. We're all servants of the music!' Only a man who has a basic serenity, as distinct from a turbulent spirit, can talk like that.

And this, in the life of the Cardinal, goes back over the years. As I have said, at Rome facets of the institutional Church which would have scandalised some—driven them possibly out of the Church, left Léon Suenens not unconcerned but unperturbed.

Serenity and good sense have something in common: an ability to see things in proportion, to avoid extremes.

A while ago, without mentioning the Cardinal's name, I related to a distinguished psychologist (Mrs. Hertha Orgler, for many years the friend and colleague of Dr. Alfred Adler) one of the Cardinal's earliest memories: how, when left behind in the pew at church, he took his place at his mother's side at the Communion rail and, as the priest approached, said: 'Me too, please!' The psychologist's immediate reply was: 'He must have been a very *sensible* little boy. Many children would have made a scene.'

I told her a couple more of his memories. Commenting on them collectively she said: 'I *like* his memories. He sees himself *with* other people—not in isolation. These are what are called "We" as distinct from "I" memories. They denote a good "life-style"—an interest in others.'

In the quiet of the cathedral I reflected on the goodwill the Cardinal had shown me, and his many kindnesses.

It was thanks to him that I was here, in Malines. Writers have their idiosyncracies. To me it is essential to set a character in the context of his or her background. To write about Teresa of Avila I had to travel up and down Spain. To write about Charles de Foucauld I had to go to the Sahara. It was no less important to see the Cardinal against the background of Malines, within the setting of his diocese. For the Cardinal, I hope I have shown, is not a world figure who merely happens to be Archbishop of Malines. It is the other way round. He is, first, Archbishop of Malines—Brussels, and his many activities undertaken on a world-scale are polarised around his diocese from which he sets out and to which he returns.

Evening was closing in.

It was growing dark in the cathedral. The pillars rose like great trees, their tops lost in the shadows of oncoming night. A cluster of tapers flickered before a smoke-stained ikon of the Blessed Virgin framed in gold.

A light shone upon the figures in the crib. The Virgin's cloak was as blue as a pane of glass from the window of *Notre Dame de la Belle Verrière,* at Chartres. St. Joseph's tunic was striped with broad, alternating bands of crimson and emerald. Straw made a carpet of gold. I heard a faint rustling sound. A cat, lifting its paws delicately, was making itself a bed in the straw, its tortoise-shell coat providing a camouflage.

Outside, the city was wreathed in fog through which I glimpsed coloured lights festooning the streets.

Later, when I visited the Cardinal I found him the friendly out-going person that at heart he is.

He gave me a Christmas prayer which he had written himself in Flemish, French, German and English, to be distributed in his diocese and sent abroad:

> *Give us, oh, Lord,*
> *eyes for seeing,*
> *a heart for loving,*
> *breath for living.*

Give us eyes for seeing,

give us, we beg, your eyes,
to see through them
the world and all mankind,
to see their history and our own
as you see them.
Grant us to think your thoughts
day by day,
hour by hour.
Help us gradually to become
that for which you created us;
let us adopt your view of things,
your way of seeing things.
Make us responsive to your Word
which can enlighten and transform
the life of each of us.

Give us a heart for loving,

a heart of flesh and not of stone
for loving God and Man.
Give us, we beg, your heart,
that we forget ourselves
in perfect love.
We need to exchange our heart for yours,
our heart so slow
to love all others but ourselves.
Let it be you, oh Lord,
who loves through us.
Give us a heart to love Our Father,
to love Mary our Mother
and to love your brothers
who are also ours;
to love even in this world
those who have gone before us in the next—
easier those to love, of course—
and to love, too, those
we walk beside on earth
who jostle us now and then,
whether deliberately or not.

Give us the breath of life
that we pant not on our way,
that our lungs be constantly filled
with life-saving breath and air
to help us walk towards tomorrow
without a backward look or thought of effort;
to prepare for
all that men, and therefore you,
expect from us;
to draw fresh hope
as if, this morning, life began;
to struggle against winds and tides,
sustained
by your presence and your promise,
carrying as we do, in us,
men's hopes and all their fears.
Give us breath to live, your breath
that you send from God the Father;
your Spirit, the Breath
that blows where it will
in gusts or sudden winds
or that light touch
with which you call us to follow.
Breathe on us,
inspire in us
out of the depths
that prayer which rises from you within us,
calling for you to come in glory,
reaching out to the fullness of God.

Lord, I need your eyes,
give me a living faith.
I need your heart,
a love to withstand any test.
I need the breath of God,
give your hope
to me and all your Church
that the Church today
bear witness to the world,
that the world may know
all Christians

by their look of joy and serenity,
a warm and generous heart
and the unfailing optimism
that rises
from that secret, everlasting spring
of joyful hope.

This is a prayer, Lord,
for all times,
but on this Christmas eve
I ask
for me and all my fellow Christians,
as for all men and women of good will—
seeking anxiously—
eyes to recognise
the smile of God
on the face of the newborn Child.
Give us a new heart
to welcome him,
to grasp his message
and translate his life
into our daily lives;
then give us
long and life-giving breath
to travel with the Lord,
following in his footsteps
day by day,
in the year to come.

CHAPTER 4

Expectavit anima mea Dominum.

PSALM CXXIX :6

FOR A YOUNG MAN of a reflective, intellectual cast of mind to find himself transported from the rarefied atmosphere of university life to a school classroom is an unnerving experience. It is one thing to have scholarly tastes, to be versed in the abstract thinking that is requisite for the study of theology and philosophy, quite another to teach handwriting, French, and mathematics to small boys.

Such was the fate of Father Suenens in September 1929, when, after completing his studies at Rome, he returned to Brussels. It was, possibly, all the more difficult because he had grown up without brothers or sisters, mainly in the company of persons older than himself. The Cardinal does not pretend that this period at the Institut Sainte-Marie, where he had himself been educated, was to his liking. He has no illusions as to his ability in handling little boys. 'It wasn't really fair on the class,' he says, somewhat ruefully.

After six months things took a turn for the better.

Appointed professor of philosophy at the seminary at Malines, where he was to remain for the next ten years, he was in his element. In teaching ethics, the history of philosophy, epistemology, and the science of education, he was free to develop ideas he had formulated while in Rome; to present fresh interpretations; approach the various aspects of his teaching from the cultural viewpoint, thus opening the minds of his pupils, enlarging their horizons. Granted reasonably intelligent, receptive hearers, he was, as a lecturer, first class, and is remembered as such by many who were among his students.

But what of the person, as distinct from the teacher? Was he likeable, approachable, friendly? A colleague who was with him on the staff says he had all these qualities. And his relations with his students? His teaching, as I have implied, met with unanimous appreciation. As to his personality, he was respected, indeed much liked. True, there were certain reservations: some of his pupils, particularly those from country districts—as distinct from their more sophisticated companions brought up in a town or city—felt at times overawed by a man upon whom, in their eyes, intellectual distinction conferred an Olympian remoteness which, in its turn, accentuated in them a feeling of inadequacy. Nevertheless, despite this gulf existing, in some instances, between professor and student, it was an acknowledged fact that no young man (intellectual or otherwise) assailed by doubts or difficulties would, if he confided in Father Suenens, be turned away without a sympathetic hearing.

During those ten years at the seminary many students passed through his hands, enriched by his breadth of vision, his aspirations for the future. He too, on his side, learnt much that was to prove of incalculable value when, later, he became Auxiliary Bishop of Malines.

Mobilised in 1939, after the outbreak of the Second World War, Father Suenens was chaplain for some weeks to a detachment of the 9th Artillery Regiment. Then in May 1940 he was appointed to the Recruitment Centre of the Belgian army in Southern France.

In the autumn the Belgian episcopacy appointed him Vice-Rector of the University of Louvain. To this period belongs an interesting episode. One day the Vice-Rector was summoned to see the Kreis-Kommandant, the German in command of the district. Over an hour passed. The Vice-Rector had not returned. It was feared that he, too, had been arrested. The truth was otherwise. The Commander, Graf von Thadden, Bismarck's grandson, spoke for a few minutes about the grievances of the German authorities towards the University. Then for an hour he talked about the over-riding need for Christian unity. A protestant, interested in ecumenism, totally (and courageously) out of sympathy with Hitler, he said, 'What matters most is that we should experience together the Communion of the Holy Spirit.'

Léon Suenens has never forgotten the conversation. 'My motto *In Spiritu Sancto* was an outcome of this encounter,' he says.

For Léon Suenens the most difficult period covered the last fifteen months of the war. The Rector having been imprisoned by the Gestapo, the Vice-Rector assumed full responsibility. Moreover the situation was an inflammatory one in which the slightest incident could assume enormous proportions. Efforts to save students from being conscripted by the Nazis for forced labour involved the

Vice-Rector in difficult and delicate negotiations with the Army of Occupation. A contemporary remembers him at this time as a man who was always capable, calm, optimistic. 'He never,' it was said, 'dramatised things.'

At Louvain his mind was not solely occupied with problems posed by the war. While he was Vice-Rector he was struck by the absence in the University of any serious religious teaching for the laity. He therefore worked out with a group of professors a plan to establish an *Institut des Sciences Religieuses*.

In 1945 Léon Suenens was named Auxiliary Bishop to Cardinal Van Roey, Archbishop of Malines, and remained such until the Cardinal's death in 1961. It was on being appointed bishop that he chose for his coat-of-arms the motto *In Spiritu Sancto*.

As time went on it fell to him to take over, more and more, the Cardinal's functions—carrying out his public duties; representing him; speaking on his behalf. This was to be expected. But it brought difficulties, in that Bishop Suenens found himself in the position of having, as spokesman of the Cardinal, to support activities and ideas with which he was more than once out of sympathy.

Léon Suenens had been ordained priest, it will be recalled, in 1927. This means that some thirty-four years elapsed between his ordination and his consecration as Archbishop of Malines on December 15th 1961, followed just three months later by his nomination as Cardinal on March 19th 1962. They were crowded years. They included two years (after his ordination) spent on higher studies in Rome; ten in the seminary at Malines; four at Louvain; and sixteen as Auxiliary Bishop.

In retrospect—in the light of the role filled by Cardinal Suenens in the Second Vatican Council and afterwards—this preceding period, especially his years as Auxiliary Bishop, presents itself as a time of preparation: a time of waiting. For waiting is the very essence of life: whether it takes the form of a joyous expectation or a darkness in which we wait, scarcely knowing for what it is we wait—the darkness in which, St. John of the Cross teaches, the soul, illuminated by the merest glimmer of faith, waits upon the will of its Creator: *Expectavit anima mea Dominum*.

To wait is more difficult for some than for others. Persons of imagination, ideas, and enterprise chafe when hemmed in by restrictions; when they want to see their horizons widen, their dreams become a reality. Winston Churchill, during a bleak period of his life,

E

when he could see no future ahead, no scope for his talents, confessed to his wife his despondency at the thought of 'the narrow sphere' to which he was confined; 'the restricted experience'. Yet, by sheer will-power and the exercise of his intelligence he lived through this darkness in such a manner that, when the moment presented itself, he was in readiness to use his gifts to the full.

In like manner Bishop Suenens, instead of yielding to a negative passivity—a condition that can be mistaken for resignation to God's will—looked about him and, seeing what opportunities presented themselves, availed himself of these. His attitude is indicated by a Chinese proverb he quotes in one of his books: 'A journey of a thousand leagues begins with a single step.'

It was while he was Auxiliary Bishop of Malines that he learnt about a lay apostolic organisation (at that time little known on the continent) called the Legion of Mary, founded in Dublin in September 1921 by an Irish civil servant: Frank Duff. Impressed by what he heard, Bishop Suenens paid six visits to Dublin to study the movement, and was instrumental in having it established in Belgium. Besides this, in 1953 he wrote a biography of Edel Quinn who, in consequence of her work for the Legion, first in Ireland, then in Africa, was acknowledged as the heroine of the movement.

In the dioceses of Nairobi and Dublin the cause of her canonisation has been taken up—indeed the 'process' is under way at Rome with the approval of Pope Paul.

This straightforward, unpretentious biography reflects something of the writer as well as the girl about whom he writes: it is a matter of selection of material, emphasis, or a mere nuance. Courageous himself, yet diffident, Léon Suenens stresses these qualities in Edel Quinn. Setting store, too, by responsibility, he admires the resolution with which this girl made decisions and despite opposition carried them out. The son of a warm-hearted mother, he appreciated the welcome that Edel's family extended to all—including the stray cat she found one night on the quays by the Liffey. He mentions, too, the qualities he likes in the people of Dublin: a sense of the poetic; humour; fun; an awareness of God that does not display itself in platitudes and 'edifying' clichés.

His imagination is stirred by thoughts of the Celtic saints who, setting forth from their wind-lashed, wave-washed island (some of them, legend has it, used no oars, the better to be guided by God's will) founded, far afield, monasteries renowned in later years: Annegray, Luxeuil, Bobbio—two hundred monasteries in all; or, voluntary exiles for God's glory, *propter nomen Domini,* roamed from place to place spreading the Gospel message. He liked Dublin as a city—which is to be expected, since Dublin and Brussels have something in common. Both, despite modern developments, retain an air of faded elegance. Both are cosmopolitan. Again, neither is too large. 'Dublin,' the Cardinal wrote, 'is a capital of the right measure for man; in it one feels neither crushed nor lost.' He liked its spacious parks, gulls circling overhead, and the tang of the sea.

In 1953 Bishop Suenens published a small, closely-packed book *Théologie de l'Apostolat de la Légion de Marie* (in English, *Theology of the Apostolate of the Legion of Mary*) which has been translated into thirty languages—its formidable title sometimes shortened to *Theology of the Apostolate.* A kind of handbook or *vade mecum* for members of the Legion, it contains much that is intended for 'all who work side by side', as the author puts it, 'in the vineyard of the Lord'.

Moreover in a booklet also written by himself, but without mention of his name, he explains what, basically, the Legion is.

A movement within the Church that finds its inspiration in the very heart of the Creed, *au coeur du Credo,* it believes, he says, with the Church and as the Church, that Christ, by the power of the Holy Spirit, was born of Mary, her consent freely given—furthermore that this same Christ continues to be born mystically in our own day, in a like manner, in each one of us.

The spirituality of the Legion, therefore, like so much else that colours the Cardinal's thought, is orientated towards the Holy Spirit.

The Cardinal is aware of certain objections that can be raised against the Legion, particularly in regard to its 'military' vocabulary, as well as expressions in the handbook that are now outmoded. Even before Vatican II he stressed the need for greater collegiality and co-responsibility in the structures of the Legion (particularly at the higher levels of authority)—all the more desirable now that the Legion had become an international movement functioning in five continents. Moreover after Vatican II he said publicly on a number of occasions that an *aggiornamento* of both handbook and structures was needed.

Despite these reservations, Cardinal Suenens remains consistently grateful for the good done by the Legionaries in their numerous activities, as well as for the inspiration he has himself derived from their example of faith and courage. Speaking in praise of Frank Duff, he has called him 'a giant in the field of the lay apostolate'.

To revert to the thinking that is at the heart of *The Theology of* the *Apostolate*. If the reader is not deterred by certain pages written specifically for members of the Legion, he or she will find emerging a theme that not only has relevance for any Christian, but recurs like a refrain through the Cardinal's writings and addresses. It concerns the mutual love that can exist between God and man, and how this relates to the Incarnation.

God is love. From him all things come into being and, in the fullness of time, God will be All in All. God first loved us. And this love, because it has its source in God and is independent of anything we do or fail to do, cannot falter.

The Spirit which in the beginning brooded over the face of the waters—this same Spirit overshadowed Mary. Thus God's love came down upon Mary, and from her, by grace of the Holy Spirit, there went up a response of love. Here, let it be said, is a paradox that' can be resolved only on the plane of faith—in that Mary is at the same time motivated by the Holy Spirit (she is the chosen one, 'full of grace'), yet acting with a freedom that is total.

Thus divine love, in the person of the Holy Spirit, and human love in the person of Mary, meet in Christ, the Word made flesh, who as T. S. Eliot has put it, is:

> The point of intersection of the timeless
> With time,

the God-Man in whom

> the impossible union
> Of spheres of existence is actual.

The union between Mary and the Spirit is the prototype of the union eternally realisable between creature and Creator. Mary's consent was given, St. Thomas Aquinas says, in the name of the entire human race: *loco totius humanae naturae*.

The Cardinal, in emphasising and clarifying this basic truth, anticipates the point stressed in the Conciliar *Dogmatic Constitution on the Church, Lumen Gentium*; namely, that true devotion to the Mother of Christ is of necessity Christo-centric. It is rooted in the Incarnation. It is directed to Mary as the Mother of God, the *Theotokos*: the Mother of the Word become flesh, 'the star', as the Akathistos hymn has so beautifully put it, 'which never more will set'. Devotion to Mary that lacks this solid foundation is sentimental, anaemic. In the Cardinal's words, it wilts, 'like a hothouse plant exposed to a breath of wind', instead of being as 'a tree that, planted near running waters, puts forth its fruit in due season'.

The Cardinal has much to say on the subject of the Blessed Virgin. I could quote from his book *Quelle est Celle-ci?* published in 1957 and translated into English under the title *Mary, Mother of God*. I have, however, confined myself to a few points which are, I believe, likely to be intelligible, if not always acceptable, to many outside the Church of Rome. And this is important. Indeed, relatively few Catholics have any idea of the difficulties presented to non-Catholics, not only by pious traditions and practices associated with Mary but by major doctrines such as the Immaculate Conception and the Assumption. There is, as Vatican II has acknowledged, a hierarchy of truths—that is to say, certain truths, at a given time of history, are not more true, but more important, than others. This being so, it is reasonable to highlight those which, in particular circumstances, are likely to bring people to a closer understanding rather than to set them apart.

As well as two works of somewhat specialised interest—*Que Faut-il Penser de Réarmement?* 1953, (in English, *The Right View of Moral Rearmament*) and *La Question Scolaire,* 1956—Bishop Suenens published in 1956 *L'Eglise en Etat de Mission*. This last (in English, *The Gospel to Every Creature*), described in the introduction by Pope Paul—then Archbishop of Milan—as 'courageous', 'disturbing' and 'optimistic', reveals its writer as a man ahead of his times. Many of the suggestions contained in the book have by now, in the post-Conciliar world, been implemented. When it first appeared it was looked upon in certain quarters as somewhat *avant garde* and consequently received with reservation, even hostility. The chapter concerned with those who are called upon to help the clergy provided the scaffolding for the later: *La Promotion Apostolique de la Religieuse.*

At a first reading, *The Gospel to Every Creature* gives an impression of being written with detachment—as do all the Cardinal's books— rather than personal involvement. It is cool, clearly reasoned. In fact, however, it is very close to its writer in the sense that, while on the one hand it looks back to his childhood determination to spread the Gospel, on the other it looks ahead, touching on ways and means whereby his determination—his dream, if you will—may become a reality. One is aware from time to time of the writer's underlying feeling of frustration because things do not happen more quickly. He observes the indifference and complacency found in the Church, in contrast to the single-minded efficiency and concern shown by

Communists. Christ has bidden us preach the Gospel to every creature—yes, to every human being without exception. This is not being done. Yet it could be done if Christians bestirred themselves; if they shook off their lethargy.

The following passage concerning our obligation to carry out Christ's command is characteristic:

> It may be thought that this command does not concern us, that it was intended only for the Apostles, Christ's immediate hearers. But no—it cuts through time and space, as lightning flashes through clouds; it is intended for the Apostles and for all those who, with them or after them, share their task; it is intended for each of us, to the last among us. How could the Eleven, alone, fulfil such a commission? That there might be no misapprehension the Master added: 'Behold I am with you always.' The Apostles died: their mission lives on in us and it is by our actions that Christ works every day and in every place. Henri Bergson, while still on the threshold of the Church, wrote these words: 'What struck me in Jesus Christ was the order to go forward always; so that one might say that the stable element in Christianity is the command never to halt.' St. John Chrysostom, in his day, was already writing to Christians who tried to escape their duty. 'Go and make disciples of all nations' was not said to the Apostles only, but to us also. The promise does not concern them alone, but all who were to come after—as may be seen by the words that follow: 'even to the consummation of the world'.

Yet to take the first step in spreading the Good News is, in the Cardinal's view, a delicate and complex matter—one that calls for tact, sympathy, and respect for the individual. The Christian must not adopt a role of superiority or condescension. People should feel free to speak to one another openly and sincerely, on an equal footing. There must be friendliness and harmony. Moreover the approach must be gradual. To understand the Cardinal's thinking one would do well to ponder on an incident in *Le Petit Prince* of Antoine de Saint-Exupéry (a writer whom the Cardinal admires), in which the fox asks the Little Prince to tame him, so that the two may be friends—explaining how this must be done gently, gradually: the Little Prince must come every day, wait quietly, draw a little closer each time.

Only in such an atmosphere of courtesy, gentleness, and mutual respect can the Gospel message be spread—only then, as the Cardinal says, will 'the petals of the flower folded in the darkness of the night open in response to the rays of the sun.

Yes, this is the normal pattern. But the Spirit blows where it will. St. Paul's conversion on the road to Damascus was sudden. Let us not imagine, the Cardinal would have us understand, that it is within our power to bring others to God. All we can do is to surrender ourselves to the guidance of the Holy Spirit. We are but unprofitable servants. It is he alone who does all: he alone who can bring our feeble efforts to fruition.

During the latter part of his time as Auxiliary Bishop of Malines Léon Suenens was working on *La Promotion Apostolique de la Religieuse*, published in 1962. The title of the English edition *The Nun in the World* (it was not the author's choice), does not convey the basic message of the book.

Writing for religious engaged in active work—not for contemplatives—he stresses that prayer and the apostolate are inseparable. Activity is not a substitute for prayer. Prayer is essential, but, instead of following rigidly a pattern intended for Contemplative Orders, it should be adapted to the needs of society as it is today.

Further, customs that are outmoded and restrictive should be abandoned. Superiors should cease to foster an infantile attitude in the Sisters and, instead, encourage them to accept responsibility and to give a lead.

The book represents findings that resulted from experimentation carried out in certain Belgian convents, but the programme, planned with a view to spiritual and apostolic renewal, attracted attention far afield.

A twofold process was in fact at work. The renewal initiated by Bishop Suenens anticipated the ideas advocated in his book, while the book, which was translated into seven languages, spread the ideas. A copy of the book was sent to each Father participating in the Council.

Today there is nothing startling about the book, but in 1962 it was revolutionary.

Some nuns welcomed the proposals: they felt that in the author they had found a spokesman—someone, too, prepared to treat them as adults: responsible human beings capable of making their own decisions. They felt liberated and believed that the religious life presented in these terms had a future.

Not all, however, were equally enthusiastic. Many needed to be 'goaded on'. In 1964 Léon Suenens, now a Cardinal, when addressing in Boston 5,000 Sisters at the invitation of Cardinal Cushing, said to them: 'Don't leave one poor Cardinal to do all the fighting for you on his own! It's *your* battle!'

He had reason to speak in this way. There were many who feared change; who felt their security was threatened. They had no wish for responsibility. It was easier to say: 'Yes, Reverend Mother' or 'No, Reverend Mother'. Had they not taken a vow of obedience?

Some Superiors took pains to encourage in their convents a responsible, mature attitude. Others, even in the diocese of Malines, forbade their nuns to read a book which would have, they said, a disruptive influence.

A story which circulated during the Council, especially at the Bar Jonah where the Bishops used to meet informally, concerns a self-important, extremely conservative Mother-General who, in an audience with the Pope, told him the wonderful things her congregation was doing.

His Holiness, apparently impressed, said to her: 'And what can I do, Mother-General, that would please you?'

She thought a moment, then replied: 'Well, Holy Father, couldn't you give me on a silver salver . . . the head of Cardinal Suenens?'

Some complain that the Cardinal lives in 'a world of concepts and ideas'—that he does not come down to the level of ordinary persons.

This is not, in fact, true. It is not to his taste to remain for any great length of time on the purely intellectual, abstract plane, where some derive pleasure from 'playing' with ideas for the sheer 'fun of the thing'.

In him, one might say, intellectualism and a down-to-earth realism 'rub shoulders'. As an intellectual he sees at once the logical implications of a situation or problem. But in transmitting his conclusions into practice his approach is predominantly realistic, pastoral. He finds unfailing inspiration in the saying of Jesus: 'My words are spirit and life.' He is not, he admits, totally at ease with psychologically complicated persons. Indeed he is only completely himself with those who are open in mind and heart.

As to his not coming down to 'the level of ordinary persons', he is not confronted, it is true, as are vast numbers of men the world over, with the day-to-day problem of how to earn a livelihood, how to support a family. He is well aware of this, and it is one of the reasons why he chooses to live simply. There is no pomp, no ostentation, no luxury. He does not smoke. He rarely drinks. He eats sparingly.

The problems of social justice, the obligation of the privileged to help the underprivileged—these for him are concerns of paramount importance which occupy him on the level not only of nations but families. He has not forgotten a childhood which though happy—thanks to his mother's courage, cheerfulness and good sense—was nevertheless passed in circumstances so straitened that basic needs, such as heating and lighting, presented a financial problem. Possibly, warm memories of the home that his mother, despite difficulties, made for him, coupled, it may be, with a nostalgia, at some hidden level of his consciousness, for the father he scarcely remembers, have contributed to his preoccupation with family life.

This has found expression in different ways. When, as Auxiliary Bishop of Malines he represented Cardinal van Roey at the Brussels Health Congress in 1958, he made an appeal before an audience of over 3,000 members of the medical profession—doctors and others engaged in research—to make a concentrated effort to resolve the problem of birth-control.

Bearing in mind the traditional teaching of the Church and emphasising in that context, the responsibility of Catholic doctors, he said:

'We have not the right to ask people to keep the law [of the Church], unless we do at the same time all that is in our power to make this obedience possible. There are sins of inertia and intellectual sloth which on the day of judgment will weigh far more heavily than any sin of frailty.'

To this appeal, doctors, professors, and scientists from a wide variety of countries, inspired by the Cardinal's concern for family life, reacted favourably. A year later, in May 1959, an international symposium concerned with problems of conjugal morality was established at Louvain and has assembled there every year since. Moreover this initiative led to founding at Louvain, as part of the *Institut Universitaire des Sciences Familiales et Sexologiques*, the *Centre International Cardinal Suenens*.

The Cardinal's interest in family life is reflected in *Vie Quotidienne, Vie Chrétienne*, a series of talks given on the radio during the later years of his bishopric and published, 1961, in book form—in English under the title *The Christian Life Day by Day*.

The theme that holds the book together is love: divine and human. The Jewish philosopher, the late Martin Buber, in his beautiful study *I and Thou*, makes the point that Jesus loved each individual in a different way: his feeling for the man possessed by the devil, Buber says, differs from his feeling for the Beloved Disciple; yet the love which is the source of these feelings is one and the same. The Cardinal, developing this, distinguishes between the love of Jesus for each of his Apostles; for the woman of Samaria; for Nathaniel, when he sees him afar off, under the fig tree; for Mary Magdalene weeping in the garden by the empty tomb. But his book is specially concerned with love in the context of the family: between husband and wife; brothers and sisters; parents and children.

Moreover he quotes the findings, arrived at under the guidance of psychologists, of a survey made to ascertain what children want from their mothers and fathers. The following, addressed to parents, are based on the children's reactions which were more or less unanimous:

1. Don't quarrel in front of your children.
2. Show the same degree of affection to each one of them.
3. Don't lie to a child.
4. Parents, be nice to each other!
5. Let there be a sense of comradeship between parents and children.
6. Give your children's friends the same welcome you would give to your own.
7. Don't scold or punish a child in the presence of other children.
8. Draw attention to your children's good points. Don't emphasise their faults.
9. Always answer their questions.
10. Show them that they can rely upon your good humour and affection.

What peace and happiness there would be, the Cardinal comments, if adults could live up to the expectations—and the logic—of their children, who consciously or unconsciously are always watching their parents and passing judgment!

Again in his book *Un Problème Crucial: Amour et Maîtrise de Soi* (1961), in English *Love and Control,* the Cardinal dwells on what it means for children to grow up in a happy home: in an atmosphere of love, harmony, and gentleness. The relationship between parents 'as it appears to the watchful eyes of their adolescent children is nothing less than an object lesson, and one of over-riding importance'.

If the relationship is a happy one, he continues, the children will carry this picture in their hearts all their lives. For them love will mean to live in harmony and an affection that all can see.

The Cardinal's belief in the reality of the love that can unite the hearts of two persons joined by the bond of wedlock becomes apparent in unexpected ways.

There is the anecdote he tells about King Beaudouin and Queen Fabiola.

One day the King came to Malines to open an exhibition. The Cardinal walking at his side through the streets heard the crowds calling out, again and again, not 'Long live the King!', as he expected, but 'Long live the Queen!'.

When he expressed surprise the King explained that this often happened. 'On one such occasion', the King continued, 'a man said to me: "Do you know, Sir, why we call 'Long live the Queen!'?" not "Long live the King!"? It's because we think this gives you greater pleasure'.

Some months later, when the Cardinal mentioned to the Queen what had happened at Malines, she replied: 'Do you know what happened to *me* in a village where I was visiting sick children? A woman said to me "Your Majesty, do you know why we love you so much? It's because you make the King happy!".'

I remember, also, at Brussels Airport during a wait for a flight, a conversation I had with a young husband and wife from near Louvain.

Speaking of the Primate of Belgium with sudden warmth the young man said: 'The Cardinal is the Bishop of Bekkers of our country!'

For a moment I did not know what he meant. To me, Wilhelmus Bekkers, Bishop of Den Bosch in southern Holland, evokes a much-liked prelate of rustic stock who, immediately on reaching his parents' home, used to go out into the fields to see how the crops and the cattle were doing; and who, until shortly before his death in 1966, liked to ride through his diocese on a favourite horse. Then I recalled a phrase applied to him in Holland: 'The bishop of the married couples.'

'Cardinal Suenens', the young man went on, glancing at his wife, 'genuinely cares about people like ourselves. He *believes* in human love—and you can't say that of every cleric!'

Moreover at the close of his book *Love and Control* the Cardinal tells how he came to write some verses for two young friends of his who were to be married.

'It was at the end of a flight home: the lights of the capital shone in the darkness below like a huge Milky Way come down from the sky. Every house, every room on every floor—all contributed their dots of light: it was like a procession of motionless torches. I thought of the young couple, friends of mine, who were soon to be married and who would soon have their light that shines in the dark, a light to bring out from under a bushel. On landing, I wrote these lines for them in the hope that the words may bring to every home the eternal message of happiness and love, happiness in the love which is at the heart of Christianity.

Coming in to land,
look down on a town.
What better way of seeing men and things
in their true dimension?
Consider the meaning of each house below,
the secret of each small flat.

What's a house?
Roof and four walls
for a family,
which enclose in poverty or luxury
the unchanging reality
of the family.

What's a family?
Convergence of two loves,
a young man and girl meeting one day
after a thousand mysterious chances
which we call Providence.
I love you:
these were the simple words
they spoke.
There are no others,
they're the same in all tongues,
poor and rich say them alike—
for once on this earth absolute equality.

Why did these two meet?
Who's to say?
Wishing to appear a creature of reason
man will give himself reasons,

inventing reasons for loving
which he tells to himself and his friends,
if they'll listen—
reasons they don't really believe
and wisely too.
A woman explains nothing.
She loves because she loves, that's all.
Her love wavers less,
not resting on the logic
of doubtful reasons.

From these two loves a home is born,
a hearth where two flames burn as one,
inextinguishable in the wind.
This single flame will one day light another flame
and then another.
A home is like a grotto at Lourdes,
many tiny candles round a large one
protecting them.

This flame is love,
every candle a new source of love.
This flame is in the image of God,
for God is love.
And the real things that happen in life
in each of these houses winking in the dark
are those which touch this living flame.
Man is made only for that—
and woman also
and their children
and the children of these children.
To keep God's love
they have but fragile vessels
and the secret of keeping it lies
in spreading this love to others.

To keep love
we must keep it as we do our soul,
that is: give it,
lose it
in the souls of others

who will thrive then on this gift
for time and for eternity.
Love does not die
since God does not die,
and it is God who loves
in the heart of man.

Part II

CHAPTER 5

'There was a man sent from God whose name was John'

ST. JOHN 1:6.

THERE IS A photograph—it stands out from others taken on the same day—showing Léon Suenens making obeisance to Pope John on March 19th 1962, when he became Cardinal, just three months after he was consecrated Archbishop of Malines-Brussels.

The two men are smiling at each other. It is not the artificial, embarrassed smile at times assumed perforce by those participating in some ceremonial occasion: it is a warm smile of friendship, genuine, spontaneous.

But what was there in common between the Pope, then in his late seventies, and the Cardinal aged fifty-eight—the one nearing the end of his life; the other entering upon the most important stage in his ecclesiastical calling? It is difficult, perhaps impossible, to analyse the bond that unites two human beings. One can say there is a rapport. *Cor cordi loquitur.* And that is about all. Yet, in this instance, there are, I believe, points worth reflecting upon.

There was no question of there being between these two what has come to be called—to use a tiresome cliché—a 'generation gap'. Pope John was old in years; old-fashioned, too, in certain of his attitudes and pious practices, but he was young in heart, open in mind, resilient, shrewd, and remarkable in his capacity to appraise the modern world—the demands being made, consciously and unconsciously, upon the Church of Rome, not only by Christians of various denominations, but also by those whose ideologies are based on a philosophy of atheistic determinism.

The Cardinal, on his side—as he had shown by his writings and his actions during his years as Auxiliary Bishop of Malines—was no less aware than was the Pope of the needs of the world and the role required of the Church.

F

Again, the Cardinal since childhood was used to the company of persons older than himself, which probably contributed to the fact that he was a good listener. He had a way (he still has) of listening with a deep, at times an almost tense, concentration; then all of a sudden his face lights up into a smile.

This gave pleasure to Pope John. He appreciated having an intelligent, sympathetic listener, whose thinking, while in line with his own, was quicker, more intellectual, and more sophisticated. He also liked a smiling face: there were times when he felt weighed down by the solemnity, the gloom, not to mention the disapproval, which he encountered in Vatican circles. He liked openness, an honest expression of opinion, a natural approach. Once, the Cardinal, absorbed in what His Holiness was saying and forgetting that it was not for him to interrupt the Pope, broke in with some comment. Pope John smiled with characteristic serenity. 'You're quite right to cut me short,' he said. 'I talk too much!'

Both valued truth on every level. And by this I mean not only abstract and doctrinal truth, and what we call 'speaking the truth'. I mean, also, an acknowledgment by each, in all simplicity and indeed gratitude, of his humble origins.

Among some of the most moving passages in Roman literature are those in which the poet Horace, raised to high estate from lowly beginnings, *ex humili potens,* reverts to the debt he owes to his slave-born father. Enjoying the patronage, indeed the friendship, of the Emperor Augustus and the Emperor's adviser Maecenas, he takes pleasure in recalling the father to whose selfless efforts he is indebted, not only for the best education available, but also, he says, for any good qualities that are his. Men of lesser calibre, when filling high positions, are prone, if they are of humble birth, to attempt to conceal the fact; or to boast of how they have triumphed over unfavourable circumstances.

Pope John took pride in his beloved Roncallis—their stalwart virtues bred of poverty, hardship, a simple life and a simple faith. In a letter to his mother he tells her that he praises his family to everyone and hopes their qualities will be perpetuated. And to his brother Severio he says: 'Go on loving one another, all you Roncallis.' He wanted to be remembered, as was Pius X, as the Pope who was 'born poor and died poor'. The Cardinal, equally, makes no secret of the hardships of his childhood and the magnitude of the debt he owes to his understanding, selfless mother.

But the closest bond uniting Pope John and the Cardinal was an attitude towards the Church which each was quick to recognise in the other. Each loved the Church—not as a human institution existing for its own sake, its self-glorification, but as the means, established by Christ, to spread throughout the world, to all without exception, the Gospel's saving message of hope and joy. Each realised, independently of the other, that the Church, (though it is the Mystical Body of Christ) is in the world and consequently at the mercy of men with the frailties of such—and yet, never totally at their mercy, in that Christ has promised that to the end of time the Holy Spirit will be with the Church. And each realised that this truth, reassuring though it is, must not be used as an excuse for men to adopt an attitude of passivity, sit back and do nothing or a minimum.

Everyone, I suppose, is familiar with the story of how Pope John, to explain the purpose of the Second Vatican Council, threw open the window and said: 'We must let in fresh air.' This was precisely what Léon Suenens had been trying to do on another level, when he was Auxiliary Bishop of Malines—to throw open windows, let in fresh air where the atmosphere in the Church had become stifling.

Yes, these two men, before they worked together in the period immediately preceding the opening of the Second Vatican Council, and then during the First Session, had already been moving, each in his own way, in the same direction: or, to use a different metaphor, each had been preparing the soil, so that, when the time came, the two were ready to work together in a spirit of openness, harmony, and mutual respect.

It was towards the end of 1958 that Pope John decided to hold an Ecumenical Council. He was talking one day to his Secretary of State, the late Cardinal Tardini, when he mentioned for the first time what he called his 'inspiration'.

A month or so later, after a Mass for Church Unity celebrated at the Benedictine monastery adjoining the basilica of St. Paul Outside the Walls, the Pope, without warning, reverted to the subject. Having announced to the eighteen Cardinals present that it was his intention to hold a Council, he went on: 'I would like your advice.'

His words were received in stony silence.

Pope John later admitted his disappointment. 'I thought,' he said, 'that at least some of those present would have come up to me, if only to give me their good wishes.' Even so, he was deflected from his purpose neither by this chilly reception nor, in the months that followed, by the reiterated forebodings, to which he refers in his opening speech to the Council, delivered on October 11th 1962, in which he dissociates himself from 'those prophets of gloom, always forecasting disaster, as though the end of the world were at hand'.

While never wavering in his determination, the Pope, nevertheless, was at times bewildered by the magnitude of the task before him— after all, he was an old man; nor was there anyone with first-hand knowledge who could advise him how to set about preparing for a Council. Moreover, having asked for the views of bishops from all over the world, he had accumulated if not a mass of suggestions certainly a daunting amount of paper. The answers, indeed, sent by the bishops filled seventeen volumes, from which emerged seventy-two preparatory schemata touching on all manner of subjects without order or plan.

Already when he was Auxiliary Bishop of Malines Cardinal Suenens had been named by Pope John as a member of the Preparatory Commission which was to formulate other Preparatory Commissions, in which he explained and confirmed ideas expressed in his book *The Gospel to Every Creature*. Then, a few days after his elevation to the Cardinalate, the Pope appointed him to the Central Commission.

As a member of the Preparatory Commission concerned with the reform of dioceses he had made many journeys to Rome, but now the visits were more frequent, the stays longer. Hence the growth of an increasingly closer relationship between himself and Pope John.

While the Cardinal was a member of the Central Commission, an incident occurred which highlights two of his qualities: his courage and his sensitivity. As a gesture of sincerity, in the context of the renewal of the Church, he decided to make a formal proposal that an age-limit be set for the retirement of Cardinals and Bishops. He knew that in doing this he would lose favour among many of his fellow bishops. He knew his move was neither prudent nor diplomatic. Even so, he was undeterred, and the proposition was put to the vote.

The Cardinals rejected it, one and all. Only a very few bishops and archbishops gave a *placet* or vote of approval—the first to do so being Archbishop Hurley of Durban.

The sitting was followed by the customary break for coffee.

No one came up to the Cardinal.

He stood there, alone. Had he ever, he wondered, felt so alone? At times of deeply-felt emotion something trivial in itself can make its impact upon the consciousness with an extraordinary vividness. It can happen at a moment of crisis between two lovers, so that years afterwards the woman—or the man—will associate that moment with, perhaps, a wild rose in a hedgerow; stars glimpsed through naked branches; a pattern engraved on a wine-glass. But this heightened awareness can be experienced by anyone of sensitivity when exposed to circumstances that are in the nature of a shock.

The Cardinal was not aware of a rose, or stars, or an engraving on a wine-glass. He was aware of the spoon that he was turning round and round in his cup as he stood there, alone.

But if in making this proposal Cardinal Suenens had incurred disfavour among his colleagues, his relationship with the Pope, day by day, grew closer.

Pope John had been greatly pleased by a pastoral letter that the Cardinal delivered in his diocese in Lent 1962, on the subject of the Council: it expressed, the Pope said, just what he himself felt. And so he asked the Cardinal to give him an answer in writing to the question: 'How do you view the Council? What plan should it follow?' The Cardinal replied, in the first instance, by stating what, in his opinion, a Council should *not* be.

Then, when the Pope had intimated how completely in accord with his own views was this statement of what the Council should avoid, the Cardinal went on to develop in outline for the Holy Father the form the Council should take.

According to this proposal, the Council should gravitate round the theme of the Church. The Church should be considered in the light of a twofold perspective. First it should be viewed from within (*ad intra*) that is, in relation to, and in dialogue with, its members collectively and individually; secondly, from without (*ad extra*) in relation to, and in dialogue with, all Christians throughout the world, and finally with all human beings, without exception, regardless of their religious beliefs.

Pope John warmly approved this proposal to which he alluded in discreet terms in an address given in September 1962, a month before the opening of the Council.

The ideas put forward by Cardinal Suenens were to prove of outstanding importance. They were, in fact, the seeds from which—after a long passage of time, much arguing, much controversy, many alterations, and many amendments—there finally emerged two of the major documents of the Second Vatican Council.

The first, promulgated by Pope Paul on November 21st 1964, was the *Dogmatic Constitution on the Church*—more commonly known as *De Ecclesia* or *Lumen Gentium*—the latter being the opening words of the document, and the word *Lumen* referring to Christ the Light of the World. The second, promulgated on December 7th 1965, was the *Constitution on the Church in the Modern World* or, to use its opening words, *Gaudium et Spes*.

The Second Vatican Council opened on October 11th 1962. The procedure was at first somewhat haphazard, if not chaotic. There was no set plan as to the order in which subjects were to be treated. It was only little by little that a pattern began to emerge. A debate on the *Liturgy, Sacrosanctum Concilium,* begun on October 22nd, was followed on November 14th by one dealing with Revelation, *Dei Verbum*, in the course of which Cardinal Suenens—as well as Cardinal Léger of Montreal, Cardinal König of Vienna, and Cardinal Alfrink of Utrecht—protested against the schema as being a 'patched-up affair,' without relevance to the problems of the day.

Cardinal Suenens made the further point that, if a limit were not set to airing views, the Council would outlast the eighteen years expended on the Council of Trent. To save time, he suggested dispensing with such flowery addresses as 'Your Eminence,' 'Your Grace', 'Your Beatitude', and the like. Incidentally, he is remembered as the first speaker to raise a laugh in the Council.

He wanted to forge ahead, not dwell on platitudes and irrelevancies. According to an observer, Cardinal Suenens was able to say more in five minutes than some speakers in half an hour.

The protest against the schema *Dei Verbum* was supported with a resounding '*reiciendum est*' from Cardinal Ritter, Archbishop of St. Louis, as well as by the much-respected Cardinal Bea, who emphasised that it was the Pope's wish that the faith be presented to the world as a message of hope and loving-kindness.

Maximos IV Saigh, Melchite Patriarch of Antioch, stressed the need from the Church of a 'peaceful, positive message,' one 'worthy of the attention of our separated brethren'.

Eighty-four years old, the Patriarch was one of the most colourful, outspoken figures at the Council. Moreover he made interventions in French. In the debate on the liturgy he pointed out that Greek, not Latin, was the language of the Eastern Churches—which led to his further observation that the Greek language had been used by the Roman Church up to the third century, when it gave place to Latin simply because by then Latin had become the normal language of the faithful. He also reminded his hearers that the first sacrifice of the

Eucharist was offered in Aramaic, the language used by Christ and the disciples.

The Patriarch had further demonstrated his independence by absenting himself from the inaugural procession on the day the Council opened, thus drawing attention to a long-standing grievance (one that has since, at least in part, been resolved) whereby Oriental Patriarchs, since the fifteenth century, have ranked below Cardinals, whereas up to then they had come immediately after the Pope.

Cardinal Suenens admired the Patriarch for his fearlessness, his openness, his desire that the Gospel should be spread without distortion. But apart from that, the Cardinal has an affinity with the Eastern Churches (he speaks of them as 'the absent half of ourselves') which goes back to his friendship, as a seminarian, with the ecumenist Dom Lambert Beauduin. He appreciates the mystic quality of the Eastern Churches: the liturgy centred on Easter; a warm devotion to Christ's mother that has a firm, theological foundation; an understanding of the Holy Spirit.

In his book, *Co-responsibility in the Church* (published in 1968), he quotes words of Maximos IV spoken with reference to the Council: 'The Holy Spirit has opened doors which will never again be closed.' The Cardinal also recalls how moved he himself had been by the Chair of Peter, at the end of the *aula,* supported by carved figures of two Latin and two Greek Fathers: St. Augustine and St. Ambrose; St. Athanasius and St. John Chrysostom.

In the debate on Communication, *Inter Mirifica,* which began on November 23rd 1962, Cardinal Suenens came out with practical suggestions to the effect that, on the ecclesiastical level, a clear-cut ethos should be laid down equivalent to that governing legal and medical procedure. He urged, too, that time allotted on radio and television to religious subjects should not be wasted on the trite and banal.

The all-important debate on the Church, *De Ecclesia,* opened on December 1st 1962 with a defence of the preparatory schema by Cardinal Ottaviani. But from the beginning it was evident that the schema, as presented, would be rejected by the majority of the Fathers as too juridical, too abstract, too scholastic.

Bishop de Smedt of Bruges found it offensive in its clericalism. The Church, he said, is not a pyramid comprising Pope, priests, and laity: it is the People of God. He complained that the document smacked of triumphalism—its pompous language reminiscent of

L'Osservatore Romano: the Church was depicted as an army arrayed for battle rather than the sheepfold of which Christ speaks.

The debate was indeed making heavy weather when on December 4th Cardinal Suenens took a stand, making a clear-cut proposal that the schema *De Ecclesia* should be drafted afresh.

As the First Vatican Council had been, he said, the Council of papal primacy, Vatican II should be the Council of the Church of Christ, the light of nations: *Lumen Gentium*. In accordance with the wish of Pope John, the Church must question itself, examine itself: 'Church of Christ, what have you to say about yourself?' *Ecclesia, quid dicis de te ipso?* But it must look in two directions: within (*ad intra*) and outside (*ad extra*).

The mission of the Church, the Cardinal continued, was to search out and serve not only those within its fold, but the world at large. It was called upon to concern itself with problems at every level— not simply man's individual relationship with God, but problems posed by peace, war, justice, injustice, power, wealth, hunger, poverty, over-population. Summing up, he said that this involved a triple dialogue: with the faithful; with our separated brethren; with the non-Christian world.

So loud was the applause greeting the Cardinal's words that silence had to be restored.

On the following day Cardinal Montini, Archbishop of Milan, spoke in support of the proposals made by Cardinal Suenens. The Church, he said, was not so much a society founded by Christ—it was, rather, Christ himself using mankind to bring salvation to the world. The less we insisted on the rights of the Church, the greater likelihood there was of our being heard, especially in parts of the world where the Church was viewed with suspicion as being a colonial-minded, paternalistic institution. The scheme, as Cardinal Suenens had said, should be redrafted. Cardinal Montini spoke of the need, also, to give expression to the will and mind of Christ by emphasising and clarifying the collegiality of the bishops, as well as by establishing a truly ecumenical spirit.

The Archbishop of Milan's intervention in support of Cardinal Suenens was all the more important because it was common knowledge that this discreet, somewhat silent prelate would not have spoken with such vehemence had he not, in doing so, been expressing not only his own thoughts but those of the Pope.

Then, on December 6th, Cardinal Lercaro of Bologna, conveying his strong support of both Suenens and Montini, spoke of 'the Church of the Poor', exhorting, as had Pope John in his opening discourse, those who belonged to the Church to follow faithfully in the steps of Christ who, stripping himself of all things, had for our sakes chosen on earth a life of poverty.

A shadow was cast upon the last weeks of 1962 by the recurring illness of Pope John. Yet, ill though he was, he had read in advance, and warmly approved, the intervention made by Cardinal Suenens on December 4th. He had even written in the margin some pencilled notes which were included in the final text.

Throughout the Council Pope John had created among the non-Catholic observers an atmosphere of confidence and goodwill. An Orthodox lay theologian said the Pope had treated him and his associates as brothers, without any attempt to force them into submission or water down the Catholic position as to the papacy. 'This', the theologian added, 'I call true diplomacy—a Christian diplomacy made up of goodness, patience, and theological competence.' Moreover the Pope endeared himself to non-Catholic visitors by sitting among them, as though he were one of themselves.

The Pope had shown that he was the friend of all, and his aspirations world-wide. Before the opening of the Council he said that Catholics must not behave as if the Church were a museum filled with antiques. The Church was for here and now. As well as belonging to yesterday it belonged to today and tomorrow. And it was for the entire world. Truth, he stressed, must be presented in a way that would be intelligible to modern man. In saying this, he was thinking in particular of scientists, scholars, men in the world of industry—all, indeed, who are responsible for the progress of man. Moreover, the Pope's gesture in receiving Alexei Adjoubey, son-in-law of Krushchev, had far-reaching repercussions. The Soviet *Literary Gazette* and *Tass* conceded that the world-wide interest in the Council was indeed justified. They also commended Pope John for his 'unequivocal appeals' for peace.

It is small wonder, therefore, that, when an atmosphere such as this had been built up within the brief years of John's pontificate, not only genuine distress but also unease were felt both in Rome and far beyond, as one report following upon another revealed that the Pope had not long to live.

Cardinal Suenens saw Pope John for the last time towards the end of January 1963. It was an unexpected, informal meeting.

The Cardinal and Don Capovilla, Pope John's private secretary were together in St. Peter's one day, when the secretary asked the Cardinal if he would come up with him to his office: he had, he said, a small gift for him from the Pope.

It was a signed photograph, taken a few days before in the Pope's study, showing the Cardinal kneeling in front of Pope John, kissing his ring—for Cardinal Suenens had forgotten for a moment that, unlike the rest of the faithful, Cardinals do not kneel before the Pope!

The Cardinal, who was unaware that the photograph had been taken, thanked the secretary and was on the point of leaving when Don Capovilla said with a smile: 'If you'd like to know what the Pope thinks of the photo have a look at the back!'

The Cardinal did so. He saw in the Pope's handwriting *Non placet mihi*. ('I don't approve.')

Then the secretary gave the Cardinal a little note in which His Holiness protested in warm, affectionate terms that the Cardinal should not have been kneeling!

Cardinal Suenens asked Don Capovilla to thank the Pope on his behalf. The secretary, however, suggested that Suenens should himself thank Pope John. Whereupon he opened a door and the Cardinal found himself face to face with Pope John sitting up in his bedroom, in a chair, wearing his dressing-gown and slippers.

At the sight of his visitor the Pope's face lit up. Pope John kept his friend for nearly two hours. He showed him the pictures in his room, giving a little 'commentary' on each.

Shortly after this Cardinal Suenens returned to his diocese.

His association with the Pope had not, however, come to an end. On Holy Thursday, April 11th 1963, in the fifth year of his pontificate, Pope John gave to the world what one might call his 'last will and testament': his encyclical, *Pacem in Terris,* which, unlike many encyclicals, is a simple, human document, neither dull nor platitudinous, speaking in a language intelligible to men of our time.

Furthermore he asked that Cardinal Suenens, acting as his emissary, should in person present the encyclical to the Secretary of the United Nations, in New York.

The Cardinal looks back on this as one of the most moving occasions in his life—not simply because of the importance of the mission, but because Pope John had himself conferred this honour upon him.

On May 13th 1963 he handed the encyclical to U Thant at the

United Nations, New York, and afterwards addressed a thronged assembly for approximately an hour.

These are some of the points he made:

The encyclical is unique in that, as well as being addressed to five hundred million Catholics 'whose beloved shepherd is the successor to St. Peter', it is an 'open letter' to the world—to all men of goodwill.

Born of trust in God, it speaks of trust in man—in all that is best in man.

Compared to Beethoven's Ninth Symphony, it has been called 'a symphony of peace'.

Its theme is peace, and peace calls for:

Truth as its foundation.

Justice as its rule.

Love as its driving force.

Freedom as its setting.

Peace demands respect for the individual. The Cardinal quotes Antoine de Sainte-Exupéry:

'If respect for man dwells within our hearts we can devise a social, political, and economic system which will enshrine that respect.'

Peace begins in the mind, but it must spread in concentric circles to the limits of the universe.

No person of goodwill can be resigned to the fact that two out of three human beings live in a condition of undernourishment. Civilisation is not worthy of the name if it is indifferent to this collective social sin.

We are far removed from mutual understanding and a true spirit of friendship. We pass one another by, hurried and preoccupied, without so much as a handshake, a word, a smile.

Our century has discovered interplanetary space, but it has scarcely begun to explore the space which separates us from one another. It has built gigantic bridges across rivers, but it has not yet learnt to bridge the gap that separates people from people. Our century has discovered nuclear energy, but it has not discovered the creative energy of peace and concord.

In bestowing this testament of peace, the Cardinal concluded, John XXIII has one aim, one desire: to make the world a better place to live in.

After his address the Cardinal faced a barrage of questions.

Asked whether he believed that women have a role to fill in working for world peace, he quoted Lenin's words: 'Revolution without women is unthinkable.' 'If women,' the Cardinal went on, 'are necessary for a revolution to succeed, they are necessary for the establishment of peace. Women of the world, we need you!'

In reply to the question: 'Does Pope John bless Communism?' the Cardinal said: 'As a doctrine, Communism, from the Christian point of view, is unacceptable and as a movement it is, of necessity, influenced to a lesser or greater degree by its teaching. Persons are quite another matter. Persons are always deserving of respect and have a value far above the views they hold, and Pope John would be happy to bless *any* sincere human being!'

The Cardinal found pleasure in learning how much Pope John was admired and loved in the United States; and was glad to have the opportunity of making the Pope's thinking better known. He welcomed, too, the chance of renewing in the States friendships he had already made among Episcopalians, other Protestants, and members of the Orthodox churches. He was also able to make fresh contacts.

To appreciate what this mission meant to the Cardinal, to appreciate what he is doing in the world today, we must remind ourselves—for this is too easily forgotten—that, like Cardinal Mercier, Léon Suenens, as well as being Primate of Belgium, is a universal figure. He cares deeply about his diocese—especially in the matter of implementing on the local level the directives of Vatican II. Yet his aspirations extend beyond the confines of any diocese. And paradoxically, because this is so, he is able to enrich his diocese to a degree that would not otherwise have been possible.

I have said this before. And I offer no apology for saying it again. I have taken to heart the advice of the late Cecil Day Lewis, Poet Laureate, novelist, and director in a firm of publishers. 'Don't be afraid to repeat yourself,' he told me when reading a typescript of mine. 'Half the readers *don't* read! They skim the pages. If you want something to sink in, *repeat* it—in different words if you like, but *repeat* it!'

There are, and always have been, persons who, if they are to make full use of their gifts; if they are not to be as birds whose wings have been clipped, cannot be confined to one locality. It is not difficult to single out instances where Providence has seen fit that such persons should live on two levels: the local and the universal.

It would be absurd to draw a close parallel between a sixteenth-century Carmelite nun and the present Primate of Belgium. Even so, there is a point worth making.

St. Teresa of Avila—a saint whom the Cardinal admires for her common sense and her humour—when planning her reform of the Carmelite Order, visualised herself as spending her life in contemplative prayer within the walls of St. Joseph's, the small convent in Avila, that was her first foundation.

In fact, without neglecting St. Joseph's, without neglecting her life of prayer, she travelled distances that, in her day, were stupendous, braving storms, snow, floods, drought, robbers—not to mention filthy inns—making friends and acquaintances who ranged from King Philip II to the lowliest muleteer. The Papal Nuncio was only one of those who berated her, calling her a 'restless, disobedient, contumacious gadabout' and much else besides.

Yet she would have wilted had she been confined her life long within the four walls of a convent—and Providence foresaw it. Equally, the Cardinal's gifts would be stunted if he never set foot outside his diocese—and the diocese would be the poorer.

Soon after the Cardinal's return from the United States, Pope John died. It was the evening of June 3rd 1963, the Monday of Pentecost.

John Moorman, Anglican Bishop of Ripon, in his book *Vatican Observed,* recalls how, on going one day into St. Peter's just a month before the Pope's death, he saw a group of crippled children near the High Altar. Presently the Pope was brought in on the *sedia gestatoria.* He spoke to the children, the Bishop relates, in a clear firm voice, but afterwards, as he was taken away, looked pale and tired. A student from Trinity College, Dublin, also in St. Peter's on that day, remembers how Pope John, smiling at the children, said something which amused them: they laughed in response, and a little girl clapped her hands.

Pope John XXIII was mourned the world over. In the words of Cardinal Suenens: 'He was mourned as a dearly loved father is mourned by his children.'

CHAPTER 6

'We must have a living, serene
faith in the Holy Spirit working
within the Church yesterday, today,
and tomorrow.'

LÉON-JOSEPH CARDINAL SUENENS

POPE JOHN was mourned by rich and poor, old and young, intellectuals and simple persons. He was mourned by those who had worked with him side by side; those who had served him in high places or in some humble capacity; by those who saw him daily close at hand and those who knew him from television or radio or photographs in the press. It was as if a light had gone out, as if a star had set. There were, it is true, those who, though they probably did not acknowledge it even to themselves, felt a certain relief that Providence had thought fit to call to his rest this well-intentioned yet tiresome old man who in the brief span of four and a half years had turned everything upside down: now that he was out of the way, things, it was to be hoped, would revert to normal.

But what is done cannot always be undone.

Less than three weeks after John XXIII died, Cardinal Montini, Archbishop of Milan, was elected to the papacy. He took the name Paul VI. The next day he made public his intention that the Ecumenical Council would go on in the spirit in which it had begun under his predecessor. On the following day he appeared on the balcony outside the window of his library. With him was Cardinal Suenens, whom he introduced to the cheering crowds in the piazza below. On the Pope's part it was a spontaneous gesture of friendship, and the Cardinal appreciated it as such. Apart from that, the Cardinal makes light of the incident. 'I just happened to be with the Pope,' he says, 'so he made me come out with him.'

But the occasion caught people's imagination. They talk of it to this day. Moreover at the time it had particular significance for those who recalled how, in Pope John's lifetime, when the schema *De Ecclesia* was being debated in the First Session of the Council, the then Archbishop of Milan had given unqualified approval to proposals made by the Cardinal Suenens.

On September 15th 1963, two weeks before the opening of the second Session, Cardinal Suenens was appointed by the Pope as one of the four Moderators. The others were Cardinal Döpfner of Munich, Cardinal Lercaro of Bologna, and Cardinal Agagianian, who for many years had been Patriarch of Armenia. Of these the first two were said to be forward-looking men, while the third, regarded as more traditional, was likely to serve as a bridge between Rome and the Churches of the East. The Fathers in the Council used to call the first three the 'synoptics' to stress the affinity between them—thus distinguishing them from Cardinal Agagianian (the fourth Evangelist, as it were!), who was a member of the Curia.

In his opening speech in St. Peter's on Sunday, September 29th, Pope Paul emphasised that it was not the role of the Pope to work alone, but in co-operation with the episcopacy. Pope John, he said, had wanted to remove the impression created by Vatican I in the minds of many that the supreme powers conferred by Christ on the Roman Pontiff were in themselves sufficient to govern and revivify the Church, unaided by ecumenical councils—as though the Pope, alone, must direct the Church, the bishops being representatives of the Pope solely and not of Christ himself.

He went on to say that the Church must become aware of its true nature, then learn how best to convey this awareness to the world—not in the form of a new dogma, but rather by an explicit and authoritative declaration. There must be, he continued, renewal and reform within the Church, not by overthrowing its present way of life nor by breaking with what is essential and worthy in its tradition, but by stripping away all that is defective. Ecumenism must have high priority: sincere relations should be established between the Church of Rome and other bodies of Christians. Finally, the Church must forge bonds with the world at large, having regard in particular for the oppressed, the poor, the afflicted. In words that echoed those of his predecessor, he said that the role of the Church was not to condemn, but to comfort and to serve.

Moreover it was on this occasion that—again in the spirit of John XXIII—Pope Paul publicly acknowledged that the Church of

Rome must accept its share of responsibility for past dissensions among Christians. Turning to the tribune of Longinus in which the non-Catholic observers sat, he said: 'If we are in any way to blame for the fact that we are separated, I humbly beg God's forgiveness, and ask pardon, too, of our separated brethren who feel that they have been injured by us'.

Among his listeners those who had been conditioned to think of the Church as being, already here on earth, 'without spot or wrinkle', were shocked. Others felt he had not gone far enough. In the light of the uncompromising attitude hitherto adopted, the words were courageous. Moreover in the following morning, when the Council assembled to resume the debate *De Ecclesia,* Cardinal Frings of Cologne congratulated Pope Paul for having admitted—not because it was tactically a good move, but because it was true—the fact that the Church of Rome must not shirk its share of responsibility for a divided Christendom.

In the course of the ensuing debate *De Ecclesia,* Cardinal Suenens made three major interventions.

The first, on October 8th 1963, concerned the restoration of a permanent diaconate, open to married as well as unmarried men: he wanted this ministry, which functioned in the early Church, to be restored in its own right, instead of existing merely as a stepping-stone to the priesthood. The second intervention, on October 22nd, concerned the charismatic dimension of the Church: that is, gifts bestowed by the Holy Spirit on the faithful—the laity no less than priests and religious. The third, on November 12th, was about the resignation of bishops.

In opening his first intervention the Cardinal stresses the sacramental character of the diaconate as demonstrated in the New Testament, in the early Fathers (especially Clement of Rome and Ignatius of Antioch), in tradition, and in liturgical writings both of the East and the West. The diaconate, by reason of this sacramental character and the charisms conferred upon it by the Holy Spirit is, he maintains, an enrichment to the universal Church and consequently to any Christian community in which it may function.

True, the laity are recipients of grace conferred by the Sacraments and by the free action of the Holy Spirit, and as such could carry out some of the tasks suggested for deacons. But this is no argument against making available in the world today a ministry that goes back to the early Church. Now, no less than formerly, 'the Christian

G

community has the right to profit from gifts that are part of the Church's heritage'.

In answer to objections raised against the restoration of a permanent diaconate, the Cardinal makes clear that it is not his intention that it be foisted on areas where it is not wanted and would serve no useful purpose. It should, however, be available in places where the local authority considers it would be beneficial.

The need for the diaconate, the Cardinal believes, is indeed evident, particularly in areas where a small Christian community is forced to live more and more in a *diaspora*—separated, that is, from other Christians because of different religious views, vast distances, or political ideologies. There is a need for it, too, in sprawling industrial or suburban areas, where there is little awareness of the Church as a family. Different solutions would be applicable in different areas: 'The good of the faithful must be the final criterion.'

It is unnecessary, in the Cardinal's opinion—indeed undesirable—that the diaconate should be confined to those living a celibate life. Nor is there reason to suppose that the admittance of married men to the diaconate would mean a reduction in vocations to the celibate clergy of the Western Church: 'The valuable witness given by clerical celibacy should certainly,' he says, 'be protected, in accordance with the ancient and venerable practice of the Latin Church. A diaconate with a clearly-defined relaxation of the law of celibacy is not in opposition to a celibate priesthood.

'Instead of the negative results which some fear, one may hope, indeed, for certain advantages.'

'To say that the restoration of a married diaconate,' the Cardinal continues, 'would reduce the number of vocations to the priesthood is an *a priori* assumption. On the contrary, such vocations might well increase in communities welded more closely together by deacons; helped by them; and vitalised by their charisms. As a consequence, priestly vocations would be more sincere, more genuine, and better attested. Finally, chastity embraced solely for the kingdom of heaven will shine with a greater lustre and thus afford a richer witness.'

Cardinal Suenens was supported by the Maronite Archbishop of Beirut, Ignatius Ziadé, as well as by Cardinal Döpfner of Munich and Cardinal Richaud of Bordeaux. On the other hand, Cardinal Spellman dismissed the proposal as unnecessary: when told that bishops in Latin America (hard pressed to find priests for their enormous dioceses) thought differently, he remarked tersely: 'Let them think what they like'. Cardinal Bacci of the Curia took a particularly gloomy view. Vocations to the priesthood, he said, would without a doubt decline, since 'the young always choose the easy way out.' 'Permit a mere spy-hole,' he added grimly, 'and presently you have a wide-open window: a *finestrella* can quickly become a *finestra*'.

That the Holy Spirit works in and through the Church at every level is a theme dear to Cardinal Suenens. Not surprisingly, therefore, his intervention on the *Charismatic Dimension in the Church* was one of the outstanding contributions to Vatican II. Moreover, its presentation, as distinct from content, illustrates his ability to gather up, as it were, much of the Council's most valuable thinking, co-ordinate and present this in a concise, acceptable manner. In his view, charismatic gifts, or gifts freely bestowed by the Holy Spirit, are not something odd or peripheral but are at the very heart of the Church. The Holy Spirit is in, and with, the pilgrim Church on earth, purifying the People of God, shedding upon them life and light, leading them, despite faults and frailties, into the fullness of truth. The Cardinal's thinking follows closely that of St. Paul to whose Epistles he reverts again and again.

The Holy Spirit, far from being the prerogative of bishops, priests, or religious, is for one and all: 'Know you not that you are the temple of God and that the Holy Spirit dwells within you?' In the sacrament of baptism all Christians receive the Holy Spirit. All are 'living stones', whereby a spiritual dwelling is constructed. The Holy Spirit reveals himself in the Church in the diversity and richness of his gifts.

In St. Paul's time some of these were extraordinary, even marvellous. But not all the gifts of the Holy Spirit, the Cardinal emphasises, are spectacular: St. Paul speaks of the charism of wisdom, knowledge, faith; the charism of teaching, helping others, giving guidance, distinguishing false spirits from true. The Church, so presented, is not a rigid administrative organisation. No, the Spirit permeates the whole, bestowing his gifts, different in kind, on every member.

All Christians are not the same: some are lettered, others are unlettered; but each has his role. All, St. Paul says, must have one aim: to build the Church of God. It was not only in past ages, in the time of St. Thomas Aquinas or St. Francis of Assisi, that the charisms of teachers and prophets were needed. They are needed today.

And this brings the Cardinal to speak specifically, about the laity: 'Do we not all know among the laity in our dioceses men and women

who are called by the Lord to do a particular work? It may be catechetical work, or charitable work. The possibilities, in the realm of the Holy Spirit, are endless.' He continues: 'Charisms in the Church, if entirely independent of the ministry of the clergy, would indeed be disorderly, but, *vice versa,* the ecclesiastical ministry without charisms would be poor and sterile.' It is the duty of the clergy—both those in charge of local, individual churches and those responsible for the universal Church—to discern, through a kind of spiritual insight, the charisms of the Holy Spirit, foster these and encourage their growth. It is also the duty of the clergy to listen, with open minds, to the laity and repeatedly to engage with them in a free exchange of views. Each of the laity has been given particular charisms and often has a greater daily experience of life in the world than is possible for the clergy.

Again, it is the duty of the clergy themselves to aspire to greater charisms. For while it is clear that the faithful, even those endowed with the highest gifts, are disposed to revere and obey their clergy, it is also true that a like attention and reverence is due to the charisms and inspirations of the Holy Spirit bestowed, very often, on members of the laity who have no position of ecclesiastical authority. St. Paul is speaking to all Christians, priests included, when he says: 'Do not quench the Spirit. Do not despise prophetic utterances, but bring them all to the test and keep what is good.' These manifold gifts and charisms can be put to use and serve to build the Church only through the freedom of the sons of God, which the clergy, following St. Paul's example, should protect and foster.

Ending on a practical note, the Cardinal proposed that 'in order to manifest both in the Council itself and before the world, our faith in the charisms granted by the Holy Spirit to all believing Christians', the number and the range of lay auditors should be increased. 'Women, too,' he added, 'should be invited as auditors: unless I am mistaken, they make up one half of the human race.'

In the debate that followed, there were no allusions—with one exception—to the proposal that women should be admitted as auditors. Presumably the Fathers were somewhat taken aback or did not wish to commit themselves publicly.

The exception was Bishop Hakim of Israel who, after remarking that clearly certain speakers in the Council had no knowledge of what was taught by Churches other than their own, went on to say that some of the comments made were insulting (though not intended as such), particularly on the subject of married clergy. Then, expressing his support for Cardinal Suenens, he said that the place of women in the Church should receive public recognition. Further, the Council should give attention to the role of women, who, in many parts of the world, are not treated with the respect due to them.

Predictably, the mention of women by Cardinal Suenens provided a scoop for *Il Borghese,* a sensational weekly which manages to steer a course between pornography and extreme right-wing Catholicism. An article headed *Il Feminismo di Sua Eminenza* conjured up the horrors that must ensue if women were allowed to meddle in ecclesiastical matters. Another Pope Joan was visualised. So were furtive encounters as in Boccaccio's *Decameron Nights*—not to mention a Parliament of Women straight out of the *Lysistrata* of Aristophanes.

The most delicate of the Cardinal's three interventions was the third. It was no easy matter to make a plea in favour of introducing an age limit for bishops and Cardinals—inviting them (or making a law to this effect) to retire at the age of seventy-five. In standing up to make this suggestion Cardinal Suenens was reverting to a similar proposal made by him the previous year (when he was a member of the Preparatory Central Commission) and overwhelmingly rejected. The situation, however, was now somewhat different, in that he was addressing the entire Council. True, only the day before, Bishop De Vito of Lucknow had dismissed the idea of the retirement of bishops as 'outrageous'—indeed, 'as preposterous as attempting to change the course of the moon'. On the other hand, Archbishop Mingo of Monreale, Sicily, referred to what he called 'a harsh but necessary law': *'dura lex sed necessaria'*. Whatever one might think, the matter called for delicate handling: no one wants to be reminded that, as far as his work is concerned, his 'time is up'.

The intervention is, in fact, clear-cut, realistic, compassionate in so far as such a subject permits, and touched with humour. At the outset Cardinal Suenens dismisses in a few words two objections raised against the compulsory resignation of bishops.

The first concerns 'the perpetual role of the bishop as father of his diocese' whereby, the argument runs, his office is, in its very nature, permanent. But in a family, the Cardinal points out, sons, as time goes on, take over more and more the direction of affairs that formerly had been the responsibility of the father.

As to the second objection—that the bishop is bound to his diocese by a bond as indissoluble as that of marriage—'if this indeed be so,' the Cardinal adds, 'then, since it is by no means uncommon for bishops to change their sees, there are, here in the Council, among those listening to this intervention, a number of "divorced" bishops—some of them "divorced" for a second and third time.'

The vital question, he goes on, is this. What is best for the faithful? What is best for the diocese? The need for a clear-cut procedure is obvious. Pious exhortations are as unavailing as words written on water. The Second Vatican Council will go down in history as the Council concerned with bishops: this involves the responsibility of bishops in relation both to the universal Church and the diocese of each. In the world as it is today, the functions of a bishop have taken on new dimensions. His role is to revivify and co-ordinate apostolic work: to be the leader, indeed the soul, of the *pastorale d'ensemble*. He is the source of initiative, providing guidance for the faithful entrusted to him—laity, priests, and religious—that they may work in unity and harmony to enable the Church to spread the Gospel.

The pace of life becomes faster and faster: 'Every day fresh problems present themselves. The bishop must be constantly on the alert, ready to meet new needs. This calls for a man young in mind and body, so that he can understand the adaptations that are necessary and put these into practice.'

We must face reality, the Cardinal continues. We have only to consider conditions in dioceses administered by men who are too old. Again, a bishop, for the good of a parish, is sometimes faced with the necessity of asking an ageing priest to retire. How can a bishop do this if he is not himself prepared to set an example? Moreover, the faithful watch their bishops closely. They look to them for a sign of sincerity in the field of pastoral renewal: 'We should be on our guard against scandalising the faithful, especially since in our day there is in the secular world, in every sphere, an age-limit, lower, indeed, than seventy-five: in universities, in industry, in the civil and diplomatic services. If this is necessary in a secular society, why should it not apply where the goal is man's supernatural good? It is true that there is a difference between a purely human office and a sacramental one such as that of a bishop, but the laws of psychology remain the same.'

The Cardinal's interventions, it will be noticed, are all three practical—concerned, that is, with how, under the guidance of the Holy Spirit, the members of the Church (whether deacons, laity, or bishops) may be so deployed that the Gospel can in the best possible way be not only preached but lived.

Moreover all three have left a mark. A greater number of lay auditors were subsequently admitted to the Council, and these included a sprinkling of women. The permanent diaconate has been restored. Charismatic gifts of the Holy Spirit are being treated with a seriousness unknown, perhaps, since the early Church. As to the retirement of bishops and cardinals, the battle lost by Cardinal Suenens at the Council was won later when in 1966 Pope Paul in his *Motu Proprio*, *Ecclesiae Sanctae*, took the initiative of making it obligatory that bishops should offer their resignation on reaching the age of seventy-five.

During his third intervention Cardinal Suenens had said that Vatican II would go down in history as complementary to Vatican I—which was the Council of the Pope—as being the Council which stresses the role of the bishops. Certainly what came to be known as the 'collegiality' of the episcopacy was the subject which perhaps more than any other occupied the minds of the Fathers. As many as 191 speeches were made dealing with this from the practical, the theological, the juridical, and the ecumenical standpoint.

At the First Vatican Council in 1870 the role of the Pope had been defined but, because the Council was brought to a precipitous end by the Franco-Prussian War, the implications of the doctrine of Infallibility in so far as it related to the bishops was barely touched upon. Hence the need at Vatican II to clarify the role of the bishops. In this context the word 'collegiality' came to be used in reference to the bishops when, as a body or group (whether assembled in one place, as at Rome during the Council, or scattered over the globe in their respective dioceses), they work in union one with another as the successors of the Apostles and at the same time (this is vital) in union with the Pope, the successor of Peter—that is to say, *'cum Petro et sub Petro, sed nunquam sine Petro'*: 'with Peter and under Peter, but never apart from Peter.'

The bishops, therefore, are spoken of as forming a *collegium*. The English word 'college' is an unfortunate one, carrying pompous overtones associated with educational institutes—and not even remotely suggestive of the Twelve wandering from place to place over the countryside of Galilee in the company of their Master. There is a story—whether true or apocryphal—that Cardinal Cushing, bewildered during one of the Conciliar debates (his Latin was not all it should have been), asked a Father what the discussion was about.

'The college of bishops,' was the reply. Whereupon the Cardinal

103

rejoined: 'Fine! If that's what they want, tell them I'll raise the million dollars to build it.'

Collegiality, dealt with at length in what is now the third chapter of the *Dogmatic Constitution on the Church* or *Lumen Gentium,* gave rise to a lively exchange of views at the Council.

Cardinal König, Archbishop of Vienna, maintained that, far from being the new-fangled idea that some supposed, collegiality had been accepted since the time of the Apostles and was, in fact, upheld at the First Vatican Council by those who supported the promulgation of papal infallibility; moreover it was the response to the hopes expressed by Pope Paul in his opening speech, when he asked that the episcopate and its functions should be examined more fully.

In a similar vein the Bishop of Bruges argued that collegiality had always existed in the Church and, furthermore, that today there was a greater need than ever that Peter should not only strengthen his brethren but be their point of unity.

The Patriarch Maximos IV Saigh said that a 'college' of bishops was essential—if only as a counter-weight to those who appeared to be under the impression that the Church comprised solely the Pope and the Curia.

Cardinal Liénart, Bishop of Lille, reminded his listeners that Christ made a special choice of the Twelve, but, within that group, conferred a primacy on Peter. Peter, he said, was not outside the Twelve nor in opposition to them. 'We cannot,' he continued, 'deny the divine institution of the apostolic college, nor did this body die with its original members.'

Cardinal Alfrink, Archbishop of Utrecht, said that what was needed was not a juridical definition but a declaration of Catholic teaching, to the effect that all bishops 'gathered with the Pope in Council or dispersed throughout the world (but in communion with the Pope) represent the supreme authority of the Church'.

Others, however—a resolute and tenacious minority—were totally opposed to the idea of collegiality. Cardinal Ottaviani declared that there was no precedent for it in Scripture and that, furthermore, the bishops, no less than the rest of the faithful, were 'sheep' and as such, must follow their shepherd: the Pope. Indeed, he was so disturbed by the debates on this theme that he made a complaint to Pope Paul and even suggested resigning.

Today, over ten years after the Council, collegiality is still much in people's minds. Its existence—or its non-existence, some would say— is a source of tension within the Church. But where there is tension there is life. Some fear that authority given to the bishops is synonymous with authority taken away from the Pope. At certain periods of English history the diminution of a monarch's power meant increased power for the barons, with the consequence that people found they had exchanged one form of autocracy for another; that instead of submitting to a king they were the servants of an oligarchy. It is however a question not of a rigid 'either—or,' but of striking a balance. Cardinal Suenens brings this out in his book, *Co-responsibility in the Church*, published after the Council was over.

Pope Paul when addressing some bishops he consecrated in March 1966 said: 'The Ecumenical Council, when it proclaimed the powers of the bishops, recalled at the same time their duties.'

The Cardinal quoting in his book these words of the Pope comments:

An opposition is all too easily established between the Pope acting alone and the Pope acting as the head of the Church within the episcopal college . . . If the primacy is, in fact, a prerogative of the sovereign Pontiff there can be no question of his governing the Church without the co-operation of the episcopacy. And this means, the more each individual church will be able to develop its particular spiritual personality, all the more will the Christian people mature in a greater diversity of rites, theologies, disciplines and customs and the papal primacy be free to exercise in full its specific role of assuring the fundamental unity and cohesion of the Church.

The *Dogmatic Constitution on the Church* [the Cardinal continues] tells us: 'The Roman Pontiff, as the successor of St. Peter, is the permanent visible source and foundation of the unity both of the bishops and of the faithful collectively.' This is the *raison d'être* of the Primacy. During the next few generations, as the different regions in the world expand in all their variety and diversity, in accordance with the desire expressed by the Conciliar decrees, the true role of the Papal Primacy will reveal itself to us as both providential and necessary. This same primacy will show itself as both the protector and guarantor of unity.

For a week and a half, beginning on Wednesday, October 16th 1963, there was a debate carried on with some heat on what was then chapter III of the schema *De Ecclesia*, concerning the People of God. At a suggestion from Cardinal Suenens, which was put before the Fathers in a booklet of *Emendationes*, chapters II and III were reversed. The chapter on 'The People of God', therefore, immediately followed the opening chapter entitled 'The Mystery of the Church' and preceded the one on the hierarchy. That the faithful should come before the hierarchy was indeed an innovation: one which, in Conciliar terminology, was referred to as the 'Copernican Revolution'. Cardinal Jäger in his book, *Le Décret de Vatican II sur L'Oecumenisme*, Casterman 1965, (I quote from the French edition), speaks of Cardinal Suenens as having reached a happy solution: '*Ceci s'avéra une solution particulièrement heureuse*', in that, as the author goes on to explain, the emphasis on the People of God in all their diversity paved the way for the decree on Ecumenism.

The Council was a period of ups and downs, tension and controversy, sometimes between the bishops, sometimes between the bishops and the Pope.

In the midst of this there intervened an occasion of respite and calm, when for a few hours differences were forgotten.

It was the morning of October 28th 1963, when the Fathers assembled in St. Peter's to participate in a Solemn Requiem Mass for Pope John XXIII. At the invitation of Pope Paul, Cardinal Suenens delivered the eulogy.

In the thronged basilica the words of the Cardinal—clear, resonant, restrained, yet betraying the speaker's warmth of feeling—fell upon a silence heavy with expectancy. He did more than pay a fitting and moving tribute to the man who had been his Pope and his friend and whom the vast majority of his hearers had known and loved—he evoked his presence. Pope John, the Cardinal said, 'is here in our midst in a profound mysterious way.' Indeed, he spoke of the late Pope's personality in language so direct, so simple, that many who were listening felt that Pope John was not only with them, there and then, but would continue to be with them, giving them hope and inspiration in the difficult times ahead.

The Pope thus evoked was warm of heart; a lover of peace and harmony; concerned not with what separates but with what unites; a friend to all; a man whose words—when he spoke of God, brotherhood, justice, and peace—came to his listeners as a challenge to their better selves, making them think of God: 'For, whether they know it or not, men are always in search of God, and it was the reflection, as it were, of God that they sought when they lifted their eyes to the countenance of this ageing Pope who loved them with the love of Christ.'

When bidding goodbye to Bulgaria in 1934, after he had been Papal Representative for some years, the then Monsignor Angelo Roncalli had promised, the Cardinal recalled, that, should he be at the ends of the earth, he would hold out a welcome to any Bulgarian absent from his native land, be he Catholic or Orthodox—that a candle would be burning in his window, like the lighted candle placed in a window in Ireland on Christmas Eve to give welcome to Mary and Joseph.

The Cardinal told of Pope John's visit to the *Regina Caeli* prison in Rome—how, when asked by a criminal what hope there could be for such a one as he, the Pope's reply had been to reach out his arms and clasp the man to his heart. At all times Pope John awakened a response; in all the vicissitudes of life he found an occasion for hope and joy. When, after a prolonged and painful illness, his end was drawing near, he bade that there should be no sadness. 'Let all rejoice, not grieve,' he said—and thus turned his death into an 'Easter Liturgy'. He was gone from our sight, but he had left men closer to God and the world a better place. His holy, gentle memory would live down the centuries.

The address as well as being moving was skilful, in that Cardinal Suenens linked past and present. The spirit of Pope John, he said, breathed again in the words of Pope Paul's opening address to the Second Session of the Council. In each of these pontiffs the Holy Spirit was speaking. Each offered an invitation to openness, to an interchange of ideas, to doctrinal and pastoral charity. Each had spoken words that contained a positive, constructive message. Each was eager to bring the Gospel alive for man as he is today. Echoing Pope John's words, Cardinal Suenens said: 'We have no cause for fear: fear comes from a lack of faith.'

When the address ended, all rose to their feet and a great round of applause rang out. As required by protocol, the Cardinal, his text in his hand, walked across to Pope Paul, who was standing by his throne, to receive the blessing of the Holy Father. The Pope, smiling, reached out his arms and warmly embraced the Cardinal. Another burst of applause rang out, as if to confirm the meaning of the Pope's gesture.

It had been, indeed, a human occasion. At the beginning of the Mass which had preceded the Cardinal's address, Pope Paul, who as

Archbishop of Milan was used to the Ambrosian rite, faltered when saying the opening prayers. It was a trivial incident, but it endeared him to many: they felt that this man, whom they were disposed to look upon as the correct cleric, the polished diplomat, was, after all, human. Moreover Pope Paul lent another human touch at the end, during the recessional. To the consternation of the Master of Ceremonies, the Pope, without giving any indication of his intention, stepped out of the procession to shake hands with two elderly men with weather-beaten faces: they were Pope John's brothers.

It cannot be denied that a mood of disenchantment had begun to settle upon the Council towards the end of the Second Session. Things, it was felt, were moving too slowly. Moreover people missed the cheerful, reassuring presence of Pope John. And no one, perhaps, was more aware of this than Pope Paul. But, for all his goodwill, he could not change himself into a different person. He did not exude the optimism, the confidence, the hope, that had characterised his predecessor. On public occasions he gave the impression of speaking from the intellect rather than the heart. But then, he was very much the intellectual, the diplomat, the cleric. 'He's every inch a Pope, but what is he like as a *man*?' a pilgrim murmured one day as he came away after an audience at Castel Gandolfo.

No one could ever have asked such a question of Pope John who, as he rose higher and higher on the ecclesiastical ladder, remained to the end Angelo Roncalli, the shrewd, open-hearted peasant from Sotto Il Monte. But it was not so much Pope Paul's personality that troubled people—it would have been unreasonable to expect a second Pope John. What troubled them was the apparently slow pace in getting renewal in the Church under way. Some of the bishops felt they would be better employed at home in their dioceses. Others feared that the Pope, though he had shown himself capable of independence, was allowing himself to become more and more the prisoner of the Curia: the victim of a system.

If Cardinal Suenens shared such misgivings he gave no indication that this was so. On December 1st 1963 he delivered a lecture at the Canadian College in Rome, which was attended by Canadian bishops as well as priests and students belonging to the College. Much, he said, had been achieved; nor did he see any reason to share the disappointment felt by those who had hoped for quicker results. He went on to speak of seminary training and the ever-recurrent theme of the collegiality of the bishops.

Seminary training had occupied his thoughts already when he was himself a seminarist at the Belgian College at Rome and again when he was lecturing at the seminary at Malines. Since becoming archbishop—indeed already when he was still Auxiliary Bishop to Cardinal van Roey—he had begun a study into the training for the priesthood from the time of the Council of Trent, tracing its effects during the past four hundred years.

Having called upon the help of ten lay experts and questioned the *alumni* of the Malines seminary, he investigated the situation in his own diocese. In doing so he found that the pattern for a seminarist's training, as laid down by the Council of Trent, had not changed to any appreciable degree. In this field all kinds of possibilities lay open. It was most important, he realised, to strike a balance. As things were, preparation for the priesthood was almost entirely spiritual and intellectual. More attention should be paid to pastoral and practical aspects.

As to collegiality, little progress might, on the surface, appear to have been made. Even so, the Cardinal took an optimistic view. The victory, he believed, was already won to the extent that collegiality had, in principle, been accepted. There were bound to be setbacks, but it was only a matter of time.

The Cardinal also emphasised that although collegiality was of the utmost importance, it was still more important that there should be no question of one group 'scoring off' another as a result of differing views in the debates: all must be open and free—with the freedom of the Holy Spirit.

On December 4th the day on which the Second Session of the Council came to an end, Pope Paul announced his forthcoming pilgrimage to the Holy Land.

From the flat roof of the convent of Our Lady of Sion in the Old City of Jerusalem you can look down on the Via Dolorosa climbing steeply to the Church of the Holy Sepulchre which encloses the traditional sites of Christ's Passion and Resurrection. In the opposite direction you can see the pale slopes of the Mount of Olives and glimpse a little to the north a white building: the residence of the Patriarch Benedict, where Pope Paul called upon Athenagoras, Patriarch of Constantinople.

If, as some say, the Pope's pilgrimage was no more than a gesture, it was nonetheless a splendid gesture. The first Pope since St. Peter to walk Jerusalem's streets, on Saturday January 5th 1964 he made his way up the Via Dolorosa, jostled and hustled by crowds straining to get a glimpse of him, reaching out their hands to touch him—at moments sweeping him off his feet.

Later, when the two prelates met, Pope Paul gave Athenagoras a golden chalice, and the Patriarch gave him an *encolpion,* or chain worn by bishops of the Eastern Churches. The Pope, with the help of the Patriarch, put the chain around his neck. Then they read aloud, from the Gospel of St. John, Christ's prayer that 'all may be one', using a New Testament in which the Latin and Greek texts were on opposite pages. They read alternating verses: the Pope in Latin, the Patriarch in Greek.

What has this to do with Cardinal Suenens? More than might be supposed. The Cardinal is a visionary, a dreamer. And one of his dreams is that the day will come when a Second Council of Jerusalem will be held in the city that is the cradle of the Church; and that participating in it with the Pope will be the Patriarch of Constantinople and the Primate of England.

A dreamer dreams his dream. He does not know by what precise means the dream will become a reality. Emboldened by faith he is as one who follows a star, and when the star is hidden waits for it to shine again.

The Cardinal's dream is of a Church that is visibly one, even as Christ prayed to his Father: 'that they may be one even as we are one'. Yes, the Cardinal, despite his preoccupation with practicalities both in his diocese and in the universal Church, is a dreamer.

But he is also a theologian. Moreover his theology is orthodox— too much so to please some. He does not 'water down' the primacy of Peter. 'I love the Church and I love the Pope'. He has said these and other such words many times, and he means what he says. He loves the Church, and he loves the successor of Peter—not just John XXIII or Paul VI, but whomsoever the Holy Spirit has permitted to occupy the see of Peter.

When the Cardinal talks about his dream he uses the language of a dreamer, a visionary. He no more talks in terms of theology than does the prophet Isaiah when he says:

> *The People who walk in darkness*
> *Will see a great light.*

The dreamer dreams his dream. But when the moment comes—and the Cardinal is confident it will come—for the dream to be transmuted into reality, then the theologian will have a vital role. For, in the Cardinal's view, there can be no visible unity which conflicts with allegiance to the Pope as the divinely appointed successor to Peter. Does not this present an unsurmountable barrier? The Cardinal does not think so. He believes that in the power of the Holy Spirit what is impossible today can become possible tomorrow.

CHAPTER 7

'No generation can claim to
have plumbed to the depths the
unfathomable riches of Christ.
The Holy Spirit has promised to
lead us step by step into the
fullness of truth.'

LÉON-JOSEPH CARDINAL SUENENS

THE THIRD SESSION of the Vatican Council opened on September 14th 1964.

More happened at this session than at any other.

The debate on the schema *De Ecclesia* was completed and, on December 8th of that year, the amended version was promulgated under the title the *Dogmatic Constitution on the Church,* or *Lumen Gentium.* Thus the proposal made by Cardinal Suenens to Pope John in 1962 that the Church should examine itself (*ad intra*) had flowered into this Christo-centric document, vast in its Biblical and historical range, treating of the People of God to whom Christ, their Redeemer, their guide, and their final end, communicates himself in a relationship of boundless love.

On September 16th, in concluding the section concerned with eschatology, Cardinal Suenens criticised adversely not canonisation, but the process involved. Not only was it complicated, he said, and vastly expensive, but it discriminated against the laity and non-Europeans: eighty-five per cent of canonised saints came from religious Orders and ninety per cent from thirteen European countries.

This intervention was one of the many indications of the Cardinal's concern for the laity. He shows a like concern during a debate on Catholic Action—a term which was used, he felt, in too narrow a sense. Valuable work, done for the Church by the laity, often went

113

H

unrecognised, he pointed out, because it did not fall within the scope of Catholic Action as the term is officially understood.

The Cardinal's attitude to the laity, it is worth noting, is echoed by his friend Archbishop Helder Camara who, in reflections written during the Council, says: 'Let us integrate the laity once for all—in theory and in practice—into the structure of the Church. In difficult times as in easy, where there is a shortage of clergy and where there is a surplus, let us recall that the layman has his own mission which is not for us to exercise.' *Pour Arriver à Temps* (Desclée de Brouwer. Brussels, 1970).

In October 1964 the schema on the Blessed Virgin, instead of standing alone (as had been originally intended) became, under the title *The Role of the Blessed Virgin Mary, Mother of God, in the Mystery of Christ and the Church,* the eighth and final chapter of the *Dogmatic Constitution on the Church.*

Some of the Fathers wanted her to be given the title Mother of the Church. This was in fact conferred upon her not by the Council but by Pope Paul in his closing address at the end of the Third Session.

Cardinal Suenens commended the text because it was ecumenically sensitive and also because it was presented in Biblical terms, supported by the relevant verses from both the Old Testament and the New.

He had reservations, however. He felt something was lacking: a richness and depth. He would have liked more about the maternity of the Mother of God in communion with the saints in heaven. Further, to the Cardinal the link between Mary and the apostolate is supremely important. The theme recurs in his writings and his addresses: Mary gave Jesus to us—and this, in a different but none-theless real sense, is what the apostolate is doing: giving Jesus to the world.

Lastly, the emphasis in the Conciliar text veers to the past. The Cardinal, on the other hand, feels that the connection today between the spiritual maternity of the Church and that of Mary should be emphasised—this, of course, in terms of a Christo-centric theology.

On Tuesday, October 26th, the debate opened on the schema that was finally to emerge as what Pope Paul called 'the crown of the Council's achievements': *The Pastoral Constitution on the Church in the Modern World* or *Gaudium et Spes.* This document was to be complementary to *Lumen Gentium* in that (again in accordance with the suggestion put to Pope John by Cardinal Suenens) the Church, as well as looking at itself (*ad intra*), should look beyond (*ad extra*) to the world at large. At this stage the Fathers were presented with only a rough draft: a framework or scaffolding on which to construct a treatise that would reflect the Church's attitudes to burning problems of the day.

Bishop Guano of Livorno struck the right note when he said that the Church could not remain closed in upon itself, 'a fortress, concerned solely with defending its own interests'. Cardinal Lercaro, commending the schema for its positive approach and its lack of condemnations, advocated an airing of opinions from every standpoint, care being taken not to view things solely from the European angle.

Cardinal Silva Henriquez of Chile was glad that the schema afforded scope for the consideration of humanism, especially atheism, on the lines laid down in Pope Paul's encyclical *Ecclesiam Suam*. Atheism, he reminded his listeners, derives its strength from its concern for the temporal order, the problems experienced by innumerable people every day; it was essential, therefore, that the Church should be able to meet atheism on its own ground.

Cardinal Suenens, reverting to points he had made in his book *The Gospel to Every Creature*, went on to say that more thought should be given to the subject of militant atheism. Why, we should ask ourselves, are men atheists? Is it because we live and speak about our faith in a manner which instead of revealing God obscures him?

The necessity that man should accept responsibility both on his own behalf and that of his fellowmen permeates the Cardinal's thinking. And in the Council similar thinking was voiced by Maximos IV Saigh, who stressed the need for the Church to develop in its members a sense of responsibility. As if echoing Pastor Dietrich Bonhoeffer's phrase: 'man come of age', he spoke of modern man as having 'grown up'—by which he meant that laws cannot any more be imposed in an arbitrary fashion: reasons must be given if laws are to be acceptable. 'A new attitude is essential,' he continued. 'The commandments have been laid down for the sake of love. We should not, therefore, give orders. Modern man rebels against the employment of force.'

The Patriarch was supported by Bishop Méndez Arceo of Cuernavaca, Mexico, who noted that, in view of the growth of a sense of responsibility in the world at large, the Church must be seen to be the defender not only of religious freedom but of the principle of freedom. Rigorism must be shunned. To heap up penalties under threat of mortal sin brought the Church into disrepute. According to certain manuals a woman may do embroidery on Sunday, but should she knit for several hours, that could be an offence against the holiness of the Sabbath and, as such, a serious sin. 'This attitude,' the Bishop added, 'turns people into sinners!'

On the whole, the reception given to the schema that was to become *Gaudium et Spes* was favourable. A minority, however, were suspicious—taking the view that the Church was becoming involved in matters outside its range.

At the end of October 1964 the subject of marriage came to the forefront. Cardinal Léger of Montreal deplored the all too common negative, pessimistic attitude to human love, which stemmed not from the Scriptures but from certain pre-Christian philosophies. Married love, he went on, should be recognised unequivocally as good in itself, apart from the procreation of children. The two ends of marriage: the love between husband and wife and the procreation of children, should be acknowledged as 'equally holy and good'.

Then Cardinal Suenens spoke. He proposed that the small, secret commission appointed by the Pope to study birth control should be enlarged by new members; that their names should be known—to assure credibility and enable the widest possible information to be put at their disposal.

To cast doubt on the traditional teaching of the Church, the Cardinal said, would be unwise. 'Nevertheless, are our hearts fully open to the light of the Holy Spirit so that we may understand the truth in all its plenitude? This is a question we should put to ourselves.' 'The Bible,' he continued, 'is always the same. But no generation can claim to have plumbed to the depths the unfathomable riches of Christ. The Holy Spirit has been promised to us, to lead us step by step into the fullness of truth. The Church is not required to repudiate a truth that it once has taught, but in the measure that the Church progresses in a deeper study of the Gospel it can and must integrate this truth in a richer synthesis. In this way the Church draws from its treasure things both new and old.

'This having been established,' the Cardinal added, 'it is important to ask whether we have maintained in perfect balance all the aspects of the Church's teaching on marriage. Possibly we have stressed the words: "Increase and multiply" to the extent of obscuring another text: "The two will be one flesh." Both truths are central to our belief, both are Scriptural; they must illumine each other in the light of the truth revealed in our Lord Jesus Christ. St. Paul, indeed, has seen in Christian marriage a counterpart of the love bestowed by Christ on his Church. The "two shall be one" is a mystery of a union between persons that is sanctified in marriage. It is a union of such profundity that divorce cannot separate those whom God has joined together.

'Furthermore, it is for the Commission to tell us whether we have emphasised the first end in marriage, procreation, at the expense of another end no less important: growth in union between husband and wife. Likewise the Commission should confront the immense problem arising from over-population. The subject is a difficult one, but the world, whether consciously or not, waits for the Church to give expression to its thinking and thus be "a light to the nations".

'No one', the Cardinal stressed, 'should say that in doing this we are opening the way to moral laxity. The problem does not arise because the faithful want selfishly to indulge their passions. On the contrary, thousands try in anguish to respond to demands of a two-fold loyalty: fidelity to the teaching of the Church and fidelity to the demands made by love between husband and wife, parents and children.

'It must be asked,' he went on, 'whether the doctrine on marriage, as set out in manuals, has taken sufficient account of knowledge put at our disposal by the advancement of science—the apparent conflicts, for example, between the biological and the psychological, the conscious and the subconscious. These factors can help us towards a deeper understanding of the unity of man. We have made progress since Aristotle and Augustine, and as a consequence are better able to realise what accords with man's nature and what does not.'

Then, speaking with particular emphasis, he said: 'I beg you, my fellow bishops, let us avoid a new "Galileo affair". One is enough for the Church'.

A breathless silence followed the Cardinal's words.

There was no question, he continued, of giving way to 'situational ethics'. Doctrine, however, while remaining the same in its principles, must take into account contingent factors and changes brought about in the course of history. This, in fact, was what Popes did when they composed such encyclicals as *Rerum Novarum, Quadragesimo Anno* and *Mater et Magistra.* They were attempting to give expression to un-changing principles in terms more in harmony with the days in which we are living.

He concluded with words that echo the Scriptures: 'The truth, both natural and supernatural, will set us free.'

Prolonged applause greeted these words.

Some days later Cardinal Suenens was supported by the Patriarch Maximos IV Saigh, who spoke even more strongly on the gravity of the problems facing married couples who felt caught on the horns of a dilemma presented by conflicting imperatives: conscience as formed by the traditional teaching of the Church, and normal married life. He went so far as to say that possibly a 'bachelor psychosis' coloured the thinking of those committed to a life of celibacy.

Cardinal Alfrink, while emphasising that the Church must preserve the divine law, stressed that it must nevertheless be open to human problems: it would be disastrous were the Church to lag behind, offering no guidance in a sphere that cried out for pastoral solicitude.

On the other hand Cardinal Ottaviani, speaking *ex abrupto* (that is, out of turn—for he was due to speak the next day) dismissed as untenable any idea that married couples should determine the number of their children. He continued: 'The priest addressing you is the eleventh of twelve children whose father worked in a bakery—I say *worked*, because he did not own the bakery. My parents put their trust in Providence.'

Then Cardinal Browne spoke at length on the scholastic teaching on marriage, stressing the distinction between the primary and secondary ends. Moreover, two days later Cardinal Ottaviani in a world-wide television interview assured his interrogator that the Church's teaching on marriage could not be subject to any kind of change, because, he argued, it was based on the natural law and on a number of Scriptural texts.

Compared with the words spoken by Cardinal Suenens and others of similar thinking these interventions made little impact.

Indeed many Fathers had come to Cardinal Suenens in the *aula* and in the bar to thank him for what he had said, some with tears in their eyes. 'We have waited years', they told him, 'to hear such words.'

On November 11th the Council debated *The Adaptation and Renewal of the Religious life; Perfectae caritatis.*

Cardinal Suenens opened his intervention with a clear-cut: *Schema non placet.* He went on to enlarge on points he had made in his book *The Nun in the World*—stressing in particular that those engaged in active work must, without abandoning the essentials of their religious calling, free themselves from the mentality of the cloister. Theologians should work out a spirituality of the active life. The Cardinal was not criticising contemplatives, but to 'cloister' an active Order was, in his view, to impede, if not to nullify, its apostolate. Not only theologians and canonists but nuns themselves must devise a means of changing a system which breeds an infantile attitude among the Sisters and, among Superiors, a maternalism which fosters in subordinates an incapacity to make decisions and accept responsibility. A similar view was stressed by Father Buckley, Superior of the Marist Fathers, who said that the so-called 'crisis of obedience' stemmed, in his opinion, not from the religious *en masse* but from Superiors who fail to realise that the young of today are not as ready, as were those of certain earlier generations, to see the will of a Superior as being *ipso facto* the will of God; they can accept an intelligent obedience, but they see no virtue in blind obedience as such.

During this third session the schema on the *Declaration on Religious Freedom, Dignitatis Humanae*, gave rise to a twofold crisis.

On October 9th fourteen Cardinals signed a letter addressed to Pope Paul, beginning with the sombre words: '*Magno cum dolore*' ('With deep distress') in which the writers protested that the Declaration, though approved by the majority of the Fathers, had, contrary to Conciliar procedure, been entrusted for further consideration to a select committee of which three members were known to be in opposition to the views clearly expressed in the Council.

'This,' the letter ran, 'causes us extreme anxiety and disquiet. Countless persons throughout the world know that the Declaration has already been prepared; they know also the sense in which it has been drafted. In a matter of such importance anything that appeared to be a violation of the rules of the Council and its freedom would, in the light of world opinion, be prejudicial to the whole Church.'

The name Léon-Joseph Suenens was included on the published list of the fourteen Cardinals. At the time, however, he was absent, to preside in Belgium at the funeral of the Queen Mother, Elisabeth. He consequently did not know of the initiative, which met with his approval and was endorsed by him *post factum*.

For a moment it seemed that the crisis had been averted: that it was a matter only of some weeks' postponement. This was not so. In November it was announced that the promulgation of the *Declaration on Religious Freedom* was once more to be deferred—to the chagrin, in particular, of the American bishops who had received a telegram from Cardinal Cushing (he had gone back to Boston) telling them to bring the Declaration with them when they returned at the close of the session.

A further letter was therefore addressed to the Pope begging with respect, but also with 'urgency, extreme urgency, indeed, all possible urgency', ('*instanter, instantius, instantissime*') that the final vote on Religious Freedom be taken before the end of the session, 'lest the confidence of the world, Christian and non-Christian, be lost'. Cardinal Ritter of St. Louis, Missouri, Cardinal Meyer of Chicago, and Cardinal Léger of Montreal, delivered the letter in person to the Pope—despite attempts of functionaries to bar their way. His Holiness received the Cardinals with graciousness and expressions of sympathy, but declined to intervene. He gave an assurance, however, that the *Declaration on Religious Freedom* would be dealt with immediately the Fourth, and final, Session opened in the autumn of 1965.

That same afternoon, during a 'Little Conclave' (a meeting in the Pope's study of a small number of Cardinals), Cardinal Suenens took the opportunity to remark that, although legally it was possible to postpone the *Declaration on Religious Freedom*, the 'psychological effect' could only be deplorable.

While there was sympathy from Catholics and non-Catholics for the frustration felt by the majority of the Fathers, there was also a certain amount of cynicism. 'What else could one expect?' someone was heard to murmur, 'the Roman leopard does not change his spots'. Moreover the delay explains the glum mood—in part disillusion, in part disappointment—that prevailed at times during the last weeks of the session.

If one may compare the lesser with the greater, '*Si licet exemplis in parvis grandibus uti*', to follow the various stages of the Council is like reading a history of the Church down the ages. The wheat and the cockle grow side by side. There are good days and bad; achievements and setbacks; courage and cowardice; interest and lethargy; enthusiasm and boredom; elation and gloom; patience and impatience; openness and guile. No bishop, as far as I know, physically attacked another, as happened at the Council of Trent! But there was controversy, wrangling, ill-humour—indeed all the reactions that are to be expected in a gathering composed of persons holding conflicting views, and holding them strongly.

After all, there had been trouble at Vatican One. As Cardinal Suenens recalls in *Co-responsibility in the Church,* the Jesuit Father Ballerini described the work of some of his colleagues as a '*moles indigesta'*, 'an undigested mass', an *'opus de novo conficiendum'*, 'a work that must be done all over again'. Another participant, an archbishop, demanded that the schema *De Fide Catholica* be sent back to the commission responsible for it, *'non ad corrigendum sed ad sepeliendum'*, 'not to be corrected, but to be buried'.

The bishops participating in a Council are, let us remember, the successors of the Apostles. When the Holy Spirit came down upon the Twelve at Pentecost he gave them strength to be able, despite their faults and failings, to carry out their mission. He did not, however, at one stroke, change them into flawless beings. Consider Peter. He was no less impetuous than he had been in former times. If he did not literally strike Ananias dead he frightened the man so much that he fell dead! And his wife Sapphira fared no better! Did Christ ever behave in this way? Not at all. Christ came to heal, not to destroy; to give life, not to take it away. Or consider Paul. Christ, when struck in the face, held his peace. Not so Paul. Turning on the High Priest he shouted: 'God will smite you, you whited wall!'

Small wonder, then, if at the Council all was not smooth going. Small wonder if Cardinal Ottaviani—a man of brilliant intellect but now old and set in his ways; obsessed, too, with the idea that nothing in the Church must change—was ready at the least provocation, to suspect heresy or a betrayal of tradition. Basically, tiresome though he was, there is something pathetic about this prelate who, quick to accuse others of disloyalty to the Holy Father, was loud in his protestations against changes in the liturgy approved by Pope Paul. There is something pathetic in his admitting to the Pope, towards the end of the Council: 'After all, I was always in a minority'.

But it was Pope Paul who towards the end of the Third Session came in for the most stringent criticism. And no one knew this better than he. On the one hand he was blamed for being influenced by 'false progressives' who were betraying the Church. On the other hand he was said by his very temperament to be incapable of carrying through any reform—of completing the work begun so auspiciously by Pope John. How could he up-date the Church, since he was unable, it appeared, to take one step forward without taking two steps back?

Despite his sincerity, his good intentions, his tireless efforts, Pope Paul seemed, by and large, to please no one. And to make it worse, he had a bad press. It was all too easy to compare him unfavourably with Pope John who was a man of totally different temperament.

It was all too easy to surmise what Pope John would or would not have done had he lived.

It is ironical, but nonetheless true, that appreciation of Pope Paul came, at this period, less from members of his Church than from an unexpected, external sources—from a journalist, for example, writing for a Communist Indian paper at the time when, after the close of the Third Session, the Pope was in India for the Eucharistic Congress. Many important persons, this journalist wrote, had come to India— President Eisenhower, the Shah of Persia, Marshal Tito, President Nasser, and the Queen of England. 'Yet,' he concluded, 'this humble pilgrim and Vicar of Christ met with a reception which surpassed them all.'

Pope Paul thought of his journeys as being, each one of them, in the nature of a pilgrimage—himself a humble pilgrim, bearing witness to Christ: 'an apostle on the move'. And it cannot be denied that he has given to the papacy a new perspective, a world perspective— the papacy can no longer be thought of as an antiquated museum piece, an embarrassing encumbrance, hindering rather than encouraging the spreading of the Good News.

'An apostle on the move.' The words are no less applicable to Cardinal Suenens. One has only to reflect how, stage by stage, his ideas and aspirations for the Church have assumed world proportions, so that the boy whose horizons seemed at one time to be limited to little beyond Square Riga, Brussels, is in manhood equally at home whether it be Malines Cathedral, the corridors of the Vatican, or the vast expanses of the Arizona desert.

CHAPTER 8

'Lo, I have opened a door!'

REVELATIONS 3 :8

ON OCTOBER 28th 1964, in the course of the Third Session, Cardinal Suenens had said—to the consternation of some of his hearers, to the satisfaction of many more—that one 'Galileo case', was enough for the Church.

The following January Pope Paul, during a Eucharistic Congress at Pisa, went out of his way to 'rehabilitate' Galileo unobtrusively but publicly—three hundred years after the humiliation by the Inquisition of this brilliant astronomer whom Father James Broderick, S.J., in his book *Galileo, the Man and his Work*, describes as 'one of the brightest spirits in human history'. It is significant, too, that it was only in 1964 that a biography of Galileo, written thirty years earlier by the late Monsignor Paschini, was allowed to be published, having previously been impounded by the Holy Office.

In any case, like Pope Paul's earlier avowal that the Church of Rome must accept its share of responsibility for a divided Christendom, the words he spoke at Pisa about Galileo were a sign of a genuine desire for openness, truth and simplicity.

Simplicity was evident, too, in the ceremony which, on September 14th 1965, opened the Fourth Session of the Council. There was little pageantry—no lackies dressed in crimson, no elegantly clad chamberlains. Pope Paul came into St. Peter's on foot, wearing, not the heavy papal mantle and the tiara, but a cope and a mitre, like any other bishop.

Then having concelebrated Mass with twenty-four of his fellow bishops he delivered a homily in which he emphasised the need for charity—love of God; love of the Church; love of humanity. He refrained from any reference to matters which were to be discussed in the Council, lest he should appear to be curtailing freedom in the expression of ideas. Towards the end of his discourse he announced his intention to visit in October the United Nations Assembly in New York, to make a personal appeal for world peace. Finally, he disclosed his decision to establish at Rome a Synod of Bishops, in accordance with the wish of the majority of the Fathers present at the Council.

Warm applause greeted his words.

Far from being an innovation, the idea of a Synod of bishops to advise the Pope was a return to a form of ecclesiastical government recognised in the Church down the centuries.

The first matter to be dealt with at the Fourth Session was, as Pope Paul had promised, the *Declaration on Religious Freedom*. During the heated debate, remarks made by Cardinal Cardijn, based on over sixty years' experience among young workers, were particularly apt. The Declaration, he said, could not fail to give hope to the young—adding, furthermore, that a Church when it is in a minority cannot expect religious freedom unless, when it is itself a majority, it allows others a similar freedom.

On September 21st the motion was carried—though not formally proclaimed until December 7th. In view of Pope Paul's coming visit to the United Nations this was all-important. A world aware of Pope John's encyclical *Pacem in Terris*, in which it was made clear that the dignity of man rested on the concept of freedom, could only have been disillusioned had there been ambiguity as to the Council's views on this vital matter.

The principle of religious freedom having been established, the Council went on to the debate (begun in the Third Session) on the schema that was to become the *Pastoral Constitution on the Church in the Modern World*.

It was a unique document in that (in accordance with the suggestion made by Cardinal Suenens to Pope John) the Church was not only talking to its own members (*ad intra*), but to the world at large (*ad extra*)—indeed to all mankind. It was unique, too, in being the sole Conciliar document to be presented, in its original form, not in Latin but in French: it was felt that a decree steeped in modern thought ought to be presented in a modern language. The French, in its turn, was translated into other languages.

The 'official' version, nevertheless, as Archbishop Felici was at pains to point out, was in Latin, but it was Latin translated from French—the reverse of the normal procedure whereby the original documents, composed in Latin, were translated into a modern language as occasion required. The document in its essential lines was the fruit, to a large degree, of the theological thinking of the distinguished American Jesuit, Father Courtney Murray, who took an active part in the preparatory drafts.

Again, the schema was unique in that the emphasis was on man: man living from day to day, facing the pressures and problems presented by life in the modern world. Hence the emphasis on community life, socialisation, respect for every human being—the need to dispense with distinctions artificially created by race, religion, colour, sex. Hence, too, the importance attached to advancement in culture and, in particular, science. Man, through the means put at his disposal by modern discoveries, was called upon, in the light of the Holy Spirit, to reform the world. The Church must not stand aloof. It must insert itself in history. It must become for the world the Sacrament of Unity. In words used by Pope Paul, that have in them 'a Teilhard de Chardin ring', Christ must be 'the focal point of the aspirations of history and civilisation'.

As was to be expected of a document as challenging as this, reactions varied. Some complained that it smacked of naturalism; others, that the passage between Scylla and Charybdis had not been successfully charted; or, again, that its tone was 'too optimistic'. Bishop Jordan of Edmonton, Canada, however, praised it for its realistic, humble approach: it dispelled, he said, the errors of those who think that 'the Church and her ministers have all the answers to the problems of this century'; on the contrary, he continued, it represents the Church as a humble servant, seeking in all sincerity to approach the source of divine and human knowledge and, in doing so, welcoming the help of others.

Reverting to the theme of marriage, on which he had spoken in the Third Session, Cardinal Suenens said it was wholly desirable that there should be serious research in the domain of sexual behaviour. Man, the Cardinal said, should be studied in all his complexity, especially on the level of sexuality and marriage. Hitherto, enough had not been done on this level: Catholics who had undertaken research in this sphere had not been given enough encouragement. There was a lack of co-ordination. Were the Council to invite research of such a nature, this would prove an effective stimulant. Catholic universities should encourage research by offering scholarships.

Then, moving from the scientific to the personal he suggested that it might prove valuable if, as is done in the case of baptismal and religious vows, a special day could be set aside for husband and wife to renew their marriage vows. An Italian daily paper took this up and, under the headlines 'Marriage should be renewable', proceeded to insinuate that Cardinal Suenens was advocating divorce. As the attack involved the Church, the Cardinal insisted that the insinuations made in the press should be withdrawn. This was done but in a half-hearted manner. A protest was therefore published by *L'Osservatore Romano* to dispel any misunderstanding.

The Cardinal's views received strong support from Bishop Reuss, Auxiliary of Mainz and head of one of the most forward-looking seminaries of that time—a member, too, of the Papal Commission on Birth Control. The Bishop stressed that marriage is not just an institution for the procreation of children. Greater emphasis, he said, should be put on responsibility: the responsibility that falls on married persons and the manner in which it is exercised determines the nature of married life.

In the Third Session difficulties in the missionary field had been discussed; and, closely allied to this, the difficulties confronting not only priests but seminarists. In an interview in 1964 Cardinal Suenens had said it was not so much that the world did not want to listen— it was rather that the clergy were not ready to talk to the world— possibly because they were uncertain how this should be done and, as a result, shelved responsibility instead of boldly carrying out the commandment of Christ: 'Go forth, and preach the Gospel to all nations.'

In the Fourth Session the same points came up. Cardinal Alfrink complained that the formation of seminarists was such that one would suppose a priest never left his sacristy or his church. Cardinal Léger complained that priestly holiness was presented in a too unworldly, too unrealistic, manner.

John Moorman, Bishop of Ripon and observer at the Council, in his contribution to Canon Pawley's *The Second Vatican Council* (a collection of studies by Anglican observers), remarks that, as in many other Conciliar questions, Cardinal Suenens got to the heart of the problem.

Quoting the Cardinal, the Bishop says: 'In the world today, and particularly in the West, there has been a progressive loss in the sense of the sacred. Priests are becoming more and more strangers in the world. The difficulty of their work frightens them. They are looking for dialogue and searching for contacts, and this makes them keenly aware of the paradox of their mission: that while being at the heart of the world, they must keep apart from it in order to be at the service of the Gospel. Priests have come to question, because of the increased emphasis on the role of the laity, their own specific role in the Church.'

The Cardinal—with realism, not pessimism—was facing up to a critical situation in the Church. The solution would be found, he believed, in discovering how best to emphasise the bond uniting priests and laity, one with the other and both with Christ.'

No one who either participated in the events leading up to Vatican II and the four sessions that followed, or who has studied the records of what transpired, could deny the importance of the role played by Cardinal Suenens. He not only helped Pope John in the preliminary stages by suggesting ideas for the schemata that were to become respectively the *Dogmatic Constitution on the Church*, *Lumen Gentium* and the *Pastoral Constitution on the Church in the Modern World*, *Gaudium et Spes*. He also, by perseverance coupled with diplomacy, overcame the opposition to these decrees that was at work (specially in Curial circles) both in public and behind the scenes—in particular, the numerous attempts to sabotage *Gaudium et Spes*.

But as a man, a human being, what impression did Léon Suenens make on those who knew him during this period? 'How did he strike you as a speaker?' I asked a fellow Cardinal of his. The reply, which came without hesitation, was the more impressive because it was from a prelate who was not wholly in sympathy with Cardinal Suenens: 'He was a superb speaker, his thought logical and precise, his French polished, his Latin worthy of Cicero.' That his Latin should be described as 'worthy of Cicero' causes Cardinal Suenens some amusement. In reality, to make himself intelligible, he spoke, he says, 'bad Latin'. The complex, sweeping 'periods' of Cicero would have been lost on many who were listening.

The story goes that Demosthenes, the great orator of the ancient world, overcame his stammer by forcing himself to declaim on the seashore, above the howling of the wind and the thudding of the waves, his mouth crammed with pebbles. Léon Cardinal Suenens had no defect in his speech, but he had to fight his innate diffidence, his *timidité*: a disinclination, too, to cause pain or distress to his listeners. 'He never tried to "corner" an opponent or to "score a point",' an Anglican told me and went on to say that there were times when the Cardinal suffered 'anguish' before he could bring himself to make an intervention, because, in doing so, he would, he knew, cause pain. Only a few persons close to the Cardinal were aware of this. To the majority he appeared unemotional, self-possessed.

If the Cardinal does not like to hurt others, neither does he like to be hurt himself. In reply to a question put by a television interviewer in July 1972 he said: 'It's never a joy—it's always suffering —to be misunderstood. To be thought of as a rebel is suffering.' The Cardinal is not a 'superman'. He is not a Stoic philosopher. He is a very human person, sensitive to atmosphere, and this does not diminish his stature.

The Anglican whom I have already mentioned remarked on the Cardinal's spontaneity and openness—his capacity, also, to make good use of time. He recalled how, once, when the two men were driving together from one quarter of Rome to another, the Cardinal asked his friend to enumerate, while they were in the car together, not the advantages but the disadvantages of a married clergy. The Anglican, a happily married man, did what was asked as fairly and as dispassionately as he could.

The Council was drawing to its close.

In so far as one may generalise, the mood was one of restrained optimism. What mattered, Cardinal Suenens said, was not whether the *aggiornamento* had become the reality which Pope John had visualised, but whether firm foundations had been laid. Then again, drawing his imagery—as he often does—from nature, he said: 'True, we have not yet reached May. Rather are we in April, when there are still frosts at night. Yet of this we can be sure. Spring has come, there can be no return to winter.'

Pope Paul has a sense of occasion. An example was the inter-denominational service, the Liturgy of the Word, held on December 4th 1965, in the Basilica of St. Paul Outside the Walls, four days before the closing of the Council's final session. The Lessons were read in English, French, and Greek by respectively a Methodist minister, a French priest, and an Orthodox priest. The Pope, like the rest of the participants, joined in the singing in English of the seventeenth-century Lutheran hymn, 'Now thank we all our God', using a simple leaflet, instead of the customary buckram-covered booklet stamped with the papal arms.

In a moving address he said to the non-Catholics: 'We would like to have you with us always.'

Serious theological differences divided these groups of Christians who had come together: Roman Catholics; Orthodox; Anglicans;

Cardinal Léon Suenens

The Cardinal at a First Communion, 1965

Leon Suenens: a seminarist

Pope John receives the homage of Cardinal Suenens, March 22nd, 1962

Cardinal Suenens with King Beaudouin and Queen Fabiola on the occasion of the
Cardinal's jubilee on December 11th, 1970

Cardinal Suenens and Brother Roger Schutz, Prior of the Taizé Community

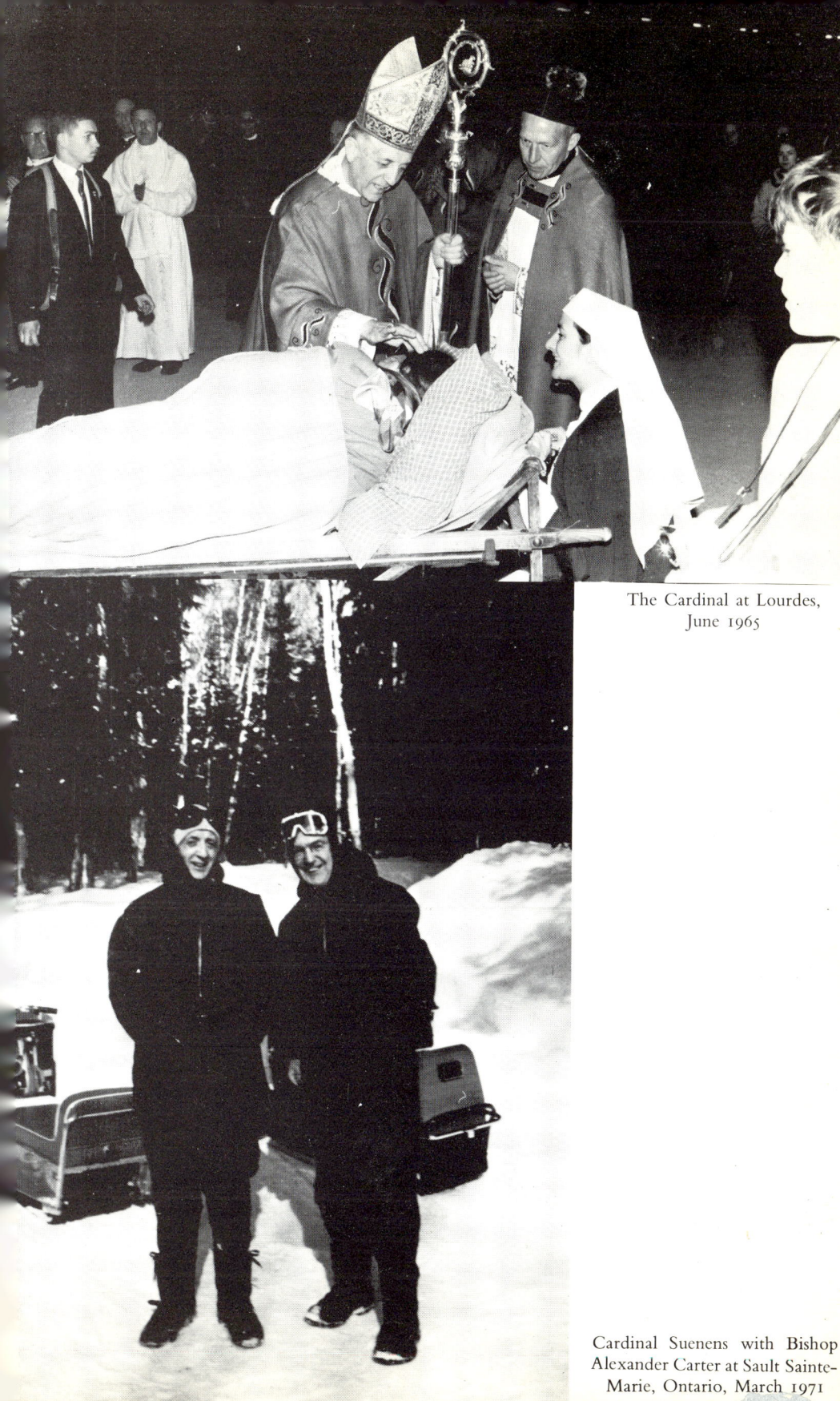

The Cardinal at Lourdes,
June 1965

Cardinal Suenens with Bishop
Alexander Carter at Sault Sainte-
Marie, Ontario, March 1971

Cardinal Suenens with Dr. Coggan (then Archbishop of York) and Mrs. Coggan, Malines, May 1971

FATHER
RICHARD
CENTER

Cardinal Suenens with Archbishop Helder Camara,
May 1973

Cardinal Suenens with Ralph Martin, edit
New Covenant, at the Presbyterian Confe
Michigan, 1973

Pope Paul VI and Cardinal Suenens

Cardinal Suenens in the garden of the Archevêché, Malines, 1970

With Dr. Michael Ramsey, former Archbishop of Canterbury

Cardinal Suenens in his study, Malines, 1970

Methodists. To pretend the differences no longer existed would be less than honest.

Yet something had happened.

A great gust of wind—the breath of the Holy Spirit—had swept aloft these worshippers to a dimension where, for a fleeting moment, all were at one—at one with each other in the presence of God.

On December 8th 1965, after four sessions, the Second Vatican Council ended. The bishops dispersed. Some were glad to go: they had come to Rome from a sense of duty, not of their own volition. Many were glad to return to their dioceses—some in the hope that, the Council ended, things in the Church would revert to what once they had been; others eager to set to work to implement the Conciliar decrees. A Roman resident remarked: 'Even here, where there's a perpetual coming and going, we'll miss these bishops; they have come with such regularity!'

Yes, with the regularity of a great flock of migratory birds, for four years they came and went. And yet their departure at the close of the Fourth Session was not a *finis* written at the end of a story. Vistas reached ahead. God, despite our failings, weaknesses, our reluctance to respond to his invitation, had confirmed the work begun by John XXIII and continued by Paul VI: 'Lo I have opened a door that never again will be closed to you.'

I

CHAPTER 9

'I am convinced that there is a
great liberating force in the
honest expression of what one
profoundly believes to be true.'

LÉON-JOSEPH CARDINAL SUENENS

The end is where we start from. This can indeed be so for those who
have determination, courage, vision. There are men and women who
on perhaps some public occasion speak out fearlessly on behalf of
others, then, giving as it were a sigh of relief tell themselves: 'That's
that. I've done my best.' It is not, however, of these that I am
thinking, deserving of credit though they are.

The persons I have in mind are of a different calibre. Knowing
that words spoken today can be forgotten tomorrow, that saying and
doing can be separated by a great gulf, they have no choice but to
begin again, and yet again, in pursuit of what to others may seem
an unattainable goal, an unreachable star. They are persons whose
faith is such that the impossible becomes possible—who, even if they
do not see the fruit of their labours, renew the face of the earth.

Archbishop Helder Camara, writing about the post-Conciliar
period in *Pour Arriver à Temps*, says:

> It would indeed be a pity if Vatican II managed to produce
> extremely fine decrees, but these decrees remained dead letters and
> were never applied. They would soon be covered in discredit and
> ridicule.
>
> However, we are not under any illusion: it is easier to hold
> a Council than to put its decisions into practice. Only someone
> convinced and enthusiastic will succeed in transmitting the flame.
> We shall have to fire with the spirit of the Council our clergy
> and our laity, exhorting them to be, with the aid of divine grace,
> the missionaries of Vatican II.

Cardinal Suenens, having at the Council done all he could do, having said all he could say, returned to his diocese, resolved to do this very thing—to transmit the flame. He set up pastoral councils and priests' councils, to which members were elected by a free ballot. He decentralised his sprawling diocese, delegating the work to six vicars-general who exercised full authority in their respective areas. There were times when he knew it was his duty to assume entire responsibility himself—in which case he conferred with those concerned and explained the reasons for his decision.

He also travelled abroad.

This entailed making a choice: indeed a series of choices, weighing one course of action against another.

Here is an example.

In the months ahead there are ten days during which he can either go from village to village, confirming children in his diocese; or he can accept an invitation to the United States to engage in ecumenical discussion and address an audience of some 5,000 nuns on how to implement Vatican II.

He has no hesitation. It is a matter of priorities. He can deputise the confirmations. He cannot deputise the work awaiting him abroad.

His role, I repeat, is twofold. There is no discrepancy. His diocese is the focal point from which he sets out and to which he returns, bringing with him the richness of his experience—whether it be Charismatic Renewal or Marriage Encounter from the United States, or ideas voiced at a Synod of bishops at Rome.

The first Synod in the post-Conciliar Church was held in the autumn of 1967. It was the direct consequence of Pope Paul's *motu proprio, Apostolica Sollicitudo*, which was subsequently inserted into the first chapter of the *Decree on the Bishops' Pastoral Office in the Church: Christus Dominus.*

Concerned primarily with doctrine, the Synod opened on October 5th, when a draft document, bearing the formidable title '*On Dangerous Modern Opinions and Atheism*', was rejected almost unanimously as totally inadequate on both pastoral and theological grounds. The Pope, who was present until the coffee break at 10.30 a.m., heard Cardinal Suenens give his views.

'The document,' the Cardinal said, 'lacks historical perspective. It does not relate to contemporary conditions; it does not explain the present crisis in the context of the history of the Church as viewed in its entirety.'

'It fails to distinguish between real errors and unhappy or imprudent formulations.

'It lacks judgment as to the extent and geographical diffusion of the errors and their causes.

'Indeed, the text underestimates the objective difficulty presented by many problems—a difficulty which arises from the nature of things and not from ill-will or lack of obedience. We try to express the mystery of divine revelation in human terms which are always capable of improvement. Much requires to be said on this matter. In short, the document lacks any precise distinction between those things which truly and irrevocably belong to faith and those which are a theological elaboration.'

The Cardinal concluded with a proposal that an International Theological Commission should be formed.

His criticism of the draft document was supported by Cardinal Heenan, who objected that the title was negative. Referring to the *Syllabus of Errors* promulgated by Pope Pius X, he said: 'A new syllabus of errors would do great harm to the Church.'

On the following day Cardinal Bea criticised the alarmist tone of the draft: 'It does not serve the good of the Church simply to fix one's eyes with fear and trepidation upon the dangers to faith. Dangers there have always been from Apostolic times, as St. Paul bears witness'. Cardinal Bea, too, was in favour of an International Theological Commission.

Cardinal Suenens spoke also about seminaries. Peter Hebblethwaite in his book *Understanding the Synod* (Gill, 1968) summarises the Cardinal's words:

The seminary problem is inseparable from the priestly ministry in the Church. The seminarian of today is the priest of tomorrow and is preparing himself for his world and the future. His ministry must be in harmony with this new world which is being born, and yet must maintain profound continuity with the past. This calls for important changes in seminary structure. Gone are the days in which the priest was regarded as a Jack-of-all-trades. Today's and tomorrow's priest must be specialised. The priest of the future must feel perfectly at home in the modern world. Just as there is no such thing as one type of priest, so there can be no such thing as one type of seminary.

Moreover, Cardinal Suenens had something to say about mixed

marriages. He was in favour of preserving the existing canonical form of marriage, the bishop of a given diocese having authority to grant dispensations. He did not think this would prejudice ecumenism. On the contrary, it would provide an opportunity for discussing the sacraments of baptism and marriage. He urged, however, a thorough study of marriage both as a human institution and as a sacrament and sign of the Church.

The Cardinal's suggestion that an International Theological Commission should be set up was adopted. The work he did for this Commission provided the material for the sixth chapter (concerning the role of theologians) in his book *Co-responsibility in the Church*, published the following year, 1968.

A title should indicate the content of a book, and the Cardinal is not to blame if the title he chose is somewhat unwieldy. The fault emanates from the strange fact that neither the English language nor indeed the French has a euphonious word conveying adequately the idea of persons, regardless of rank, nationality, age, or sex, working together in harmony to attain a common end—in this instance the spreading of the Gospel by the Church that Christ founded.

A commentary, in a sense, on some of the most important issues debated in Vatican II, the book maps out the co-operation that should exist at every level in the Church: co-operation between Pope and bishops; bishops and priests; priests and deacons; clergy and laity. Without minimising the need for authority (absence of authority would mean anarchy and be contrary to the Gospel), while at the same time making clear the distinction between authority and authoritarianism, he emphasises the vital need in the world as it is today for a sharing of responsibility.

The following excerpts convey the tone of the book:

> In every field today team work is the predominant characteristic. Whether it be a matter of an Apollo space programme, medical research to find a cure for leukaemia, or a question of military, economic, or social organisation, the task of the leader has become so complex that his role is in fact more to co-ordinate or to lead—in the manner of a conductor leading an orchestra—than to know the answer to everything, solve all problems. Today's pastoral effort must be a team effort—else it will be neither pastoral nor effective . . .

> Men have discovered the meaning and value of a common

united effort. They have understood that it "takes many to be intelligent" and we must avail ourselves of this insight . . .

Theologians must work together with those who are competent in other scientific disciplines. Those who teach in seminaries, colleges and universities should try to co-operate with men well-versed in other spheres of knowledge . . .

Just as in ancient cathedrals buttresses were placed against the transverse arches, so theologians work together within the Church when, in varying ways, they stress complementary views. We must combine a concern for unity, doctrinal continuity, and the demands of tradition, with a desire for direct contact with the currents of thought in the modern world. The balancing, one against another, of various points of view is beneficial to the Church and profitable to all. Theology lives out its life within the Church and the Church is at one and the same time a reality of the past, an actuality of the present, an openness to the future. In this sense the Church is both "memory and prophecy" . . .

The emphasis throughout the book is on what unites men: how they can work one with another of their own volition—not herded in blind obedience to a remote authority, but each, in freedom, making his unique contribution to the good of the whole, each respecting the other.

Cardinal Suenens, however, is not writing as a sociologist. The Church, for him, is not a 'spiritual Red Cross'. While it has a tremendous responsibility in the matter of man's temporal welfare, it is first and foremost a supernatural mystery: a 'mystery of communion, of which the roots are in eternity'. Yet the Church addresses itself to man living in time, in a world perpetually evolving, so that there must be a continual theological and pastoral adaptation without, however, any blurring of the edges of revealed truth.

Stressing the need for the laity to develop their faith by prayer, reading, and study, the Cardinal suggests there should be in the Church a place for the lay theologian. In the early centuries of Christianity, he reminds his readers, lay theologians were by no means rare. There were men such as Justin the Martyr, Lactantius, Didymus the Blind, Aristides of Athens. Why, in the Latin Church, he asks, has theology become the monopoly of the clergy? In the Orthodox Churches lay theologians occupy chairs in the universities. The layman, whether in this or in another sphere, should make his contribution towards the enrichment of the Church; he would do well to ponder on words addressed by President John Kennedy to the young: 'Don't ask what your country can do for you, but what you can do for your country'.

The Church needs, the Cardinal says, the competence of administrators, the knowledge of those engaged in the legal profession or in education, the talents of writers, the insights of sociologists. It needs, too, in the face of family and marriage problems, the skill of doctors, psychologists, and psychiatrists. In brief, the Church needs, on the part of the laity, a widespread exercise of apostolic co-responsibility.

As the Church moves forward into the future, while at the same time maintaining continuity with the past, it must also be receptive to the values that await us in the days to come, to the riches of a world yet to be born, so that Christ, the king of the ages, may take these to himself and lift them on to the plane of the supernatural, the eternal. And this he will do for each of us to the extent that we are receptive to the working of the Holy Spirit: the more the Holy Spirit lives in each one of us, the more will we be able to reveal to the men of tomorrow—that is, the youth of today—'the freshness and the power of the Gospel.'

Co-responsibility in the Church is a straightforward, down-to-earth book, written by a man endowed with exceptional intelligence, intellectual honesty, clarity of thought, and a sense of history. It deals primarily with practicalities: how the institutional Church may function most effectively. Yet there is no suggestion of a dichotomy between the practical and the spiritual. St. Catherine of Siena and St. Teresa of Avila, 'mystics dedicated to the highest degree of contemplation', were at the same time, the writer reminds us, 'at the heart of the problems of their time'.

Moreover, the Cardinal quotes from a discourse addressed by Pope Paul to the Carmelite Fathers on June 22nd 1967:

'You must be willing, as was St. Teresa, to acknowledge the needs of the Church and the sufferings of society that these may provide you with motives, not for fleeing from the world but for spiritual concern. You must understand your dedication to the love of God as an exercise in the love of your neighbour . . . From being good Carmelites who know nothing of pastoral work you must become excellent pastors and, if it should happen, worthy bishops—as indeed has already been the case, to the honour of your Order, the building up of the Church of God, and the glory of the Lord. We know that this is not your vocation, but it can become so when the authority and the charity of the Church ask it of you.'

The Cardinal, as so often, reveals his concern for justice. His attitude to women is a case in point. It must be admitted, he says, that the ecclesiastical world has not yet recognised the full contribution made by women to the Church.

Having commended an acknowledgment of this fact in Pope John's *Pacem in Terris*, as well as a declaration made by the Third World Congress of the Lay Apostolate, held in Rome in October 1967, he writes:

> The role of woman is not yet fully recognised; it is a goal yet to be attained. Still, the situation is improving. We have only to think back to the tremors produced at the idea of inviting women as lay auditors to the Council and the resistance that had to be overcome—by recourse to the highest level—before women were allowed to receive Communion along with men at the Mass celebrated in the Conciliar *aula*.

The Cardinal's personality—his sensitivity, imagination, and powers of observation—is revealed in his writing, not because he speaks of himself (he remains in the background) but by a nuance, a turn of phrase, an image suggested by the Belgian countryside or by a carillon of bells, a thought taken from Antoine de Saint-Exupéry, a line from T. S. Eliot.

The book could be described as being exploratory. This is not to say the writer is in doubt as to his destination. Not at all. His objectives are clear; but how precisely these are to become a practical reality—on this level he is an explorer. Like Odysseus, he is a traveller who knows where he is going, but knows, too, that on the way there will be obstacles to overcome, difficulties to surmount. That the book is exploratory rather than dogmatic in tone, that the writer does not say 'the last word' but rather by implication invites comments and suggestions from the reader, is another way of saying that it is itself, by this very fact, an exercise in, and an invitation to, co-responsibility.

Co-responsibility in the Church made a considerable impact. There was hostile criticism, but approval far outweighed disapproval both in the press and in the numerous letters received by the Cardinal.

When the English translation appeared, Rosemary Haughton commended the author's charity, forthrightness, and vigorous hope. She wrote: 'Here is a man whose ideals and aims are clear and explicit.' In the Cardinal, she continues, we are confronted with someone who, if he can, will avoid antagonising others 'not only for tactical reasons but because he sees others in the Church as co-responsible with himself in the work of Christ'.

The fact that the book invited questions; that, by implication, it asked readers to apply their intelligence, use their minds—this, more than anything else, gave rise to what has come to be known as 'the Suenens interview', in the course of which, on May 15th 1969, the Cardinal answered questions put to him by José de Broucker, then editor of *Informations Catholiques Internationales*.

At the outset the Cardinal made it clear that, while he was willing to speak about his ideas in terms of trends, functions and institutions, he was not willing to speak in terms of persons. 'The intentions of individuals,' he said 'are not in question.'

If *Co-responsibility in the Church* is a commentary on aspects of the Council, the interview is a commentary on the book. Again he takes up the subject of papal supremacy and the collegiality of the bishops —which, in his view, far from being opposing ·concepts, are two sides of the same coin. True, the Cardinal has bold things to say, but if these are read in the context, not taken in isolation; if indeed the interview is studied in its entirety, not in snippets, it is clear, beyond all question, that the Cardinal's purpose, far from diminishing papal authority, is to strengthen it.

Emphasising the necessity of taking into account the needs and demands of the local churches united under the See of Peter, he says that encyclicals and other important documents emanating from the Holy See should be presented as being ultimately the expression of co-operation between Rome and the individual churches, yet in such a way that the supreme authority of the Pope is unimpaired.

'This,' he writes, 'could only serve to strengthen our bonds with the Pope, whose authority is an incomparable advantage to the Church. But his role, in all its aspects, can only be understood in relation to the Church, in it and for it—never apart from it or above it.' He adds (and this is all-important):

I do not mean that the Pope is merely a spokesman for the Church, nor that he needs its legal consent to validate his actions. Certainly not. But the Pope is never outside or apart from the people of God: the head is never cut off from the body. To those who spoke at the First Vatican Council in favour of isolating the Pope from the Church, so as to make his role more important, a bishop exclaimed: 'We refuse to have Peter beheaded again!'

The Cardinal, reverting to the Pope's right to act or speak alone, continues: 'the word "alone" never means separately or in isolation. Even when the Pope acts without formal consultation with the bishops —as he has a legal right to do—he is still acting as their leader.' And, quoting from the Acts of the Apostles, he recalls how Peter 'standing with the Eleven', lifted his voice and addressed the people.

The papacy, the Cardinal believes, if freed from the over-centralised system (that is, the Curia) which at present envelops it 'like a cocoon', will be better able to carry out its incomparable, universal mission, in that 'the inalienable and unique charism of the Pope is indeed the charism of unity, of communion'. The Pope, he says, is 'at the heart of the communion between the Christian churches'.

Then, having expressed his appreciation of Pope Paul's visits abroad, first to Jerusalem, then to Geneva, he goes on: 'It was magnificent to see Paul VI at the United Nations, pleading so eloquently the cause of disarmament and peace and embodying in a unique way a Church which is at the heart of a great human family— Gaudium et Spes incarnate: this the whole world could see.'

The Cardinal quotes Arnold Toynbee, an agnostic:

When Pope Paul VI landed at Amman Airport in the course of his pilgrimage to the Holy Places in Jerusalem, he was met and greeted by a welcoming crowd which must have been about ninety per cent Moslem. When on a later journey he arrived at Bombay to take part in a Eucharistic Congress he received another warm-hearted welcome from a crowd that must have been about ninety-nine per cent Hindu. The reason, we may guess, why the Pope touched the hearts of crowds whose religion was not his own was that they recognised that the Pope's concern was not limited to the members of his own flock, but embraced all human beings of all religions—as Pope Paul had shown and has continued to show in his untiring labours on behalf of world peace. [The Times, April 5th 1969.]

The Cardinal, having reiterated that the authority of the Pope is not in doubt, having declared that we must be more than ever united to Peter, emphasises that a Christian is a man of faith, and faith develops outwards into hope. 'The Church,' he says 'is for the world and, that being so, it must overcome its own inner tensions so as to take up its task in relation to all men and the vast problems they face.'

To speak about papal primacy and the collegiality of the bishops involves speaking about the Curia. Nor does the Cardinal mince his words:

> It is not the authority of the Pope which is in doubt among the faithful sons of the Church, but the 'system' which holds him prisoner and involves him in the smallest decisions made by the Roman Congregations, whether or not he has actually signed a given decree. What is needed is to liberate everyone, even the Holy Father himself, from the system—one which has been a source of complaint for several centuries, and yet we have not succeeded in really loosening its grip or reshaping its structure.
>
> For while popes come and go the Curia remains. During the Council a Curial prelate was quoted as saying: 'Let the bishops have their say—they'll go home in the end: we shall stay and put right all the damage they may do.'

The Cardinal has something to say, not against Canon Law as (life in the Church, as in a secular society, can function only in a context of order), but against a petty legalism taking the form of prescriptions labelled *sub gravi,* which means technically that the transgressor is in a state of mortal sin and therefore in danger of losing his soul. He cites offences which have fallen within this category:

Sub gravi . . .	reading a book on the Index (Descartes, Flaubert . . .)
Sub gravi . . .	omitting (in the case of a priest) to say one of the *Little Hours* of the Office.
Sub gravi . . .	One could go on and on.

And how often, he points out, these sanctions were applied unjustifiably to protect, not the law of God but a discipline established by the Curia.

One could make quite a catalogue of sins which, declared to be 'mortal' over the centuries, have gradually vanished as we attained a greater understanding of man, psychology and real life. It would indeed be wrong to conclude from this that the Cardinal is denouncing Canon Law.

If particular laws are out-dated or ineffectual, or positively harmful, they should be changed or abolished. But if laws are merely ignored, anarchy sooner or later will follow. Hence, the *fait accompli* policy, although it may appear to provide a solution, is undesirable.

The role of the Canonist, in the Cardinal's view, is not to impose burdens, but to give form and direction.

He quotes with approval the words of the Redemptorist Canon Lawyer in Rome, Father van Biervliet C.S.S.R.: '*Soyez torrent, nous vous ferons un lit!*' 'Release the floods, we (the Canonists) will channel their course for you!'

Throughout the interview the Cardinal speaks with candour. There is no façade, no piosity. He acknowledges the faults in the Church, for he knows that only when faults are acknowledged, when an honest appraisal is made, do we allow the Holy Spirit to renew the Church. The prevailing mood is one of hope. Difficulties confront us, but all shall be well. The Holy Spirit will not forsake his people.

The interview, which was translated into twelve languages simultaneously, created a sensation.

René Laurentin, writing in *Le Figaro,* called it 'a cry of faith'. Norman St. John-Stevas in *The Times,* speaking of the Cardinal's profound loyalty to the Pope, commended his courageous criticism of the structures of the Church. He went on:

> The Cardinal's manifesto will encourage and strengthen the many Roman Catholics throughout the world, zealous for reform and renewal, but who have been losing faith in the episcopal hierarchy as an instrument by which these ends can be carried out. For them the significance of the interview will lie as much in its authorship as in its content; if such views can be expressed with frankness by one who is both a leading pastoral prelate and a prince of the Church, there is hope for the ecclesiastical establishment yet . . .
>
> Cardinal Suenens will doubtless be accused of being disloyal to the Pope in expressing himself as he has, but the truth of the matter is precisely the opposite. Not the least of the merits of what he has written is that he has rendered a signal service to the Holy See by pointing the way it must follow if it is to retain its position and prestige in the contemporary world.

Bishop Butler wrote: 'The interview with Cardinal Suenens is one of the most important contributions to the contemporary discussion in the Catholic Church. . . His frankness and prudence should serve to provide a rallying point for all those who share his own position "at the extreme centre" of the post-Conciliar Church.'

Adverse criticism, on the other hand, came from Cardinal Léger, former Archbishop of Montreal, who, interviewed by *La Corriere della Sera,* said: 'I do not find it right that the Archbishop of Malines-Brussels should spread abroad his opinions in the press.'

In Vatican circles disapproval of Cardinal Suenens found expression mainly through rumours, gossip, and insinuations. Then, after approximately a month had elapsed, three Curial Cardinals—Cardinal Tisserant, Cardinal Villot, and Cardinal Garonne—wrote personal letters to Cardinal Suenens, conveying their displeasure. Cardinal Tisserant's letter was particularly bitter: it suggested that the interview had been defamatory, disrespectful, even slanderous.

And Pope Paul? What were his reactions? We have little to go on: only his reply to good wishes conveyed to him by Cardinal Tisserant for June 24th, the feast of St. John the Baptist. To those of us—I speak, I believe, for the majority of the laity—who are unversed in the obscure phraseology, the innuendoes, the ambiguities that have for many generations characterised the utterances emanating from the Vatican, Pope Paul's words are baffling. I can only give my own reaction.

The Pope, it seems, is both puzzled and hurt. Not merely sensitive but hyper-sensitive, he interprets criticism made against the Curia as being directed against himself. It is his wish, however, to reflect upon the criticism with 'a humble and tranquil objectivity'. As to those 'sons of Holy Church' (Cardinal Suenens is not mentioned by name) from whom the criticisms emanate, their motives—though it would have been preferable had they kept silent—are, the Pope believes, 'entirely sincere', nor will he cease to have confidence in their loyalty.

It is unlikely that the Pope's words can have satisfied members of the Curia who wished ill of Cardinal Suenens—those, in brief, who hoped that the interview would prove the downfall of a man who had already (rumour ran) displeased Pope Paul, first by his famous 'One Galileo case is enough for the Church', and secondly because he had flown from Brussels to Rome in a final, unsuccessful attempt to deter the Pope from proclaiming the encyclical *Humanae Vitae.*

Cardinal Suenens is a man of peace.

When personal attacks, as I have said, are made upon the Cardinal—on television, on the radio, in letters, from public platforms, from the pulpit—he remains silent. If, however, the Church, is involved, he speaks out. Hence, his two statements in the summer of 1969.

The first, made on June 23rd, received wide publicity. It was a reply to the 'onslaught', made by Cardinal Tisserant, in which he asked Cardinal Suenens to 'retract' what he had said.

Taking up the accusation that the interview was 'defamatory, disrespectful, even slanderous', with regard to officials of the Curia, Cardinal Suenens replied:

> Difference of opinion is quite normal in the Church. But I cannot accept that my intentions are in question and that a discussion about ecclesiastical structures should be regarded as an attack on persons.
>
> I had attempted, at the beginning of the interview, to anticipate such criticisms, emphasising that I would speak only in terms of tendencies, functions, and institutions as distinct from persons; in any case the intentions of individuals are not in question, and to classify them *en bloc* would be an over-simplification. . .
>
> I therefore consider totally unacceptable the accusation made against the interview, that it was defamatory and slanderous. Consequently I see no cause for a retraction . . .
>
> Frank, open, and constructive dialogue, inspired by a love of the Church and its head, is a sign of vitality and strength. It is normal and healthy that there should be open discussion about vital problems which concern the whole Church—the more so when these problems are felt in their acuteness and urgency over the entire world and are publicly discussed in the press, whether we like it or not. Intolerance of public discussion concerning these differences, under the pretext of preserving unity, is, in my opinion, harmful in the present day. . .
>
> To conclude, it would perhaps be useful to read again the words of Paul VI with which he invited the members of the Roman Curia on September 21st 1963 'to receive criticism with humility, reflection, and even gratitude. Rome has no need to defend herself by turning a deaf ear to suggestions coming from honest voices, more especially when they come from friendly and fraternal ones.'

The second statement was made in the cathedral at Brussels on the evening of June 28th, during a Mass celebrating the anniversary of Pope Paul's coronation, in the presence of Archbishop Cardinale, recently appointed Nuncio to Belgium:

I am the more happy to speak on behalf of the Belgian bishops, priests, and people, because some—I am glad to say few—seem to fear, in consequence of my recent interview and the repercussions in the press, that I am seeking to minimise the Holy Father's authority. I have already answered the distortions, not only of my intentions but my words. If the text were read again objectively and attentively these criticisms, I believe, would end.

I am happy, moreover, to thank all those who, by means of the innumerable letters I have received, have shown their understanding. They are here with me in a special way today to welcome the Nuncio with joy, enthusiasm and respect.

To say that authority should be exercised in the Church—as in society—in a manner different from that of former times is not to say that it should be suppressed or lessened. If we face facts we cannot but observe that an irreversible trend has taken possession of the people of God, filling them with a longing for renewal, joy, change, progress, and freedom within the Church. Some thought they could obstruct this change by pretending it did not exist. Facts, on the contrary, show that there is a most urgent need to give it support, so as to be able to direct it aright.

Rapid, numerous and constant changes characterise civil institutions today. How, then, can the Church do other than adjust to the rhythm by which its members are living? The principle of authority remains unshaken. Only the way in which it should be exercised is at issue. . .

In reply Archbishop Cardinale said: 'I greet your Archbishop, Cardinal Suenens, with joy and sincere affection. I appreciate his profound love of the Church and his loyalty to the Vicar of Christ.'

Perhaps the silliest comment on the Suenens interview came from a prelate quoted in *Le Monde* as saying: 'God does not act like that.' Is he suggesting that God does not wish his servants to speak the truth as they see it, in all honesty and sincerity? If that be so, we should, presumably, close our ears to the voices of the Prophets, the voices of the Apostles—as well as many of the saints down the centuries.

What kind of logic is this? No one raised a storm when Cardinal Ottaviani, Cardinal Léger, Cardinal Felici, and Cardinal Daniélou (to mention but a few) publicised their opinions in the press, on radio, and television. Why, when Cardinal Suenens does the same, is he hounded—like Orestes pursued by the Furies?

Why is he accused of disloyalty to the Pope? The answer is not far to seek. His loyalty is of a kind not always recognised as such. Loyalty is not necessarily the simple thing it may appear to be. It is easy to march in step, to beat an outdated drum. But there are times when loyalty demands something more: an honest and fearless expression of dissent. Loyalty, like love—it is a facet of love—requires that we be concerned for—more than that—responsible for the other. Now, when that other is the Pope—any Pope—our loyalty pertains not solely to him, but beyond him to the Church: the Church today and the Church as it will be in the years that are to come. Loyalty to the Pope demands, then, that both for his sake and that of the Church, we serve him with the utmost courage and truth. It is not enough to bow before him in silence, wings folded, like the seraphim.

The distinguished theologian Karl Rahner, S.J., assessing the Suenens interview, wrote in the German weekly *Publik*:

> Nobody can possibly say that Cardinal Suenens has offended in the slightest degree against the Church's understanding of her own essential nature. But if that is so, one has to ask why there should be in certain quarters such a negative and hostile reaction to this interview.
>
> Perhaps the explanation is that a Catholic or a Cardinal should not discuss such matters in public? One can easily answer this objection. Those who resort to it should first of all ask themselves whether or not they raise the objection, consciously or unconsciously, as a tactic for avoiding discussion and any serious treatment of the real questions at issue. Anyone who has no other objection should, as soon as possible, set to work on the matter in hand and attempt to find along with Cardinal Suenens a solution of the problems he has raised . . .
>
> Why so many complaints about these questions being discussed publicly? What has happened to public opinion, which Pius XII said was essential in the Church? It is perfectly reasonable to concede that every public discussion in the Church leads to a certain amount of 'pressure' on those ultimately competent and responsible

for the changes that are proposed. But why should pressure of this kind not be exerted? Are Church authorities not sensible and courageous enough to withstand such pressure when it can be seen, objectively, to be moving in the wrong direction? Finally, secret policy-making behind locked doors is no longer practicable today.

The basic problem posed by the debate on the interview can be put in another way. Many persons sincerely believe that it is not legitimate to raise questions about issues on which the Pope must finally decide. But when we realise that, in a sense, there is never a final word, not even in *ex cathedra* definitions, which are always open to subsequent interpretation, and when we leave aside the question about the need for openness in discussion, then one must ask quite simply: "Because the Pope has the last word, must he therefore have the last but one?" And the answer is "No". Furthermore, anyone who, as a responsible Christian sharing in the life of the Church, makes a contribution and speaks the last word but one, cannot be said to be acting in a manner disrespectful to the Pope or the papacy. This is true even when he says things that are contrary to the opinion of the Pope . . .

Father Rahner quotes St. Thomas Aquinas on the conflict between Peter and Paul as recorded in Galatians 2.14:

This incident gives an example, first of all, to ecclesiastical authorities, showing them they should have the humility to allow themselves to be criticised by subordinates. Secondly, it shows the zeal and sincerity subjects should have, so that they are not afraid to rebuke their superiors, particularly when the matter is public and threatens many.

It is quite clear that Paul did not ask Peter for permission to rebuke him. One can argue about whether the rebuke was justifiable or not. But one cannot argue about whether one may or may not say something critical to the highest authorities in the Church without first having been invited to do so.

As to the incident about Peter and Paul, Archbishop Roberts, S.J., in his book *Black Popes,* makes the further point that the man who rebuked the first Pope was 'certainly not St. Paul at that moment, but a convert notorious for a campaign of savage persecution'.

Cardinal Suenens has no need, then, to defend either his beliefs or his actions. In both he is completely orthodox. His interview takes its place in a long tradition of public criticism addressed to the Holy See in a spirit of loyalty and devotion. Paul stood up to Peter; St. Jerome to Pope Damasus; St. Bernard of Clairvaux to Eugene III; St. Bridget of Sweden to Gregory XI; St. Catherine of Siena to Gregory XI; St. Philip Neri to Clement VIII.

This tradition of outspokenness is woven into the history of the Church. But those who resort to it, whether in relation to the Pope or other ecclesiastics, must accept the consequences.

Luis de León (1527–1591), poet, and professor of philosophy at Salamanca University, one of the most brilliant intellects in the Church, spent five years in prison under the Inquisition—his spirit unbroken. Cardinal Newman, anguished yet not despairing, derived comfort at a time of intense personal crisis from the thought that: 'Truth defends itself and falsehood refutes itself'. Teilhard de Chardin, 'impatient of any unjustified yoke on the intelligence' (I quote from his letters to Léonie Zanta), 'frustrated by obtuse and pharasaical minds', delated to Rome, forbidden to allow his name to go forward for the Collège de France, bowed beneath a weight of suspicion ('they could do anything if only they would trust me'), did not, for a moment, consider leaving the Society of Jesus, still less the Church. And in our own day we have only to think of the cloud of suspicion that has overhung such men as Yves Congar, Henri de Lubac, and Edward Schillebeeckx. Those in high places do not always want to hear the truth:

> *human kind*
> *Cannot bear very much reality.*

Pope Leo XIII said that some people would 'suppress, if they could, the facts about Judas and the triple denial of Peter'.

The Jesuit theologian Cardinal Billot, having come into bad repute because he expressed views differing from those of Pope Pius XI, resigned his Red Hat. He wrote:

If you say nothing and do nothing, you will escape criticism.
I have not escaped, but we must not dramatise the shocks we get. . . I have not yet been accused of heresy as was St. Basil before Pope Damasus; nor condemned as a heretic, then deposed, as was St. Cyril by a council of forty bishops; nor accused of witchcraft as was St. Athanasius; nor of vile immorality as was St. John

Chrysostom; nor have I been condemned and deposed by the Holy See as was St. Joseph Calasanctius who died in disgrace in Rome at the age of ninety-two. [*Black Popes,* Archbishop Roberts, S.J., Longmans, 1954.]

Cardinal Suenens had no illusions. He realised that for many he would be 'a sign of contradiction'. He accepted this as the price of loyalty. He was well aware of the misunderstandings, the hostility, he would arouse. We have his own words: 'I know I will be attacked. But I love the Church and the Pope, and I am ready to pay the price.'

One of the most uncalled-for attacks made upon the Cardinal occurred in August 1971, when, as the Representative of Pope Paul, he was presiding at the Marian Congress at Zagreb, Yugoslavia.

All were assembled at the shrine of Marija Bistrica for the closing ceremony when, suddenly, before the massed congregation of Croats, Cardinal Šeper launched from the pulpit a virulent diatribe directed against the publication in the review *Glas Concila* in Yugoslavia of the Suenens interview. He did not mention Cardinal Suenens by name, but everyone understood to whom he was referring.

The result, however, was not as Cardinal Šeper intended. His eloquence was wasted on the bewildered Primate of Belgium who, not knowing the Croatian language, could not follow what was being said.

The truth dawned on Cardinal Suenens only later, when journalists and others gathered round him to offer apologies and sympathy.

CHAPTER 10

'With you I am one of the faithful,
for you I am a bishop.'

SAINT AUGUSTINE

WHILE THE INTERVIEW given in May 1969 to the editor of *Informations Catholiques Internationales* was still very much 'in the air', a hundred bishops from European countries had assembled at a symposium at Chur in Switzerland to exchange ideas and discuss problems—in particular those concerning the priesthood.

A hundred or so indignant priests had also assembled at the other end of the town. It was an ironical situation. The bishops were embarrassed by the unexpected presence of the priests, with whom they had no wish to communicate. The priests were enraged at being excluded from discussions which were, they felt, of vital concern to them. And as well as priests and bishops there were two hundred journalists avid for news, vainly to-ing and fro-ing.

It was only at the closing session on July 10th 1969, that the symposium was thrown open to the priests and the journalists.

Cardinal Suenens was present.

It was his first public appearance since the interview in May. Would he, in the company of his fellow bishops, it was wondered, stand by his opinions? Would he be faithful to the 'logic of the interview'—the 'logic of Vatican II', with its emphasis on co-responsibility at every level?

Yes, he was faithful to the 'logic of the interview'. In the words of a layman, quoted by Henri Fesquet in *Le Monde,* 'the Cardinal saved the symposium from mediocrity'.

In the course of a speech on 'The Priest as the Servant of God' he read aloud a letter written to him by the theologian Hans Küng, in which the latter, having expatiated on the problems of priests, stressed that problems of this kind could be solved only by discussion between bishops and priests — that any solution arrived at independently of the bishops and therefore against them would be disastrous.

The Cardinal's speech was remarkable for its depth of thought, its historical perspective, its humour, and its wisdom. Quoting the memorable words of St. Augustine: 'With you I am one of the faithful, for you I am a bishop', he identified himself with the listening priests, while at the same time showing them that here was someone in high places whom they could trust, who understood their aspirations, who, when the appropriate moment came, would stand by them.

And the extraordinary thing was that the Cardinal did this without loss of face among the bishops. Granted, there were a few who felt he had taken advantage of the symposium to air his own opinions. But the vast majority could only respect his courage and consistency.

Indeed Chur provided a surprising spectacle when the priests, after denouncing the bishops *en masse,* applauded the Archbishop of Malines–Brussels with overwhelming enthusiasm.

Bishop Butler wrote in *The Tablet*:

> The highlight of the symposium was Cardinal Suenens's address at the public closing meeting. This was in no sense an agreed résumé of the symposium. It simply gave the Cardinal's own view on the flexibility of the Christian priesthood throughout history, on the present crisis, on the basic functions of the priest, and on the challenge presented to the whole People of God (and not only the hierarchy) to reflect upon the future evolution of the role of the priest in a renewed Church. . .
>
> Such a brief and bald account gives no idea of the impassioned oratory, the deep concern, and the high Christian hope, of this great religious leader.

Cardinal Pellegrino, Archbishop of Turin, without mentioning Cardinal Suenens by name, left no doubt as to where his sympathy lay: 'We have lost,' he said, 'too much time in Byzantinism, in subtlety and groundless fear. Now, after the Second Vatican Council which put before us a new manner of living, a new spirit, it is no longer possible to behave as before. Today when someone lifts his voice to say that we must go forward, many cry "Scandal!" But it is a scandal that is beneficial.'

The first Synod had taken place in the autumn of 1967. The second opened on November 11th 1969.

Karl Rahner, commenting on the Suenens interview, had said that it would provide subject matter not only for this Synod of 1969, but for others in the future.

As a result however of the interview the Cardinal, in the eyes of many, was the *enfant terrible* of the Church, and even those who were strongest in support of him feared that what he had to say would not carry much weight.

In fact, it turned out differently. For it soon became apparent that the majority of the bishops were in substantial agreement with his ideas, which at the opening of the Synod he expressed calmly and frankly in the presence of the Pope.

'All of us in this assembly,' he said, 'are at one in affirming, with a like fidelity, that the Church is directed by the college of bishops, with Peter and under his authority.

'We do not disagree as regards either the primacy which places us under Peter or the collegiality which unites us with Peter. Our differences come to light in the way we understand how the primacy should be exercised according to the will of Christ. . .

'There are some who insist so strongly on the role of the primacy that they easily come to present the papacy as an absolute monarchy, in the *ancien régime* style, in which everything depended on the sovereign good pleasure of the monarch. A unilateral insistence of this kind leads in practice to the negation of collegiality. The "*sub Petro*" eclipses the "*cum Petro*". In such a perspective the danger is serious and the hopes raised by Vatican II vanish.

'We must frankly recognise that there is uneasiness in the Church on this subject. The fact, patent to all, is public and discussed among the people of God.

'We must, therefore, with serenity and clarity, become aware of the tension, at the very heart of our common faith, between the tendency called monarchical and that which is called collegial. At the root of this tension are two different theologies of the Church. There is also a difference of mentality and of sensibility to the signs of the times in a world in which participation in the making of decisions (decision-making, not decision-taking) is seen more and more as a normal exercise of co-responsibility, a *sine qua non* for the proper use of authority.

'In the study of these questions we must absolutely avoid mutual suspicions or excommunication. No one has the right to present himself as the sole defender of the Pope; we all profess the same deference and fidelity. But we should have the courage to recognise our disagreements, unless we are to be bogged down in ambiguity . . .

'Principles are often affirmed, they are less often applied . . . Making my own the proposal of Cardinal Döpfner, I am asking the Synod to refer these problems to the International Commission of Theologians for study and examination. And I suggest that our Eastern brothers should take part in this: their ecclesiology can teach us a great deal about communion and collegiality . . .

'Let us believe in the Holy Spirit who, according to the role of each, is actively present in the Sovereign Pontiff, in the bishops, and in the faithful.

'Let us believe in the Holy Spirit who speaks to us through the signs of the times.'

It has been said, not without truth, that Cardinal Suenens came into his own in the Synod of 1969. Certainly his influence was a major one. Many of his proposals were enthusiastically endorsed. Out of 145 Fathers, 130 favoured a revision of the structure of the Synod, as originally presented, to allow the collegiality of the bishops to be exercised more effectively on the level of the universal Church.

All this is common knowledge. But only those who were on the spot—and by no means all of them—were aware that October 1969 was for the Cardinal a time of intense personal suffering. Echoes of Cardinal Ottaviani's dictum during the Council: 'He who criticises the Curia, criticises the Pope' had not died away. As well as being the target of virulent abuse and the recipient of insulting letters, Cardinal Suenens was the object of scurrilous, unfounded attacks in the less worthy elements of the Italian press. To all this he submitted in silence.

Nor today does he talk of these things. It was I, not he, who 'brought up' the matter one day in conversation, angered by what I had learnt from reliable sources. 'You'd think,' I said, 'the *Osservatore Romano* at least would have made a stand for you. It is usually quick to defend the honour of a prince of the Church.'

He smiled, shrugging his shoulders barely perceptively. Then with a gesture of his hands suggestive of resignation rather than bitterness he said, still smiling: 'Someone must die for the people.'

The American sociologist, Andrew Greeley, said that were he asked to name the outstanding personality of the 'sixties' his answer would be: 'Cardinal Suenens, the man who did not give up.'

'The sixties,' he said, 'had ended in tragedy. Pope John was dead. The Kennedy brothers were dead. Martin Luther King was dead. Bishops and priests had given up; so had political leaders. Hippies and drug addicts had "opted out". So much had turned sour. So many dreams had faded. So many hopes had been destroyed. Yet Cardinal Suenens had stood his ground; heard himself attacked, insulted, defamed. His chances of becoming Pope—which were real— had, it seemed, vanished; it had even been insinuated that he might be asked to resign from his diocese. And yet, despite the hostility, his proposals had been inserted in the final recommendations of the Second Synod.'

Concluding, the sociologist said: 'We need men of courage, tenacity, and hope; honest, intelligent and full of humour; men to take calculated risks ... such men are rare.'

The spring of 1970 came. And again the Cardinal spoke out. On May 12th he gave an interview—not, this time, to a Catholic paper, but to M. Henri Fesquet of *Le Monde*. It was sparked off by the conflict that had arisen between the Dutch Church and Rome on the question of enforced celibacy. But it was not celibacy as such that was the immediate concern of the Cardinal; it was the matter of how the Church should be governed and Vatican II implemented. In making his points the Cardinal could not fail to mention the Pope. He was not criticising Pope Paul as such, but a method of government. Not everyone, however, is able or willing to make this distinction.

The Cardinal believes that, in the world as it now is, an open exchange of ideas is essential.

Celibacy had been one of the subjects brought up by the priests at Chur in July 1969. It was also raised by the Dutch bishops at the sixth session of their pastoral council. It had not, however, been discussed at the Vatican Council or during either of the Synods.

In his interview with M. Fesquet the Cardinal said: 'The deadlock —and deadlock there is—arises from the fact that the Pope did not allow the question of ecclesiastical celibacy to be discussed by the Fathers of the Council. And this prohibition has been maintained by his clear and repeated statements—thus excluding any collegial inter- vention as was the case some time back over the birth-control question. Public examination and discussion thus authoritatively with- held, the bishops arc not in a position to exchange views seriously on this subject either with the Pope or among themselves in episcopal congress.'

But has the Pope the right to reserve questions to be decided by himself alone? The Cardinal answers that he has the right legally and in exceptional cases, but that this should not apply in the normal government of the Church.

He quotes Monsignor Gustave Thils, a Louvain theologian: 'On the basis of the fact that the Pope may make decisions without the express collaboration of the bishops, it is claimed, as an ideal, that the Pope should decide alone. From the fact that the Pope may reserve for himself some important problems, it is considered normal that he should reserve to himself every more or less thorny or delicate problem.'

By implication the exceptional is made the norm; what is juridically possible becomes regular practice.

But to halt discussion the Cardinal believes is impossible. A ban, far from preventing discussion, gives it a fresh impetus:

'The question is brought up in congresses and seminars, in specialised reviews and in the daily press. Extensive studies are undertaken from the historical, psychological and pastoral points of view. This trend increases day by day and the echoes that reach us from the international press are only the more spectacular manifestations.'

As well as being ineffective the ban, the Cardinal continues, is unfortunate: 'In this post-Conciliar atmosphere, where people are highly sensitive to all that pertains to collegiality and co-responsibility, I am obliged to confess through love for the Church that I do not think this can be called a good thing.'

As in the 1969 interview, the Cardinal repeats in 1970 that he is concerned not with persons but with systems. Moreover he reiterates that he is concerned not so much with the celibacy of the priesthood —which in fact he favours—as with 'method and procedure'.

He remarks that at Chur the bishops were 'apparently torn between conflicting choices. They had to appear either disloyal to Rome or to be shrinking responsibility in their own Church. Loss of credit or loss of credibility.'

He disapproves of the 'drumming up' of support from Episcopal Conferences: 'Telegrams sent by bishops to Rome arouse ill-feeling, because they are sent over the heads of the clergy, without their being consulted.'

The timing of the 1970 interview with M. Fesquet was important in that it was published the day before the Secretariat met to prepare the agenda for the 1971 Synod. It was, in fact, another attempt to prevail upon the Pope to permit discussion on every level.

The first reaction took the form of an insolent reference to Léon Suenens by Cardinal Gracias of Bombay in an address of homage to the Pope. The implication appears to be that because Mahatma Gandhi had said: 'What has kept Catholicism fresh is celibacy', this was the last word; nor was there any place for 'inane dialogue or false concepts of co-responsibility'.

Then came the Pope's allusion to the same interview, with no mention of names:

'We set great store on the Council as a most precious gift of the Holy Spirit and we endeavour to show respect for episcopal collegiality. This is in sharp contrast to what has recently been said to our amazement and sorrow—and said in a way which, in our opinion, does not seem in keeping either with the fraternal style required of collegiality or the gravity of problems which, as everyone is aware, are being studied by responsible and competent persons.'

The interview with *Le Monde* took place on Tuesday May 12th. By Friday Cardinal Gracias and the Pope had made their comments. On Sunday—it was Whitsunday—during his homily in the cathedral at Malines Cardinal Suenens said:

'The press interprets the recent declarations of the Holy Father as a criticism of my suggestions made in an interview to *Le Monde*.

'Some people may be troubled by those words, and so have a right to an explanation from me. I will give this briefly, in an attempt to dispel their uneasiness.

'I would like to tell them, first of all, that if I expressed my ideas on so delicate a subject, it was because I felt obliged, in conscience before God, to assume my responsibilities as bishop. I will not hide from you the suffering this entailed, but I consider it inherent in the accomplishment of my duty.

'If I expressed publicly my thoughts on a problem that is discussed publicly in all quarters today, it is because I am convinced that in our post-Conciliar Church, as in our contemporary civil society, free and frank expression of thought is normal and healthy.

'There is nothing irrelevant in such openness: I consider it entirely compatible with the respect due to the Pope, whose right it is to take the final decision.

'As to the controversy itself, I would insist that it does not question the inestimable value of voluntary celibacy undertaken, for love of the Lord, by our priests in a sacred commitment. The discussion centres

155

round the existing legislation which links compulsory celibacy with ordination to the priesthood.

'The Holy Father having declared that the question was not open to discussion (*L'Osservatore Romano*, February 2nd 1970) I considered it necessary to ask that this decision be revoked, and the question of celibacy be studied and discussed in all serenity and objectivity, with the help of experts in councils of priests and pastoral councils. I made this request just before the Preparatory Commission first met in Rome to prepare the agenda of the Synod that was to be held in 1971.

'The Holy Father declares that these problems, because of their nature and their seriousness, are being studied by competent bodies. These do not include the bodies mentioned above. I am convinced that, in the present situation in the Church, not to engage the local churches in this examination would be seriously harmful for numerous reasons. I repeat again, that, in asking for this study at a local level, I am not advocating a solution one way or the other.

'It is unnecessary to add that this divergence of views has in no way affected my unwavering attachment to Peter and his successor, nor my profound esteem and affection for the person of Paul VI.'

The third Synod, from September 30th to November 6th 1971, once more brought the bishops together in Rome. This Synod was more important than either of the preceding ones, and received greater publicity. Moreover, the preparations had not, as previously, been entirely in the hands of the Curia. A commission of bishops elected by their colleagues had been at work; so had the International Theological Commission founded in 1967. As well as the bishops, twenty-six priests were invited, also a number of laity, including two women. Arrangements were made to provide full, accurate information for the press.

The efforts previously made by the Cardinal to encourage outspokenness and a spirit of collegiality had not been in vain.

The chief subjects under discussion were justice on a world scale—particularly the obligations of rich nations to help the Third World—and priestly celibacy, including the question of ordaining married men. The Cardinal's request for freedom to discuss problems concerned with celibacy had not been officially granted, but the subject came up spontaneously.

On October 11th, having spoken first on behalf of the Belgian bishops, Cardinal Suenens said that although the link between the priesthood and celibacy is not of a dogmatic nature, yet there is an affinity between the two, in that celibacy of this kind is a response to an invitation of Christ, and has its roots in the Gospel.

In general, he said, the Belgian bishops were of the opinion that episcopal conferences in regions where celibate priests were lacking should be permitted to ask the Holy See that married men be ordained. A small number of bishops thought this should apply even when there was no lack of celibates.

As to priests who have married, the Church, it is felt, should show greater understanding and help to find a humane solution. Nevertheless, 'as one has the right to expect the ministers of the Church to give witness to an objective fidelity', it was not desirable that these men should exercise their priestly functions. They could, however, be given certain defined apostolic functions, 'if they themselves wished it...provided they were accepted by the local community—with the permission of the bishops, and in accordance with the attitude of the universal Church'. Finally, the clergy and laity of Belgium, through priests' councils and pastoral councils, had declared themselves in favour of ordaining married men.

Then, speaking for himself, the Cardinal gave his reasons for approving the ordination of married men.

First reason:

'As bishops, we have received the *power* to ordain priests. But we not only possess the power, we have the *duty* to ordain the number that is required to satisfy the needs of the People of God.

'We, the hierarchy, have the prime responsibility if there are not enough clergy. Where there is a lack of priests, we have the duty to ask men to come forward. This duty takes pride of place over any ecclesiastical legislation that blocks the recruitment of candidates and imposes uniform qualities which the Gospel does not require.

Second reason:

'The Christian people have an inalienable right to receive the priests they need for their community. And I speak specifically of priests—not lay helpers or deacons, however valuable these may be. An authentic Christian community is built up around the altar and the Eucharistic table. As Father de Lubac has said: "The Church makes the Eucharist, but the Eucharist makes the Church." The Christian people are entitled to be nourished by the Eucharist.

'We must examine our conscience: we use the word "parish" for a community in a rural area numbering 200 persons and for urban agglomerations of 20,000. This is a nonsensical juridical fiction without human or religious significance. It paralyses and discourages our most devoted priests. We must return to the human scale of true communities. This is the price of renewing our pastoral work. And paying this price means opening the priesthood to married men from these same communities.

'Who will take care of the built-up areas of our cities? Who will celebrate the Eucharist there, if not the men who share the life of the inhabitants? Who will take care of the continents where there is a tragic lack of priests and an ever-increasing population explosion, if it is forbidden to call upon married men?

'It would be inconceivable and scandalous to refuse the priesthood to baptised persons capable of assuming this responsibility: it is only force of habit which makes it impossible for us to become aware of this. Equally, if the people have the right to the priests they need, then an immediate consequence is that the baptised have the duty to offer to the bishops candidates taken from among themselves. Just as, on the civil level, a city finds a mayor, so, *mutatis mutandis,* a parish or a region should be able to find a religious leader. These men exist in great numbers—men of generous dispositions and deeply Christian: they are waiting for the call.

Third reason:

'Over and above the right of the faithful to receive priests, there is the right of Our Lord Jesus Christ to communicate himself to his people in the celebration of the Eucharist. The master has given us his Body and his Blood as food and drink, in a gesture of homely simplicity, within reach of all.

'Why should we fear that, by making possible for Christians a full Eucharistic life, we may endanger vocations to consecrated celibacy? On the contrary, to multiply the Eucharistic centres is to multiply vocations to consecrated celibacy.

'Are we going to forget that Jesus founded his Church not on St. John whom he loved with a special love, but on a married man, Peter?

'Are we going to prevent Jesus from renewing, before our eyes, the parable of the Master looking for labourers in his vineyard, whom he calls at all hours of the day, even at the eleventh hour?'

Speaking on October 30th, the Cardinal drew attention to the link between the subjects under discussion: justice and the priesthood:

'It would be paradoxical if the Synod were accused of neglecting justice by not recognising or by minimising the importance of certain fundamental rights. I would point out three:

1. 'The right of the episcopal conferences of a region to have their legitimate differences respected in all that does not relate to the common faith.

'It would be unjust, in my opinion, to impose, for fear of "contagion", a uniform law on groups of episcopal conferences which maintain that the pastoral health of their churches calls for the admission of married men to the priesthood—the conditions to be decided upon, with the approval of the Holy See.

'One may talk of "contagion" when it is a question of cholera, but not referring to a pastoral measure good in itself and alive after two thousand years in part of the Church: a measure considered necessary for Christian vitality by the bishops of this or that country who hold the chief responsibility for the evangelisation of their people.

2. 'The right to a clear vote without ambiguity.

'If a vote of the universal scope that has been proposed is to be fair and worthwhile, the principle of justice formulated by Aristotle must be applied: "True equality consists of treating with inequality that which is unequal."

'I will explain: there is a great difference between a Father of the Synod who is spokesman for his episcopal conference and an individual Father who gives only his personal point of view. There are those who prepared for the Synod by widespread preliminary consultations among both priests and laity. Others have thought either that they could not or should not do this. Some bishops have actually experienced these problems in their own countries. Others have no sense of urgency, and yet their vote could prove decisive without their having familiarised themselves with situations totally different from their own.

'In loyalty to the Pope to whom we should give full and exact information on the real ideas held by our churches; in loyalty to our own respective churches, and to others as well as our own, we are obliged to say that a ballot which does not take into account the different value of each vote, must lack credibility.

3. 'The right to genuine discussion and an organised dialogue.

'We have been invited to present in writing our remarks about faults in the procedure of the Synod, and I will respect this. I would simply like to ask one question. Since many of the Fathers realise to what a small extent there is true dialogue even at the level of the *circuli minores* (working groups), where participants argue from totally different standpoints, could we not envisage, as indeed the rules of

159

the Synod provide, that, having had experience of 'ordinary' and of 'extraordinary' Synods, we also try the experiment of 'regional' Synods, which would permit on a pastoral level a more useful and realistic meeting?'

In conclusion the Cardinal expressed regret that the restriction imposed by Rome (to prevent the discussion of these matters) should have taken so long to be lifted *de facto*. He proposed that commissions be set up in all parts of the world, to examine the issues at stake *cum summa honestate*. Moreover the participants should benefit from the experience, positive and negative, of other Christian bodies: 'Only the episcopal conferences of the various regions can validly undertake such a study; it is their duty and right to concern themselves with everything that pertains to the concrete life of the Churches, as long as the unity of faith and communion is safeguarded.'

Commending Cardinal Suenens for his courage in speaking his mind, Dr. Theodore Hesburgh, President of Notre Dame University, Indiana, remarked: 'You can't say things like this without ruffling a little fur.'

No one knows this better than the Cardinal.

Part III

CHAPTER II

'Beloved, let us love one another,
for love is of God and everyone
who loves is born of God and
knows God.'

1 John 4:7

IT WAS A July evening in Malines, the sky suffused with a pale golden light. I was returning to England the next morning, and I wanted to look again at the painting of Cardinal Suenens that hangs in the Archevêché in one of the great spacious salons, along with, yet apart from, portraits of former archbishops of Malines.

Certain of the earlier paintings stood out, I thought, as the work of an artist endowed not only with talent but integrity, so that one was confronted not just with an eminent prelate, but a man of flesh and blood whose facial expression revealed a sense of humour, perhaps, or kindliness, or complacency, or cunning. The later paintings, on the other hand, were sometimes disappointing: the conventional product of the professional portrait painter who all too easily falls into the trap of 'glamourising' the sitter, at the expense of reality.

It is true that Cardinal Mercier, if something of the 'fire' is missing, looks down with all the dignity and graciousness that were his. As for his successor, the unfortunate Cardinal van Roey (unfortunate, that is, in the treatment accorded him by the painter of his portrait) is shown as towering aloft, right arm uplifted in a gesture befitting a Roman emperor: the epitome of pomp and triumphalism.

The painting of Cardinal Suenens has a quality entirely its own. No other Cardinal, I think it is safe to say, has been portrayed in this manner or is likely to be again. The picture is highly imaginative. The face (there is only the face) is shown as if veiled in the radiance of the dawn. But how, I asked myself, would this picture look in the evening? Evening is not the time to look at a painting: its radiance would be dimmed and my earlier impressions clouded.

I was mistaken. The evening light, itself golden, enhanced the gold of the painting. The words, too, written at the base of the left hand corner stood out: *L'Epiphanie du Visage*.

The artist, Felix de Boeck, a Flemish farmer, draws his inspiration from the vast open sky, shifting light, and cloud effects. The Cardinal did not sit for this portrait. The artist, who had seen him on public occasions and in photographs, painted not so much what he saw with his eyes, but inspired, rather, by an inner vision, uniquely his own. The result is a work that has an ethereal, mystical quality reminiscent of some of William Blake's paintings.

Moreover Felix De Boeck is a man who has known what it is to suffer. And suffering leaves its imprint on a work of art. It can find expression in bitterness, discord, cynicism, despair. Or—if we think of Mozart who wrote his gayest, happiest works at a time of personal anguish—we find suffering transmuted into serenity, joy, hope: the calm that after a tempestuous night, can come with the dawn. And this applies to Felix de Boeck's paintings.

Again, a work of art, whether a poem, a picture or a piece of music, speaks with a different voice to different persons—a voice, it may be, of which its creator is unaware.

For me, the painting of the Cardinal called to mind the motto he chose on becoming bishop: *In Spiritu Sancto*. The golden light was the *lux beatissima,* the *lumen cordium* of the hymn *Veni Sancte Spiritus*—the light that came down at Pentecost in tongues of fire.

Furthermore, the painting, in being different in technique, workmanship, and tradition, from those of the Cardinal's predecessors, in being of its very nature a thing apart, symbolised, I thought, the isolation suffered by the Cardinal not simply by reason of his high office, but because, come what may, he has pursued the course he believes to be right—spoken the truth, as he sees it, fearlessly.

It is ironical that a man whose prime purpose is to unite his fellowmen to one another and to God, should himself, on not one but many occasions, be shunned, cold-shouldered, exposed even to derision—and this among his fellow Catholics who, while under no obligation to share his views, might be expected to accord him courtesy and charity. But then, a prophet in his own country, Christ himself has told us, need expect no honour.

I went down into the garden. The fading light intensified the brightness of the flowers: crimson dahlias; scarlet geraniums; fiery red begonias. The darkness of the cedar trees was tinged with blue, and a glow as of wine seen through the glass of a decanter illumined the foliage of a copper beech. The wooden seats were a staring white above the vivid green of mown grass. The Archevêché had assumed a strange, chalk-like whiteness. On the far side of the wall the cathedral belfry, its masonry a blur of browns and greys and black, like the markings on a tabby cat, rose into the wan gold of the sky. The silence was broken only by the footsteps of a passer-by or the shrill cry of swifts swooping in mad career.

It was pleasant, I reflected, to have reached a point in this book when I could, in a sense, relax; turn my thoughts away from the complexities of the Council and the Synods: think instead, of the man, Léon Suenens, whose primary concern, in the seventies, is for the soul of the Church as distinct from its structures.

That day the Cardinal, who presided at a celebration of the Eucharist for the sick, had invited me to take part in the pilgrimage at Banneux, well known for apparitions of the Blessed Virgin said to have been seen there during the thirties.

To me, to use the words of the Abbé Huvelin, *le miracle est très antipathétique*. What did impress me at Banneaux was the concern shown for the sick. The day was theirs. It was for the sake of the sick that young people were present in numbers, carrying stretchers, pushing wheel-chairs, talking and laughing with the invalids. It was for the sake of the sick that the Cardinal with the Bishop of Liège and other clergy concelebrated Mass in a clearing set about by pine-woods—the air fragrant with resin, the foliage of the trees dark against the blue of the sky, their red-tinged trunks, planted in straight rows, forming passages that reached on and on into what seemed an infinity of green.

There was a rapport, I felt, between the Cardinal and the congregation as he addressed them in Flemish, French, Italian, and German. Moreover as he moved among the sick—among the stretchers and the wheel-chairs—giving Holy Communion, this was no routine, but rather as if, as he came to each one, his entire attention, his entire concern, was for that person alone.

Later, I followed one of the passage ways through the woods, the ground strewn with cinnamon-coloured pine-needles, glimpses of sky above, and, weaving their way among the foliage, tiny green-grey birds, whispering rather than twittering, moving so delicately as hardly to be perceptible: gold-crested wrens—the *Regulus cristatus,* the smallest of all birds, yet a king among birds, its head crowned with a flame-coloured coronet.

The pinewoods opened on to a field of corn golden in the sunlight, and, on its farther edge, more pines. Then a gust of wind blew up, bending the corn, tossing the pines this way and that. A passing cloud flung sweeping shadows. I might have been looking at a painting by van Gogh.

I was back in time to watch the Cardinal as he blessed the sick. This took place in a simple, spacious chapel, for rain had begun to fall: the window above the altar was spattered with rain-drops and, visible through the glass, the pines tossed.

The Cardinal came down the length of the aisle, between the rows of the sick, stopping every few paces as, holding up the monstrance, he made the sign of the Cross—Christ in the hands of his anointed, blessing the sick, the maimed, the afflicted, as long ago in Jerusalem, in Jericho, and in the cities of Galilee.

On the way back to Malines we stopped at the Cardinal's residence in Brussels. I wanted to look at the chapel. The Cardinal came with me. He showed me on the door a small crucifix given to him by Pope Paul—St. Peter and St. Paul standing at the foot of the Cross. Then he showed me, on the tabernacle, an impressionistic design in greens and blues and white, depicting the Four Horsemen of the Apocalypse, and to one side of the altar a fifteenth-century Madonna carved in dark wood.

The Cardinal knelt down. I knelt, too. He began to pray aloud in English in his deep, rich voice. Then I realised he was praying to the Holy Spirit for me. This spontaneous prayer would have seemed natural to some. But I was not used to being prayed for aloud: in all my life no one had prayed for me in this way. I felt as if a handful of stars had been showered upon me.

Then the Cardinal went to the altar. 'Let us see,' he said, 'what the Lord has to say to you.' He opened the Gospel at random, then read aloud the words in St. John that follow the passage telling how Nathaniel was amazed to learn that Jesus had seen him under the fig tree. 'You will see greater things than these. Hereafter you will see the angels of God ascending and descending upon the Son of Man.'

All that evening I kept thinking of the Cardinal's prayer and the words from the Gospel. I was still thinking of them in the aeroplane on the way to England.

I dwell on this episode not so much because it made an impact on me, but because it highlights the Cardinal as being not only occupied with reforming the structures of the Church—but its spiritual aspects he himself being, in the true sense of the word, a man of prayer.

'A man of prayer.' It is a somewhat platitudinous phrase (I use it for want of a better one) that can evoke a picture of a monk on his knees in the solitude of his cell, his eyes cast up to heaven. Undoubtedly in the pressures and tensions of today all of us—not religious only—need spells of solitude. But there is a more urgent need: a need to break away not from solitude but (and this is a different matter) from isolation, whether it is imposed by a psychological inability to communicate with others, or is the price many have to pay for living in vast conurbations where people mill round in thousands, yet are strangers one to another.

In saying that the Cardinal is a man of prayer I mean that his way of praying spontaneously, as I experienced it that evening at Brussels, has a therapeutic, liberating quality, a 'bringing together': 'Where two or three are gathered together in my name, I am there in their midst.'

To be able to pray aloud spontaneously, in words that are sincere, seemly, and relevant words, furthermore, that awaken a response in the hearer, is a gift. This is quite different from repeating a traditional prayer (however impressive the prayer may be) or from participating in the liturgy. It differs, too, a hundred-fold, from the sometimes garbled, over-emotional outpourings that can, if things get out of hand, make a prayer meeting an occasion of embarrassment.

The prayer of the Cardinal though extempore, was restrained, controlled: it came from the heart and from the mind alike.

For the Cardinal, to use the words of T. S. Eliot,

prayer is more
Than an order of words, the conscious occupation
Of the praying mind, or the sound of the voice praying.

Over and above the time allotted to prayer; over and above the spoken word, or words which, taking shape in the mind, remain unspoken, prayer means for him to be aware, in every circumstance, of God's presence: to direct one's thoughts and aspirations to God.

Or, prayer can be thought of as an attitude of mind and heart, whereby all things touching our lives have reference to God. To take a comparison suggested by the Cardinal in one of his books, a husband who loves his wife does not, indeed cannot, think of her continually, moment by moment, when he is concentrating on his professional duties. But this does not mean that he loves her the less. On the contrary, the fact that she is there, in the background, gives him, without his perhaps being aware of it, a heightened sense of purpose, an élan, in whatever pursuit he is employed.

Those close to the Cardinal affirm that, while he is a man of simple faith, he is at the same time an intellectual. The fact that at no stage of his life has he doubted the basic truths of the Catholic Church—as distinct from accretions that have attached themselves to it down the centuries—does not mean that he has not examined these truths critically. For him there is no incompatibility between intellectual enquiry and supernatural faith.

He goes into this in his book *La Question Scolaire*, published in 1950. 'To maintain,' he says, 'that there is a contradiction between experimental science and faith is to forget an important fact—namely, that while everything is open to critical examination, everything is not necessarily open to doubt. One can examine everything without of necessity rejecting everything: the two mental processes are by no means identical.'

Quoting from the biography of Théodore Jouffroy by the French philosopher Ollé-Laprune, he continues:

When one attempts to get to the heart of the matter, to enquire into its reasonableness, doubt, as Leibniz well says, has no place in the process. To examine is not to doubt; to raise questions, even, is not (in spite of appearances to the contrary) to doubt. Doubt destroys, dissolves, or at least clouds the outline of what one wants to examine. One can, it is true, resort to critical examination in order to overcome doubt. But to maintain that to examine something critically we must begin by doubting it, this I deny completely. On the contrary, we examine a truth because we do not know enough about it and want to know more: it by no means necessitates—nor is it always the case—that we cease to admit the reality of the matter under consideration.

In the event of genuine doubt it is, then, reasonable and proper to use one's critical faculties with a view to overcoming this doubt. But that one has to begin the examination with the assumption that the matter at issue is of necessity in doubt—this the Cardinal rejects: *Le doute détruit, dissout, ou du moins trouble la chose à voir.* These words are of overriding importance if we are to understand his attitude not only in the field of philosophy and theology but at every level, in that at all times he chooses the positive rather than the negative, the constructive rather than the destructive. His purpose is to synthesise rather than to break asunder, to stress what, as human beings, we have in common, rather than what sets us at variance.

Some, however, who have not the Cardinal's philosophical and theological expertise, might more easily grasp his meaning were they to think in human rather than abstract terms. After all, the multitudes to whom Jesus spoke would have understood little if he had addressed them in the language of philosophy or theology.

Indeed the Cardinal tells a story that has relevance here.

At Rome during Vatican II he asked an Oriental what his people thought about the Council.

'Nothing,' came the reply, 'they don't understand the way in which the Fathers express themselves.'

'Well then,' said the Cardinal, 'in what kind of language should they speak?'

'They should tell us a parable,' the Oriental replied.

Imagine, therefore (to take a concrete example) a man and woman who love each other. They exchange ideas and confidences, ask questions not out of idle curiosity but to get to know each other better. Or they are happy to be together in silence. Again, if they are apart they think of each other, recall a word, a smile, a gesture; ask themselves what they can do to give pleasure to the beloved. But let doubt find a footing—doubt as to the other's love or one's own love for the other. What happens then? The vision of a reality that before was clear and unquestioned is now clouded, distorted. Love, indeed, has to be fostered, cherished. If it surrenders to the pressures of misgivings and suspicions, it can fall asunder, disintegrate. Only belief in the reality of love can keep love alive.

Now, prayer is an expression of love. The Christian, Cardinal Suenens reminds us, is not a philosopher who has found a satisfactory explanation of the universe; he is someone who believes in a personal God. One cannot pray to an abstraction, only to a person. Hence, the psalmist can say: 'I will love you, O Lord, my strength.' And again: 'Save me, O God, for in you I put my trust.' Hence, Paul Claudel's cry on the evening of his conversion as he stood by a pillar in the cathedral of Notre-Dame: 'Lord, all of a sudden you have become for me a person!' The psalmist and the prophets could pray because they had entered into a relationship of love with God. For the Christian, relationship is closer, in that Jesus of Nazareth—who died on the Cross and rose from the dead—is at one and the same time true God and true man.

Moreover in loving God the Christian does not love in isolation. He is supported not only by his fellow-Christians, who here and now are members with him of the mystical body of Christ, but also by those who have gone before.

The Cardinal reminds us:

> At the moment of the breaking of bread the Church puts on our lips that magnificent prayer: 'Lord, look not on our sins, but on the faith of your Church.' And it is with ecclesial faith that I go to meet the Son of God. I believe with the faith of the patriarchs, the prophets, the martyrs, the doctors, the confessors, the mystics, the saints. The strength of poor, weak Christians (and such we are) is the knowledge that, through those who have gone before, we are links in an immense chain, in continuity with, and united to, our Lord and Master.
>
> It is always for me a great moment when, during an ordination, the Litany of the Saints is sung. It is good to feel united to our ancestors in the faith, whose mediation we are imploring on behalf of the ordinand. A realisation of this communion across the centuries with the Church in glory is like a fresh gust of wind, or a tonic; or pausing, as it were, on a mountain plateau, we breathe the better because we see the horizon reaching on and on.
>
> Such a prayer in full community is a source of happiness—the secret of hope and joy.

Teilhard de Chardin believed that man, despite the advance of science, was 'sad' and he wanted to free him from this *taedium vitae*. The Cardinal feels the same. 'Too many Christians,' he says, 'are lacking in joy. The greatest reproach addressed to a Christian is contained in this question: "Why are you sad? For what are you waiting? If you are waiting for Christ to come, if every day brings you nearer to him and if you are convinced that he is within you, transforming your life into light, then why are you sad?"... We must not only construct a theology of hope, we must be a presence of hope.'

John XXIII, the Cardinal recalls, radiated hope, and people were aware of this. An agnostic, speaking a few days after the Pope's death, said: 'Pope John has made my disbelief uncomfortable.' It was because Pope John loved his fellowmen that he gave them hope. We cannot give hope if we do not love. And love entails responsibility, which, in its turn, demands fidelity.

Cardinal Suenens dwells on the subject of fidelity in a pastoral issued in the summer of 1971. Fidelity, in the true sense of the word, implies, he says, 'otherness': we are faithful not to ourselves but to others or to God. Moreover fidelity has to be periodically renewed. It is not merely being true to one's word given in the past. 'Opponents,' he says, 'of the indissolubility of the marriage-bond use as arguments those hastily contracted marriages broken up for some futile reason and given publicity in the press. But these were unions undertaken only on a legal basis, without the real, mutual commitment to life-long love. It could therefore be contended that from the beginning there was no authentic marriage—that it is not a question of breaking the marriage bond, but rather of its non-existence.'

The essence of what the Cardinal says is that fidelity, whether in marriage or in a totally different sphere, is not static; it has to be sufficiently flexible to adjust to changing circumstances, yet be resolute —have, that is, an element of what the ancient Romans called *constantia,* so as not to be at the mercy of every whim, every gust of wind: 'He who, having put his hand to the plough, turns back, is not worthy of the kingdom.'

Again, fidelity must not be taken for granted. It must be nurtured, tended, encouraged to grow. And this takes time. The Cardinal quotes Antoine de Sainte-Exupéry: 'To live is to be born slowly.' And (specifically in the context of marriage), Maurice Zundel's: 'It is an ever freer choice of an ever stronger love.'

Even today, in the climate of post-Conciliar thinking, one can come upon clergy who have a grudging, if not jaundiced view of marriage. In some instances this is a defence mechanism unconsciously adopted by men who, feeling themselves called to the priesthood, accept the celibacy that in the West normally goes with it, only because they see no alternative. A negative attitude can also be conditioned by constant exposure to marital problems in the confessional or in the presbytery parlour—the pressure being the greater because these men have no personal experience of a happy marriage to help them to see things in perspective. Happily married couples rarely publicise their happiness—it is something between themselves which, as Homer put it all those centuries ago, 'they themselves know best.'

The Cardinal's attitude towards marriage is entirely positive. He sees it as a relationship of love between two persons committed for life and orientated to one end. Lifelong fidelity, in his view, is not a burden to be borne—it is something in which to take pride. He quotes Roger Garaudy: 'The joy of man is to have remained faithful at sixty to the dreams of his twenties.'

Moreover to illustrate the dignity of marriage and the nature of the fidelity that is proper to it he gives in a pastoral, word for word, 'the magnificent formula' of the English marriage ritual:

'I, N... take thee, N... to my wedded wife,
to have and to hold from this day forward
for better or worse,
for richer or poorer,
 in sickness and in health,
to love and to cherish
till death us do part,
according to God's holy ordinance,
and thereto I plight thee my troth.'

This concept of fidelity, the Cardinal believes, is valid for anyone, believer or not. But faith in God gives to it a different quality:

'A Christian can never forget that his fidelity is borne, sustained, and vivified by God's own fidelity. The divine fidelity is at the heart of ours—its firmest support.

'Through and in God husband and wife love each other not only with a human love that is personal and frail but with the love of God himself.'

The sacrament of marriage penetrates with its grace the heart of the man and the woman, raising them beyond themselves, and making eternal in them the love which brought them together—translating their aspirations into joy which is a 'flower that can open and thrive only in the nourishing soil of hope that is born in God and finds fulfilment in him.'

CHAPTER 12

L'essentiel est invisible pour les yeux.

From *Le Petit Prince* by ANTOINE DE SAINTE-EXUPÉRY

THE NOVEMBER AFTERNOON was chill and grey. In the garden at the
back of the Cardinal's residence in Brussels wizened leaves rustled
underfoot.

It was warm indoors in the Secretariat where I looked at photographs taken during his travels: Chicago, Washington, Baltimore,
Philadelphia, Atlanta . . . Rio de Janeiro, Recife, Salvador . . .
Toronto, Winnipeg, Ontario . . . London, Liverpool, York. These are
a few names picked out at random.

A photograph taken at Chicago showed the Cardinal in conversation with the late Paul Tillich, that most abstruse of theologians
who was endowed with a poet's sensitivity to nature, a poet's
mastery over words.

Another showed the smiling, compassionate face of Helder Camara,
Archbishop of Olinda and Recife, champion of the under-privileged;
a man small in stature but great in courage and charity.

Later that day I listened to some of the Cardinal's anecdotes
about Pope John. Stories about a man who already in his lifetime has
become a legend are often apocryphal. One can be sure, however,
that those coming from Cardinal Suenens are authentic, for, as well
as having been on intimate terms with John XXIII, the Cardinal is
truthful to a scrupulous degree.

Many readers will probably have heard the story of Pope John's
difficulty in going to sleep at the beginning of his papacy (so weighed
down was he by the thought of his responsibilities), until one night
an angel said to him: 'You need sleep. You *must* sleep. After all,
you're *only* the Pope!'—from which time he had no more trouble.

Less well known, I think, is another story concerned with Pope
John's difficulty in sleeping, caused this time not by his thoughts

but by the 'tramp, tramp' of feet as the sentinel on guard outside the papal apartment went up and down the corridor. Unable to endure it any longer, the Pope opened the door: 'My good man,' he said, 'if this doesn't stop, neither will *you* get any sleep, nor shall *I*!'

Then there was the audience with the Grand Duchess of Luxembourg. Asked afterwards if she had any special memory, any anecdote to tell, 'O yes,' she said, 'I'll never forget how the audience ended. The Pope stood up, escorted me to the door, took hold of the door-knob, opened the door, then hastily shut it. "Forgive me," he said, "I forgot I was Pope. I have to press the bell."'

I do not recall why my conversation with the Cardinal turned from Pope John to the cathedral at Brussels dedicated to St. Michael the Archangel. But I remember saying somewhat irrelevantly: 'I'm not sure that I believe in angels!' The Cardinal smiled. 'Oh, *don't* you?' he said, '*I* do'.

Because his tone was neither condemnatory nor condescending I felt no desire to argue... I even began to wonder if perhaps, after all, there *were* angels.

Possibly the incident would not stand out in my memory with such clarity were it not for what followed, when, an hour or so later, the Cardinal said Mass in his chapel.

The congregation comprised two nuns and myself. In the open doorway the Cardinal's little grey dog Malou lay on his side, stretched full length, motionless except for the rise and fall of his body keeping time to the rhythm of his breathing. A stubby amber-coloured candle picked out the design of the Four Horsemen of the Apocalypse on the tabernacle and accentuated the shadows formed by the drapery on the carved Madonna. In a homily which was no more than two or three sentences the Cardinal said: 'There are three of you, and myself. That makes four. And there is Christ, here in our midst. That is five.' Then, looking in my direction, a faint smile on his lips, he said (articulating the words with special clarity): 'And there are the ANGELS!'

The longer I have known Cardinal Suenens the clearer it has become to me that to him the unseen world is of vastly greater reality than anything our eyes can see.

'*L'essentiel est invisible pour les yeux.*' These words from Antoine de Sainte-Exupéry's masterpiece, *Le Petit Prince*, are the key to much of the Cardinal's thinking. Nor is it, I believe, accidental that the Cardinal was favourably impressed by the play *The Man of La Mancha* and the rock musical *Godspell*. For although as a work of creative imagination *Le Petit Prince* surpasses the others, all three have closely-related, sometimes overlapping, themes.

One of these themes concerns the nature of reality.

Reality, the fox explains to the Little Prince, is not what we see with our eyes. We must penetrate to a deeper level. It is only with the heart that we truly see: *'On ne voit bien qu'avec le coeur.'* And the Prince passes on this message: 'Our eyes are blind,' he says. 'We can see only with the heart.'

In *The Man of La Mancha* the emphasis is again on reality as distinct from appearance. Don Quixote is inspired by an inner poetic perceptivity which enables him to see in the girl Alonza not merely the prostitute she is, but a human being deserving, as such, of respect and capable of better things. And because Don Quixote can see beneath the surface, because he can believe in her, he is empowered to transform this girl who is despised by others and hateful to herself.

Again, the Jesus of *Godspell* is far other than he appears to be. Nor is he misled by externals. He understands the motives, penetrates into the hearts of those who follow him: sees each as, in truth, he is. He sees into the heart of Peter, into the heart of Judas.

Moreover in the three works the stress is on the unique quality of the individual. The Little Prince learns from the fox why his rose differs from all other roses; why this particular fox differs from all other foxes.

In *The Man of La Mancha* Alonza says to Don Quixote: 'You spoke to me and everything was different.' And the emphasis is on '*you*' as distinct from just anyone.

In *Godspell* the individuality of each Apostle is brought out most movingly when Christ, bidding farewell after the Last Supper, embraces each one of them in a different way.

Furthermore, the three works are concerned (not in a didactic manner but by the use sometimes of a nuance or innuendo) with the nature of love—how in genuine love, friendship is an integral factor. Moreover friendship is shown as something which does not just 'happen'. An effort must be made. The fox explains that the Prince, if he wants his friendship, must first tame him and this will need patience. 'I shall look at you,' he says, 'out of the corner of my eye.' The Prince, the fox continues, is not to talk—'words lead to misunderstanding'—but to come a little closer every day.

In *The Man of La Mancha* it takes time for Don Quixote to win the trust of Alonza. His words are misunderstood. Again and again she rejects him. Again and again he approaches her.

In *Godspell* the concern, the depth of love that Jesus feels for each of his followers, reveals itself in all its fullness only gradually, delicately, culminating in the unconditional gift of self: 'Greater love has no man than this, that he lay down his life for his friends.'

Friendship entails the acceptance of responsibility. The fox says to the Little Prince: 'You are responsible for your rose.' And the Prince, so as to remember the words, repeats: 'I am responsible for my rose.'

Similarly Don Quixote takes upon himself responsibility for Alonza: he feels it is his task to make her understand that she is not the worthless, unloved creature she supposes herself to be.

In *Godspell* individuals are shown as having to accept responsibility for what they do: Judas must accept the remorse that is the price of his act of betrayal; Peter, the anguish of having denied his Master. But over and above this (here is the paradox) Jesus, because he loved his own—each one separately—accepts responsibility for all without exception. Of him we can say in truth: 'He bore our iniquities and by his stripes we are healed.'

Finally, in the three works the prevailing note is one of triumph, joy. There is sadness, but sadness and joy are close to one another. This is evident in children. The laughter of children is quick to turn to tears, their tears to laughter. This is also true of adults who have in maturity preserved a childlike—as distinct from a childish—simplicity of heart. Thomas More, confronted by death, could bid his dear ones be not over-sorrowful, but think how, in heaven, they and he 'will make merry for ever and never have trouble hereafter'.

In Antoine de Saint-Exupéry's story the Little Prince who weeps is also the Prince who laughs. The desert can be frightening, but because, somewhere, it hides a well, it is beautiful. The stars can be cold and distant, but they are beautiful because on one of them invisible to eyes on earth, there is a rose. '*Ce qui est important ne se voit pas.*' When the Little Prince goes away, the teller of the story is sorrowful. The Prince consoles him: 'I shall be living,' he says, 'on one of the stars. On one of them I shall be laughing. And so, for you it will be as though all the stars were laughing.' '*Ce sera pour toi comme si riaient toutes les étoiles.*'

In *The Man of La Mancha* the joy derives from the dauntless, idealistic courage of him who chose to be dubbed 'the Knight of the Doleful Countenance', who, despite ridicule, mockery, defeat, is undefeated—his triumph all the more moving because, as death approaches, it is the girl Alonza, in whom he alone believed, who recalls to his failing memory the ideal he had set before himself:

> To dream the impossible dream,
> To fight the unbeatable foe,
> To bear the unbearable sorrow. . .
> To reach the unreachable star.

Godspell has been criticised on the grounds that the Resurrection has no place in the production. This is a shallow judgment. The Cardinal has rightly said: 'The message comes through.' Once again, what is not seen is of greater importance than what is seen. This is demonstrated more effectively than if a risen Christ had been presented by scenic devices. Through a happy correlation of colour, movement, and music, the final note is one of joy. When the body of Christ crucified is carried down from the stage through the auditorium, the mood is one not of sorrow and finality but joyous expectation.

Every human being differs from every other—even as on a tree no two leaves are alike.

Love and friendship (the two converge) call for patience: '*Il faut d'être de patience.*' They also entail responsibility of one human being for another.

Joy must prevail over sorrow, for Christ the Day Star has risen; nor can any darkness quench his radiance.

These are a few of the ideas that give a distinctive quality to the Cardinal's attitude and therefore to his words.

Cardinal Suenens is a good speaker. He is logical, uncomplicated, humorous, never repetitious. His short, balanced sentences, forged in the intellect, are spoken from the heart.

Moreover he is a quiet speaker. His voice is natural, conversational—no rhetorical devices, no 'playing to the gallery'.

His voice comes across well on the radio. Something, however, is lost if one cannot see him, for his face is expressive. It can be sombre—or perhaps I should say grave. On one occasion, as he stood in the pulpit waiting for the hymn to end before beginning his sermon, I said to myself: 'The Knight of the Doleful Countenance.' Or his expression can be smiling or whimsical. In any case, the eyes which at a distance appear darker than in fact they are command attention. He has a way, too, of using his hands—not in exaggerated gestures

M

but with the purposeful movements of a potter moulding his clay.

Fluent in Flemish, French, Italian, English, and a little less so (he says) in German, he rarely uses a script. Asked how long it takes him to prepare a sermon or address, he gave the answer that Corot gave when asked how long he took in painting a picture: 'Five minutes and a lifetime.'

His English is indeed fluent. The listener has no difficulty in understanding what is said—there is no hesitancy, no fumbling for words. But to describe his English as 'impeccable' or 'flawless' (I have seen these words in the press) is misleading. Now and then his grammar goes 'skew-whiff', or he uses a continental as distinct from an Anglo-Saxon vowel sound. But this gives character to his delivery. It would be a pity, in my opinion, if he were to correct, meticulously, these idiosyncrasies—just as it can be a pity when the Scots or Welsh or Irish exchange a pleasing intonation or lilt or idiom so as to conform to 'the Queen's English'.

René Voillaume in his collection of sermons published under the title *Retraite au Vatican* makes the point that, when preaching the Gospel, it is harder today than formerly to make an impact upon a large gathering. People like to feel they are individuals, not lost in a mass. The Cardinal is aware of the difficulty. Hence his interest, in the Focolari movement, Charismatic prayer groups, and Marriage Encounter, each of which emphasises the distinctive, unique quality of every human being.

Nevertheless, things being as they are, and time and opportunities being limited, to address large gatherings, if far from ideal, is inevitable. After all, Christ—besides talking to individual persons such as Nathaniel, Nicodemus, Zacchaeus, and the Samaritan woman at the well of Jacob; besides conversing with the Twelve Apostles, each of whom differed from the others—addressed himself to crowds, and in doing so exercised a magnetism that drew to him ever more and more followers.

One of the secrets of doing this effectively lies in presenting profound truths in words of extreme simplicity—that is what Christ does in his parables. This approach, provided the speaker is endowed with intelligence and imagination, is acceptable alike to simple persons and to intellectuals—that is, if the intellectual is genuinely such: the pseudo-intellectual likes long words and complicated arguments, whether in fact he understands or not, and is incapable of appreciating a parable in the Gospels or, in secular writings, a work such as *Le Petit Prince* or a fairy tale from Hans Andersen.

Another secret in addressing a large gathering (and this is a rare gift, a 'grace' if you will) is to make the individual listener forget he is one of a crowd. This approach can be fostered in day-to-day life by developing an increasing awareness of each person as a unique being. The Cardinal fosters this gift in his normal approach to others. Moreover when preaching, he sometimes deliberately, I have heard him say, addresses himself to one particular member of a gathering. By this, he does not mean one person to the exclusion of others, but as representing the individuality, the uniqueness, of each person present.

Above all, perhaps, this quiet, restrained, humorous speaker holds the attention of his hearers because his simple words are the expression not merely of theological competence (the theology is there as surely as are the bones that provide the framework of the human body), but of a personal experience of God, coupled with an imaginative vision of the many things which, for those who have eyes to see, ears to hear, are a manifestation of the divine, the transcendent.

Evelyn Underhill has defined mysticism as the art of union with Reality. 'The mystic,' she continues, 'is a person who is aware of and believes in such attainment.'

If the mystic be thought of in these terms and not as someone in a more or less perpetual state of ecstasy, living on a plane beyond the comprehension of the majority of mankind, then Cardinal Suenens can be said, I believe, to be a mystic. Indeed, anyone who has followed the thought of the Cardinal through the 'sixties (when he was pre-eminently occupied with problems posed by the structures of the Church), then on into the 'seventies, can hardly fail to observe that the emphasis is more and more on the invisible world—on the *Deus absconditus*, a God who, hidden from our corporeal eyes, reveals himself to the eyes of faith. When listening to the Cardinal speaking I find myself recalling the poet William Blake who, when asked if at dawn he did not see a disc of fire something like a guinea, replied: 'Oh, no, no, I see an innumerable company of the heavenly host crying: "Holy, Holy, Holy, is the Lord God Almighty!"'

I do not mean that the Cardinal speaks with the emotional intensity of Blake but the thoughts behind the quiet words are, I believe, of this quality.

CHAPTER 13

'We must all of us place ourselves
windward of the mysterious breath
of the Holy Spirit. Come, O Holy
Spirit. Come, O creating Spirit.
Come, O consoling Spirit.'

POPE PAUL VI

I HAVE HEARD it said that Cardinal Suenens resembles a bishop from
the United States rather than one from a European country.

This is meant as a compliment. But in fact the words tell us
little, since in the United States, as elsewhere, no two bishops are
alike. The Cardinal can, with justice, be compared (as he has been by
Monsignor Tracy Ellis) to Archbishop Paul Hallinan of Atlanta, in
that each of these men, once he has made up his mind, displays a
dauntless courage in pursuance of his goal: a determination that can
be shaken by no conflicting interest, personal or otherwise. On the
other hand, it is not difficult to think of bishops in the United States
who are the antithesis of all for which Cardinal Suenens stands.

One can say, however, that Cardinal Suenens has a particular liking
and admiration for the United States. He is undaunted by immense
distances. Indeed, to cover vast areas gives him a sense of exhilaration.
Moreover he feels at home in the States: he likes the people—he
finds them welcoming, friendly, outgoing, enterprising, generous.

To present Pope John's encyclical *Pacem in Terris* to the Secretary
of the United Nations, New York, in May 1963 had been, it will be
recalled, a great moment in the Cardinal's life. But even before that,
he had friends and acquaintances in the States. Moreover, a number
of his books had been published there.

During the Council he continued to widen his American circle
through contact with fellow bishops, non-Catholic observers, as well as

others who had come to Rome from the States for one purpose or another.

A photograph taken on December 4th 1965 (a few days before Vatican II ended) at the Hotel-Pensione Castel Sant-Angelo, where most of the delegate-observers stayed, shows the Cardinal at the dinner-table in the company of nine non-Catholics representing different denominations and universities—all, with the exception of one Canadian, from the United States. These Protestant pastors and professors were completely at ease with this prince of the Church: they had never met, some of them were heard to say, 'a Roman Catholic like the Cardinal'—by which they meant, not that Cardinal Suenens minimised to the smallest degree his allegiance to the Church of Rome, but that he was a man of openness and understanding, ready to listen and to accept them as fellow Christians dedicated, no less than he, to the one Saviour of mankind.

If these men were at their ease, it was also because the Cardinal had taken the trouble to acquaint himself with their way of thought.

The previous year, in May 1964, during a visit to the United States, he had addressed the Protestant Theological Faculty of the University of Chicago, as well as participating in discussions with Protestant and Catholic students and Faculty members. But even before the Cardinal's visit the Faculty had contemplated founding a chair for the study of Catholic life and thought. This, to the pleasure of the Cardinal, was now founded—since when a Catholic theologian of world renown has lectured each year at Chicago.

Dr. Jerald C. Bauer, Dean of the Faculty of Divinity, wrote:

> We were looking for someone who would combine personal engagement in a theological sense with the *aggiornamento* which characterises Vatican Council II. In Cardinal Suenens, who exceeded every expectation, we found a man extremely sensitive to the major problems of the dialogue between Catholics and Protestants. This sensitivity is not only born of a wide knowledge of the central problem, but also of humility and a sense of humour which facilitated the work greatly and gave to all participants a new vision and new views.

The periodical *Time* described how in Chicago 'the debonair and witty Archbishop of Malines-Brussels' underwent the most difficult examination he had ever experienced when he entered into argument with the 'prestigious theologian Paul Tillich'—a man of whom

Cardinal Suenens speaks with admiration and respect. But it was not only in Chicago that he made an impact. He captivated audiences in Washington, Baltimore, Jersey City and Boston.

The year 1967 opened for the Cardinal with a visit in mid-January to Atlanta, Georgia, where, at the suggestion of Archbishop Paul Hallinan, he delivered three lectures at the Chandler School of Theology at Emory University—a Methodist institution. Also participating were the Methodist Bishop Fred P. Corson and Dean (now Bishop) William Cannon. All three had associations with the Vatican Council. The Archbishop wrote the introduction to the *Decree on the Bishops' Pastoral Office in the Church, Christus Dominus*; Bishop Corson wrote the response to this, and Dean Cannon had been an observer. The subjects chosen by the Cardinal for his lectures were: 'Dialogue within the Church', 'Ecumenical Dialogue', and 'Dialogue with the World'.

The Cardinal's visit to Georgia ended with Solemn Mass celebrated in the Cathedral of Christ the King, Atlanta.

From Atlanta he flew to Austin, Texas, where on January 23rd he spoke at the Catholic Student Centre of the University on 'The Church in the Modern World'.

The tone of his address was constructive, optimistic. The purpose of the Church today, he said, was to help all men of goodwill to build the world of tomorrow—to free them from the bondage of ignorance, from the distrust which paralyses human relationships, and from fratricidal hate.

Speaking of Vatican II, he said that, as the Council progressed, it had been as though a conversation were developing between the Church and the world—as though something were happening far beyond all that was taking place beneath the great dome of St. Peter's basilica.

The contribution made by Vatican II, he stressed, was not simply a renewal of the wish to save mankind—it was the idea of being at the service of others: above all, of listening to others and thus coming to understand what was passing in their minds. The obligation of one person to assume responsibility for another was implicit throughout the Cardinal's address at Texas.

In 1968 at Berkeley, California, in the First Presbyterian Church, the Cardinal gave the three Earl Lectures (sponsored by the Pacific School of Religion) under the general heading: 'The Signs of Our

Times' and entitled individually: 'A New Approach to God'; 'A New Approach to Fraternity'; and 'A New Approach to World Justice'. The press wrote about 'this distinguished Cardinal who interspersed his highly original lectures with quotations that ranged from the theologian Paul Tillich to the poet Francis Thompson'.

From Berkeley he went to Stanford University where he spoke on 'The Catholic Church Today and Tomorrow'.

In a short address to students thronging the plaza in front of Sproul Hall, the University of California, he said it was essential there should be a free interchange of ideas between generations, nations, and religious bodies. Once more he reiterated that we must learn not only to speak but to listen.

In an interview given in California to the editor of *The Catholic Voice*, the Cardinal made the following points:

We must face the problem posed by the gap between rich and poor nations—in particular the failure of the rich to help the poor. . .

We cannot by-pass this problem as the Pharisee and the Levite by-passed the Samaritan on the road to Jericho. . .

The Church is required to give answers applicable to every generation. . .

And yet the Church must maintain continuity with the past: the Holy Spirit is one and the same yesterday, today and tomorrow. . .

The 'Death of God' thinking can be an incentive to ask: 'Who is the real God?' We speak about God glibly, cheaply. The most profound knowledge we have is that God is above knowledge. . .

Ecumenism is a matter not of scoring points, but of finding the mind of Christ. This means exchanging views openly. A Russian Orthodox observer at the Council said that the most serious problem arose from the fact that the Churches of the East and the West had not spoken to one another for nine centuries. The greatest need in the Church today is faith and a sense of humour. Or possibly we should reverse the order: a sense of humour and faith!

In January 1969 Cardinal Suenens was at Philadelphia where the Methodist Bishop Corson spoke of him as 'keeping guard at the doors opened by the Second Vatican Council'. The Cardinal, he said, was one of the 'master-minds' which had helped to bring about the 'wonderful things that had happened within the Church'.

In June the Cardinal lectured in Chicago at the invitation of Dr. Bauer, Dean of the Faculty of Divinity.

In the same month he was at Notre-Dame University, South Bend, Indiana, attending a symposium on his book *The Nun in the World*.

In March 1970 Cardinal Suenens, along with Dr. Michael Ramsey, then Archbishop of Canterbury, gave a course of lectures during a seminar at Trinity Institute, New York, attended by seventy-six bishops of the Episcopal Church. The theme was 'The Future of the Christian Church'. The Cardinal and the Archbishop each gave three lectures. These addresses, published in book form, are permeated with the Cardinal's faith in the Holy Spirit, his conviction that in the power of the Holy Spirit all things are possible:

> Day by day I experience the surprises of the Holy Spirit. . . I have confidence in statistics and respect for sociological data only to a limited degree. The Spirit of God can break through the determinism created or predicted on a human level. . .
>
> The Church is Christ among us today, Christ living today; redeeming and sanctifying humanity through his Spirit. . .
>
> Christ said to his Apostles: 'All authority in heaven and on earth has been given to me. Go, therefore, and make disciples of all nations; baptise them in the name of the Father and of the Son and of the Holy Spirit. Teach them to observe all the commandments I gave you. And know that I am with you always: yes, to the end of time'. . .
>
> Only the Holy Spirit can teach us to spread the Gospel, while at the same time respecting another's freedom of conscience. History, regrettably, presents us with examples of the message of Christian freedom imposed by force upon people who neither understood nor as yet desired to accept the Gospel. . .
>
> Christ never said: 'Force people to be converts', but rather: 'Offer the Good News in a spirit of freedom and joy'. . .
>
> When we possess a treasure that brings us joy we reveal spontaneously our desire to share this. When I say to someone: 'Look, there's the dawn!' I'm not constraining him to raise his eyes, I'm not forcing him. I'm offering him a deeper experience of joy.

Also in March 1970, at the invitation of Cardinal Dearden of Detroit, Suenens addressed first an audience composed of religious, then a general audience. On June 11th an honorary Doctorate of Law was conferred on him at Harvard University.

In 1972 a fifteen days' lecture tour in the States took him to ten cities in all, from Los Angeles to New York.

On March 7th the Cardinal addressed an audience of 1,500 in the Hollywood Stadium. While he was speaking a group of protesters of the 'integrist' type (i.e. 'ultra-conservative' as opposed to 'progressive' Catholics) stood outside, saying the Rosary for 'the conversion of Cardinal Suenens,' who at that moment was speaking about the role of Mary, the Mother of Christ!

In an interview afterwards he was asked whether the 'Tiger' of the nineteen-sixties had turned into the 'Lamb' of the 'seventies—since he was putting less emphasis on structural reforms, more on spirituality. In other words, had he shied away from the institutional reforms which he had championed during the Council? 'Of course not,' he replied. Institutional reforms were still needed, he explained, but the Church cannot be renewed by these alone: 'We have to stress also the mystical aspect of the Church'. An evangelical renewal is taking place, a rediscovery of the Gospel, a fresh insight into the meaning of Christ for this age. The Holy Spirit is preparing a new springtime for the Church. Something is dying, but something else is growing.'

On March 9th he spoke to a teeming congregation in the Church of Our Lady of Grace, San Diego. As at Hollywood, a group of people, rather than listen to him, spent an hour in what they called 'prayer of reparation' to atone for the words of heresy he would (they believed) assuredly let fall.

The loss was theirs. Had they been in the church they would have heard, Michael Newman wrote in *The Southern Cross,* 'a clear and beautiful explanation of what our faith signifies. There were no histrionics, just a minor movement of the hands from time to time. There were no heresies. There was love for the Church and the People of God who are the Church, expressed simply, but with a meaning as deep as the ocean.'

Later that evening, the Cardinal made people smile when he said: 'I don't know why you in San Diego were created, but in Belgium we're created to know, to love, and to serve God; *and* to make him known, make him loved, and make him served!'

The same evening he took up the question (posed to him a few months before) as to whether the Church today is in a state of 'revolution' or 'evolution'.

'Revolution,' he said, 'is the wrong word. Revolution implies a break with the past. One can speak of the French, Russian, Copernican, or Industrial Revolution. But the Church by its very nature preserves a continuity that reaches back to the people of Israel, the ancient covenant, the promise given to Abraham. Evolution, on the other hand, is too weak a word. The change we see in the Church at the present moment is not a gradual evolution, as when a child imperceptibly grows into an adult, an acorn into an oak.

'"Progressive" Catholics should learn to love and respect tradition. "Conservatives" should acquaint themselves with history and thus be able to distinguish what is relative from what is absolute. How many Catholics reflect that, if St. Peter had remained at Antioch instead of going to Rome, the externals and the exercise of papal primacy would have taken a different form, but the reality would have been the same?'

On leaving San Diego the Cardinal was the guest of the Franciscans at Phoenix, Arizona. The desert made an unforgettable impact upon him: the immense open sky; distant horizons; weird tropical plants; the variegated, contrasting colouring of sand and rock, changing with every shift of light; an all-enveloping silence.

On March 14th in Philadelphia, he concelebrated Mass with Cardinal Krol and the Rector of the St. Charles Borromeo Seminary.

Addressing the seminarians he urged them to make Jesus Christ the 'keystone' of their priesthood; the 'joy and the hope' of their lives. He continued: 'You have the obligation to translate God's word day by day, and we cannot understand God if we do not love. Through love you will come to understand Christ. You will be the presence of Christ in the world. And this is what the world is waiting for.'

The same evening at the Baptist Temple, Broad Street, Philadelphia, he gave a lecture—sponsored by the Pope John XXIII Ecumenical Centre and the *Journal of Ecumenical Studies* of Temple University—on 'The Church of the Spirit'.

On March 19th 1972 he delivered the John Courtney Murray Forum Lecture at the Church of St. Paul the Apostle, New York City.

Father Walter Burghardt, S.J., introducing the speaker, said: 'Contrary to what might be supposed in the case of someone as well known as Cardinal Suenens, an introduction *is* necessary—if only to show that the Cardinal is *not* the person some imagine him to be. He is *not* an enemy of Pope Paul; he is *not* turning the Church into a democracy; he holds lovingly to a past that links Catholicism with Christ. He is a Cardinal indeed, but he has transformed the meaning of the word from "prince of the Church" to "servant of man".'

The Cardinal's lecture that followed reveals a depth of Christo-centric spirituality enlivened by flashes of humour. Even the most glum listener could scarcely refrain from a smile when hearing the Cardinal's anecdotes about Pope John; about an importunate journalist; about a priest who admitted: 'When I was at the seminary I learnt an answer to every question, but unhappily no one ever asks me those sort of questions!'

It is probably true to say that during the many journeys made by Cardinal Suenens in the United States nothing impressed him more than his encounters with what is known as Charismatic Renewal.

This phenomenon began to manifest itself with the Catholic Church in 1967, taking the form of prayer groups which sprang into being one after another, particularly in the universities—among students, post-graduates, and members of the Faculty. Pittsburgh, in Kansas, for example; Ann Arbor, in Michigan; Notre Dame, at South Bend, Indiana.

As when a spark has set alight stubble and presently a whole field is ablaze, so Charismatic Renewal spread through the United States from city to city—then beyond the States, to Canada, Mexico, Brazil, Chile, Peru, Korea, and many European countries.

What was called an International Congress held in 1967 was attended solely by representatives from the United States, apart from a nun from Canada. Six years later at the Congress at South Bend, Indiana, in 1973, every continent, with the exception of Antartica, was represented.

Charismatic Renewal within the Catholic Church is distinct from what may appear to be similar phenomena outside the Church: the Classical Pentecostals, for example, who go back to the turn of the century and the Neo-Pentecostals who since the early nineteen-fifties have been in evidence in many Protestant denominations.

This is not to say there is no common ground between Catholic and non-Catholic Charismatics. On the contrary, not only was the Presbyterian Charismatic Conference, in March 1973, held at Ann Arbor, an important Catholic centre, but at the closing session on March 29th Cardinal Suenens and Bishop Joseph McKinney of Grand Rapids, Michigan, both spoke. A photograph shows them standing side by side with Presbyterian ministers, hands linked, singing:

'We are one in the Spirit.'

How, then, should we see Charismatic Renewal within the Church? Should we call it a movement?

In the Cardinal's view 'movement', in this context, is an unfortunate word in that it can give the impression of an organisation with affiliated members, specific duties, and leaders holding positions of authority. He thinks of Charismatic Renewal, rather, as 'a current of grace' sent to remind us what it means to be a Christian, what in fact, Christians are by virtue of their baptism—a current which, when its purpose has been served, will disappear. Or, using another image, he likens it to a river which, having reached its mouth and merged into the sea, is to all intents and purpose no longer a river.

Among Catholics the initiative in Charismatic Renewal came from the laity, many of them intellectuals. Later, religious and clergy were drawn to it. Eventually the hierarchy gave their approval, albeit in some cases grudgingly.

One of the highlights in the story of Charismatic Renewal was an International Congress, representing thirty-two countries held in October 1973 at Grottoferata, outside Rome—the choice of place being in itself a gesture of loyalty to the Pope.

Moreover Pope Paul in an audience given to eleven delegates indicated his approval of the emphasis on prayer and a renewed life of the Spirit within the Church. This, he said, could lead to a deeper understanding of the Scriptures, a greater dedication to Christ and to the community. He expressed his joy at learning what these Charismatic groups were doing. The spirit, he said, must not be quenched. At the same time he stressed that fidelity to tradition must be observed; that the greatest gifts of the Spirit are faith, hope and charity, and that there should be prudent guidance in union with bishops and priests.

During this congress Father Kilian McDonnel, O.S.B., in consultation with other theologians, drew up a document in which it was emphasised that while Charismatic gifts are needed to revitalise the Church as an institution, equally these gifts, if they are not to get out of hand, need the structures and leadership which only the Church can provide. Nor are such gifts, the document continued, to be regarded as ends in themselves: they are not bestowed for their own sake, but to contribute to the fullness of life in Christ and in the Holy Spirit to which every Christian is called.

Cardinal Suenens presented this document to the Pope.

It was fitting that this should have been so. The Cardinal's episcopal motto *In Spiritu Sancto* has proved more then a felicitous turn of phase. For him, these are words of life.

Moreover at the Vatican Council, it will be recalled, one of his most important interventions had concerned Charismatic gifts.

Nor is that all.

During his travels in the United States he studied Charismatic Renewal at first hand, using every opportunity to extend his knowledge. He also read widely. And because his interest was plain to see, wherever he went he was asked his impressions.

When he was at Philadelphia in March 1972, some nuns from New Jersey arrived late at night to tell him what the Holy Spirit was bringing to pass in their prayer house at Convent Station. Because they had braved a terrific blizzard to come, he felt bound to receive them and to listen to what they had to say. This was his first real contact with persons involved in Charismatic Revewal.

Back in the United States in March 1973 the Cardinal visited the nuns in New Jersey. 'Something is happening in America,' he told them, 'that will give renewed strength to our faith in a living God. There is new hope. A new star shining. You are discovering, afresh, Jesus as Lord—the Spirit of Jesus working in your midst.'

During the same month Cardinal Suenens was at the Catholic Charismatic Centre at Ann Arbor, Michigan.

Why had he come to the States, why to Ann Arbor? he was asked by Ralph Martin, Director of the Inter-Communications Office for Charismatic Renewal.

The official reason for his visit, the Cardinal explained, was to give a series of lectures to Episcopalian clergy. The unofficial reason was to see how life was lived at Ann Arbor.

Recalling words spoken by Jesus to his first two Apostles: 'Come and see', he continued: 'I wanted to "come and see". In the Church today it is not enough to give theoretical answers. We must be able to point to places where it can be *seen* that God is at work—where God and the truth of Christianity can be experienced, lived vitally.'

'By your fruits you will know them.'

Using these words as his yardstick, so to speak, the Cardinal had discovered from first-hand experience that Charismatic renewal fostered loyalty to the Church; recourse to the Sacraments; love of the Scriptures; a spirit of confidence and hope; growth in prayer—

especially spontaneous prayer of praise and thanksgiving; an awareness of God's presence—in particular, the presence of the Holy Spirit. In short, here was a means whereby many could become more closely united to one another and to God.

It is indeed in keeping with the Cardinal's personality that he should be sympathetically disposed towards a spirituality which is not only apprehended on the intellectual level but actually 'experienced'. He would agree, I imagine, with the words of Pablo Casals: 'Music must satisfy not only the intellect but the soul.'

Many who would like to understand, even participate in, Charismatic prayer are deterred by a number of considerations.

They feel, for instance, that prayer meetings of this kind could attract unbalanced persons. The Cardinal does not deny this risk, saying in his own humorous way; 'If you open the window at night when the light is on, it is always possible some mosquitoes will come in!' But this only reinforces the need, of which Pope Paul spoke, for guidance and discernment.

There is also the difficulty of terminology.

'Speaking in tongues' is a case in point. Here the Cardinal has light to shed. He does not deny that this phenomenon could on rare occasions be miraculous—if, for example, someone who had no knowledge whatever of Chinese were suddenly to speak in that language. Normally, however, he regards 'speaking in tongues' as a natural phenomenon inspired by a religous motivation: a way of reacting or expressing emotion untramelled by constraints and inhibitions which the years or custom have imposed. It is natural, for instance, for children—not exceptional children, but normal, ordinary children—to leap and dance and sing and call out, just as they feel inclined. Possibly, then, 'speaking in tongues' is a way of expressing one's feeling for God: joy because he exists; above all, joy because he loves us.

Further, the Cardinal explains, this kind of prayer may be a reminder that we are not alone when we pray—that it is not, in fact, we ourselves who are praying but the Spirit who prays within us. St. Paul tells us: 'We do not know how to pray as we ought, but the Spirit himself intercedes for us with groans too deep for words.'

The greatest difficulty, however, is presented by the phrase 'Baptism in the Spirit'. As interpreted by the Pentecostals this implies two baptisms: first, baptism by water usually, but not always, in childhood;

secondly, baptism in the Holy Spirit, at a later stage when a person may be assumed to have attained at least some degree of spiritual maturity. The Cardinal rejects this. He is insistent upon the traditional Catholic teaching of there being one sacramental baptism. There is, he says, one baptism in water and in the Spirit. There can be no second baptism.

The term 'Baptism in the Spirit' describes an experience related to baptism, but not baptism itself. Hence, to avoid misunderstanding, he believes that another expression ought to be found to describe what amounts to a realisation or insight into what took place at baptism: a heightened awareness that the Holy Spirit dwells in us and we in the Holy Spirit.

From June 1st–3rd 1973 the Seventh International Conference on Catholic Charismatic Renewal was held at Notre Dame, Indiana. Delegates came from no fewer than twenty-five countries, making in all some 23,000 persons. What began as an American phenomenon had become, as Cardinal Suenens remarked, a world-wide one.

Six hundred priests participated and eight bishops. The presence of Cardinal Suenens provided (to quote Monsignor Francis Maurovitch, writing in *The Tablet*) 'the highest ecclesiastical endorsement yet given to the movement'.

A Canadian, Joseph B. Courtney, C.S.B., from Alberta, who had not attended a Charismatic prayer meeting before, gave his impressions in *Pastoral Life* (October 1973). He had reservations—the most important concerning 'speaking in tongues', which he experienced as a 'babbling, bubbling, or gurgling' sound that from time to time broke out apparently from the entire assembly. But what impressed him most was the order, the discipline, the dignity, the 'quiet grace', the restraint, the 'spirit of happy expectancy', and singing which created 'a mood at once joyous and religious'.

The closing ceremony was, he says, particularly moving, when Mass was concelebrated by several hundred priests, some bishops, and Cardinal Suenens, who gave the homily. As the clergy, having vested in the Convocation Hall, processed across the stadium four abreast, then split into two columns, one going east, the other west, there came from the gathering a ripple of clapping, then a thunder of applause—dispelling the misconception (sometimes prevalent) that Charismatics are anti-clerical. At a loss how best to speak to this vast assembly, the Cardinal prayed for the guidance of the Holy Spirit.

The following are excerpts from his homily:

'Beloved People of God, when I asked the Lord what I should say to you, his answer was, I believe:

> Tell them why you are here.
> Tell them why you love them.
> Tell them what the Church and the world
> expect from them.

'Why am I here?

'Perhaps because some thirty years ago, when I became bishop, I chose as my motto: *In Spiritu Sancto.*

'Perhaps because during the Vatican Council one of the more venerable cardinals told me that charisms were outmoded; that they were something the Lord gave in the early days of the Church, just as parents give toys to children, to encourage them—and this set me thinking . . .

'Perhaps, because I believe in the "surprises of the Holy Spirit"—for this is, indeed, a "surprise". . .

'Why do I love you?

'I love you because you praise God not for what he gives, but for his own sake, his glory. Now, this is not merely natural, it is supernatural. If we were, ourselves, to make up the Lord's Prayer, we'd begin, I imagine: "Give us TODAY, QUICKLY, our daily bread". But *you* are asking for something greater: that the will of God, the glory of God, may become a reality. By the power of the Holy Spirit you have discovered what adoration means.

'I love you because you are faithful both to the Father and to the Son—because you understand that Christians are not followers of Jesus as a Marxist is a follower of Marx or a Maoist a follower of Mao: because you understand the Jesus whom we follow is the Holy one, the Anointed.

'What is the Church expecting from you?

'That you go forth here and now—show what Christianity means, proclaim the Good News. We say: "The time is not right. People are not ready to listen."

'In the time of Jesus were people ready? I do not think so: I have only to look at a crucifix. When Paul at Athens tried to speak about the Resurrection, were they ready? By no means. "Most interesting," they said, "but we're busy. Come back another day." If we wait till people are ready we will wait until eternity. The Church

N

is asking you to show what it means to be a Christian; to open your hearts and your arms to others, in love and joy. That is what the Church and the world are waiting for.

'Be filled with the Holy Spirit and you will renew the face of the earth.'

While the Cardinal was speaking, a young man who had graduated at Yale was listening. He did not belong to a Charismatic prayer group. He was at the conference by chance or, if you will, because Providence so ordained. He had not seen or heard Cardinal Suenens before nor, as far as I know, has he done so since. Born a Catholic, he had fallen away from the Church which, in the world today, was, he believed, no longer relevant.

As he listened to the Cardinal's address he found himself recalling effortlessly, line by line the hymn: *Veni, Sancte Spiritus,* which he had known by heart years before when he served as an altar boy at his parish church.

The words came back, verse after verse:

> *Veni, Sancte Spiritus,*
> *Et emitte caelitus,*
> *Lucis tuae radium*
>
> *Veni pater pauperum*
> *Veni dator munerum*
> *Veni lumen cordium . . .*

When the young man told me this some months ago, during a chance encounter in a train between Oxford and London, he still had reservations about the Church—even, he said, about the reality of God.

Nevertheless each day he repeated the verses of this hymn.

CHAPTER 14

'I hurry wherever I am beckoned,
in search of what can bring
men together in the name of the
essential.'

DOM HELDER CAMARA,
ARCHBISHOP OF OLINDA AND RECIFE

IN 1967 CARDINAL SUENENS was in Canada, a country to which he is warmly attached.

From Sunday August 20th to Friday August 25th he was at Toronto University, participating in a major theological Congress sponsored by the Catholic Bishops of Canada and by the Pontifical Institute of Mediaeval Studies.

The theme was 'The Theology of Renewal in the Church'. The word theology was used in the wide sense of study and research into God's dealings with man; renewal referred to the pattern or structure of change, generally called reform or *aggiornamento*; and the Church (in accordance with a usage employed in Vatican II) designated the totality of the People of God—at once, in some mysterious way, divine, human, personal, and institutional.

With this in mind forty-four outstanding theologians, as well as other men of distinction in various spheres, assembled to exchange views on matters of common concern. Those taking part were not confined to the Church of Rome. The non-Catholics included Rabbi Abraham Heschel of New York and Dr. E. L. Mascall of King's College, London. There were women, too.

The opening address was given by Paul-Emile Cardinal Léger of Montreal.

At the plenary session on the Tuesday night Cardinal Suenens spoke on *'La Co-résponsabilité', Idée Maîtresse du Concile et ses Conséquences Pastorales'*.

The congress was the occasion of the Cardinal's first visit to Canada. But already at the Vatican Council he had come to know a number of Canadians. On December 1st 1963, he addressed the Canadian College in Rome, in the presence of the Canadian bishops.

Among these bishops was Alexander Carter of Sault Sainte-Marie, North Bay, Ontario, today a close friend of the Cardinal.

Bishop Carter remembers Cardinal Suenens during the Council as a man whom even 'the least discerning would have recognised as a powerful influence for change in the Church: a man, moreover of 'resolution, lucidity, courage, and forthrightness', whose interventions were for the most part 'electrifying in what they said, in the manner in which they were interpreted and in the vision they contained'.

Alexander Carter, along with other Canadian bishops, used to meet the Cardinal from time to time, but the friendship between the two men dates from the Second Synod, in 1969, which brought together the Presidents of various Episcopal Conferences.

The Bishop writes:

> Almost from the beginning, Suenens and I discovered each other. We stood for the same things: decentralisation of structures, greater autonomy for the local church, collegiality as defined by Vatican II, co-responsibility. We met occasionally, talked these things over and found ourselves in basic agreement. Moreover both realised that, although all this was secondary to a spiritual renewal in the Church, nevertheless some changes of structure were necessary if renewal was to breathe, grow, and survive.

Even at this relatively early stage in their friendship the Bishop was aware in the Cardinal of a 'deep spiritual quality'. As time went on he became increasingly conscious of this. Moreover he was happy to be able to come out in defence of Cardinal Suenens in September 1970, when a 'silly attack' was launched against his friend as a result of an article the Cardinal had written.

'I am amazed', the Bishop comments, 'to see how even in this enlightened age of new humanism so many still prefer to attack the speaker or writer rather than answer his arguments or show the weakness of his position. Suenens has had more than his share of this sort of tactic.'

In February 1971, when, at the invitation of Bishop Carter, Cardinal Suenens paid his second visit to Canada, a growing friendship, the Bishop writes, 'blossomed into a warm, human relationship'. The visit was intended as a purely private one, but, as things worked out, it became a *tournée de conférences*.

Bishop Carter explains:

> The French-speaking priests of my diocese were in the process of updating themselves through a series of 'work-shops', some of these given by professors of Laval University in Quebec. One of the professors, a Belgian, was asked by the priests whether there was any possibility of getting Cardinal Suenens to address them. The professor smiled. 'I can see no problem,' he replied. 'Your own Bishop is the man to approach. If he invites the Cardinal, I'm confident the answer will be in the affirmative. The two are close friends.'

> And so, at the request of the priests I wrote to Suenens and asked him to come for the 'workshop' in Sudbury—and one in English for the rest of the clergy in Sault Sainte-Marie. To make his visit more worthwhile I suggested two public lectures: one in Sudbury and one in the Sault, as well as a talk to the Sisters of St. Joseph in the motherhouse of North Bay.

> I added that he could take a few days of much needed rest before returning to Belgium.

> He has a wry way of reminding me of this part of my invitation, for events turned out rather differently than was expected.

When the Cardinal's visit had been arranged, Bishop Carter mentioned this to some of his fellow-bishops one evening when they were relaxing after a meeting. Among them was Cardinal George Flahiff of Winnipeg, Archbishop Philip Pocock of Toronto, Archbishop Joseph Plourde of Ottawa, and Bishop Carter's brother, Emmett Carter, Bishop of London, Ontario. Before the gathering broke up they had each proposed in one way or another that Cardinal Suenens should visit their respective dioceses. Furthermore the Western Conference of Priests had been in touch with Bishop Carter, begging him to bring the Cardinal to talk to them and offering to schedule their meetings at a time that was convenient.

Leaving aside the many invitations which shortage of time made it impossible to accept, the Cardinal was involved in a cross-country tour—and this in mid-winter; a season of storms and blizzards. Even so, not one assignment was missed.

Wherever he went he carried a message of hope that was founded upon confidence in the presence and in the activity of the Holy Spirit in the Church and in the world. Moreover he urged the People of God to listen to the young: the young were right, he said, in feeling that there is an inhuman element at work amongst us.

Bishop Carter accompanied the Cardinal on his cross-country trip which lasted from February 26th until March 16th.

Writing in 1973, the Bishop says:

> It was indeed a moving experience. The Cardinal's talks were excellent. Young people, in particular, derived hope and courage from them. There is no doubt whatever that he did a tremendous amount of good. Here, it was plain for all to see, was a man of the Church whose belief is deep, whose hope is vigorous—who loves his Church and his Lord with all his heart.
>
> During these days I grew to love this man more dearly than ever. My entire staff were charmed and intrigued: these young priests still recall the Cardinal's visit as if it were yesterday.

The Bishop describes how, in the midst of this pressure, he 'stole a day' at his cottage, to enable the Cardinal (such was Bishop Carter's intention) to relax:

> A vast expanse of fresh, shining white snow enveloped the countryside. Suenens had never experienced anything like this, and he was enthralled. It gave us hours of calm, warm, friendly conversation: meals prepared and shared together in quiet intimacy; an exchange of thoughts, hopes, aspirations for the Church we both serve.
>
> I suggested that we should take a trip on a snow-mobile. He looked a bit appalled at the idea, but I can be as stubborn as he can. And so I invited a few friends and neighbours to join us. One of them gave some instructions to the Cardinal on how to run the machine; we suggested he should make a quick turn around the road. He looked at the whole apparatus doubtfully, touched the throttle, heard the roar and said in his resonant voice: 'I have need of further instruction.'
>
> At this, my young Vicar-General, Bernie Pappin, who was to

keep special watch over him, said: 'In simple language around here we just say: "Help".'

Finally we took off. The Cardinal looked like a man condemned, but who would do his duty, come what may. He set a certain pace and would not hurry it. With my friends I would roar down the lake and the trails, then double back to see how he was getting along. Monsignor Pappin stayed close to him. At one point, however, the Monsignor thought he would investigate a small trail on an island, with the idea that the Cardinal might like a detour.

Unfortunately the snow was soft, with the consequence that the Monsignor's snow-mobile got entangled with a tree and he took some time to extricate himself. He rushed back, to find the Cardinal desolate and alone in the quiet of the snow-covered lake, surrounded for miles by a white wilderness.

Suenens turned to Bernie and said pleadingly: 'Don't leave me again!'

Later Bernie asked him, 'What were you thinking of all alone out there?'

The Cardinal answered in sepulchral tones: 'Eternity.'

Eternity.

When the boy Léon Suenens looked up at the star-lit sky he thought about eternity.

Sixty years later, when the same Léon Suenens, prince of the Roman Church, found himself alone on the vast, snow-covered lake—only the silence and the snow reaching on and on—he thought about eternity.

As the years pass from childhood to adolescence, adolescence to maturity, maturity to age, we change with the changing years. Our appearance, our ideas, our aspirations change. Our attitudes towards ourselves, towards others, towards God, undergo a gradual transformation. And yet, at some deep level, we remain the same, unique persons we have, each one of us, always been. Something intangible, invisible, unites the self of yesterday, today, and tomorrow. The child thinking about eternity, the Cardinal thinking about eternity is one and the same.

In the words of Ecclesiastes: 'That which has been is now . . . And that which is to be has already been'.

The unforgettable 'twenty-five-mile safari in the snow' was

followed by a convivial dinner, which, Bishop Carter recalls, brought out other facets of his guest's personality:

The Cardinal was a witty, delightful companion in this relaxed informal setting. My friends still talk of him with respect and admiration, but also with great warmth.

He accompanied me, I remember, when I visited friends in hospital, especially the husband of our devoted secretary of the diocesan Chancery Office. He told me how much he appreciated the intimate relationship between our priests and people, and even expressed regret that his own role did not afford him more such occasions. Since then, during a visit to Malines, I watched him preside over a liturgy of the sick in part of his diocese and shared with him in this. It was a moving and rich experience.

The Bishop and the Cardinal meet whenever an opportunity presents itself. They met at the Third Synod in 1971. And occasionally, when the Cardinal is in America, they manage to have a day together. They 'talk by the hour, compare notes, share hopes, apprehensions, disappointments, joys.' In all that concerns the Church the two men often have different opinions on what the Bishop calls 'ways and means,' but they share the same basic positions.

Bishop Carter is a man of sincerity. In expressing his feelings of warmth and admiration for Cardinal Suenens he has no wish to cast himself in the role of hero-worshipper. He understands why some people see the Cardinal in a different light—how it is that, when feelings run high, the Cardinal can, in his zeal to give witness to the truth, appear aggressive, even overbearing. People are misled, the Bishop explains, by an image ('a false one') projected perhaps on some public occasion: 'As in all else, to know is to understand. To know the Cardinal is to understand his simplicity of heart, the depths of his humility.'

Summing up what Cardinal Suenens has meant and still means to him, Alexander Carter writes: 'In all simplicity I can say that his friendship has enriched my life and what I love most about him is the knowledge that he is an honest and honourable man, a loyal friend and true Christian.'

In 1967, immediately after the congress at Toronto, Cardinal Suenens had gone to Latin America, where, between August 26th and

September 6th, he visited Rio de Janeiro, Salvador, Recife, and São Paulo.

His purpose was threefold: to examine some of the problems facing the Church in Brazil; to study, in particular, novel methods that were being adopted in an attempt to facilitate pastoral work; lastly, to meet Belgian priests from the Latin American College in Louvain, now working in Brazil—to see on the spot the conditions in which these men were living and the difficulties confronting them.

The time at the Cardinal's disposal was shorter than he would have wished. But as well as having a quick mind and a capacity to make the best use of whatever time is his, he takes pains, beforehand, to acquaint himself with the attitudes and problems of the people among whom he will be moving.

This was particularly important in relation to Brazil: an immense geographical entity where the rich are inordinately rich, the poor inordinately poor—the two sundered one from the other by political, economic and psychological factors.

Preoccupied since boyhood with justice and outraged by injustice, Cardinal Suenens has strong views concerning the Third World and the responsibilities (too often 'shrugged off') of the rich, developed nations towards those which are poor and underdeveloped.

One way of appreciating the Cardinal's outlook in this field is to study Pope John's *Pacem in Terris* and Pope Paul's *Populorum Progressio*—documents to which the Cardinal attaches the greatest importance. Or one can study the writings of his friend Archbishop Helder Camara, a man to whom can be applied without exaggeration the words of the Scriptures: *Dedit ei Dominus latitudinem cordis quasi arenam quae est in litore maris.*

In his book *Pour Arriver à Temps* the Archbishop quoting *Populorum Progressio* writes:

If any one has the world's goods and sees his brother in need, yet closes his heart against him, how does God's love abide in him?' It is well known how strong were the words used by the Fathers of the Church in describing the proper attitude of persons who have possessions towards those in need. To quote St. Ambrose: 'You are not making a gift of your possessions to the poor person: you are handing over to him what is his. For what has been given in common for the use of all, you have arrogated to yourself. The world is given to all, not only to the rich.

How can one remain indifferent to a collective injustice which affects two-thirds of humanity? How can one not be grieved by the knowledge that millions of human creatures are living in sub-human conditions, without the possibility of using the divine gifts of intelligence and freedom? How can we not feel hard-pressed before such a vast multitude about whom Christ will say to us on the last day: 'I was hungry, I was thirsty, I was naked. . . ?'

And paying tribute to Cardinal Suenens Dom Helder Camara says:

In the first phase of Vatican II, thanks to His Eminence Cardinal Léon-Joseph Suenens, an informal meeting was promoted between the bishops of the developed world and those of the underdeveloped. Once again a Cardinal of Malines took the initiative in a dialogue which tomorow may lead to tangible consequences, as did the Conversations between Mercier and Lord Halifax.

Cardinal Suenens would have liked to travel in Brazil *incognito,* so as to cut down official ceremonial and thus devote more time to poverty-stricken, underdeveloped areas. For a figure as well-known as the Cardinal this proved not only impracticable, but impossible. Even so, by a judicious use of his time he made his journeys more than worthwhile.

At Rio de Janeiro, where he was welcomed by Cardinal Jaime de Barros Camara, he had valuable discussions on pastoral concerns. He also visited Petropolis, an hour's drive from Rio, where the Franciscans have a House of Studies.

At Salvador he participated in a national meeting of Sisters engaged in parochial works, after which he visited two parishes, Platoforma and Piraja, both of which (so great is the shortage of priests) are in the care of Sisters. He was specially interested to learn of the training being given to married men who wanted to be ordained as deacons.

On the evening of Friday August 31st Cardinal Suenens arrived at Recife where he was the guest of Archbishop Helder Camara.

In the company of the Archbishop the Cardinal was able to be among the rural workers whom he saw in their homes and at their labours: he listened to all they had to say with deep attention and a mounting compassion. He recalls as one of the most moving occasions of his tour a visit to Cabo, a district of heart-rending poverty. On Sunday he took part in the celebration of the Eucharist in the parish of Ponte de Carvalhos where the priest was trying to make the Mass more 'alive' for his congregation.

The stay at Recife was for the Cardinal the highlight of his visit to Latin America. It was a source of no less happiness to Helder Camara.

The following is a translation from the Portuguese of an assessment of Cardinal Suenens made by the Archbishop:

> When I think of the kind of faith that is intelligent, that combines absolute loyalty to the Pope with a close relationship with all God's people on earth; when I think of what I would call disinterested hope strong enough to surmount the greatest obstacles. . . When I think of authentic love incapable of hesitancy —love that is demanding, stimulating, strong, I think of Léon-Joseph Cardinal Suenens.

In the Flemish periodical *Straal* (October 1972) a journalist, describing a visit he paid the Archbishop at Recife, gives an idea of the simplicity of Helder Camara's way of life as well as his admiration for the Cardinal:

> In a small room, its walls made of rough cement, there was a table, strewn with papers, at which the Archbishop worked, and a bed. On the table, to the left, was a map of the world, a small carved stag, and between the two a photograph of Cardinal Suenens. Laughing, the Archbishop said: 'Yes, this is the only photo I keep here—*my* Cardinal. I love him! A *great* Cardinal! At Rome during the Council we worked together a lot. We bishops in Brazil are greatly indebted to him.'
>
> Some people try to make out he is a rebel against the successor of Peter. I assure you I don't know a bishop in the world more loyal to the Pope—and the Pope *knows* this. If there is one man in the whole world who is striving to liberate the Pope, to enable His Holiness to serve the entire Church, this man is Cardinal Suenens.

Archbishop Camara was in Rome during the Council, listening with wrapt attention rather than speaking, and since then he has kept himself fully informed as to the Synods and all that touches upon the implementation of Vatican II. He is aware that there have been occasions when Cardinal Suenens has publicly expressed disagreement with Pope Paul (several times in the Pope's presence)—not however on a personal level, but concerning the government of the Church.

The Archbishop's words, therefore, should carry weight, and put to shame those who are malicious enough to represent the Pope and the Cardinal as 'enemies'.

The following incident, which belongs to the year 1973, illustrates the bond uniting Cardinal Suenens and Archbishop Helder Camara.

During a visit of Helder Camara to Belgium he and the Cardinal were interviewed on the French Radio.

After an hour's exchange of ideas, as well as comments from an interviewer, questions were put by an audience in the studio.

The final question was a delicate one.

'Why,' it was asked, 'is Archbishop Helder Camara not a cardinal?'

Turning to his friend, the Archbishop replied: 'I *have* my cardinal already!'

Whereupon Cardinal Suenens put in: 'As you know, we have *all* things in common!'

On September 3rd 1967 Cardinal Suenens left Recife for Sao Paulo where he was the guest of Cardinal Rossi, President of the National Conference of Bishops. The following day he celebrated the fortieth anniversary of his ordination to the priesthood.

At São Paulo he conferred with Señor Paulo Egydio Martins, previously Minister of Commerce and Industry, who had formed groups of experts in the field of economical, political and social affairs, to work together in the hope of alleviating the problems of the underprivileged.

The Cardinal also spent a day at Vila Re, outside São Paulo, where he had informal talks with Belgian priests working in this region. The priests were delighted. Long before his visit, the Cardinal was well-known in Brazil for his interest in that country, as well as for his role in the Vatican Council. On his side, the Cardinal felt that the meeting with the priests could not have been more satisfactory.

Cardinal Suenens was due back in his diocese by September 7th.

Determined to keep to this, he changed at the request of Cardinal Rossi the programme of his last day in Brazil, to enable him to attend, in Cardinal Rossi's company, the opening ceremony of the Israelite— Latin American Convention. The assembled Rabbis were touched by this ecumenical gesture and by the words addressed to them by the two Cardinals.

CHAPTER 15

'I am doing what Cardinal Mercier would have liked to do.'

LÉON-JOSEPH CARDINAL SUENENS

MALINES. 'THERE IS music in the name.'

Over and above the many other associations the city has for Cardinal Suenens, it is first and foremost the place where Désiré Joseph Mercier, a Cardinal of the Church of Rome, and Charles Lindley, Viscount Halifax, an Anglican layman, each accompanied by representatives of his own Church, came together in a spirit of charity and with a courage which persons acclimatised to post-Conciliar thinking may fail to appreciate.

The Malines conversations were, to use a phrase of Cardinal Suenens, 'the seed-bed' of the ecumenical work that occupies so much of his time and thought today. Already as a small boy his ambition had been to preach the Gospel, but his specific concern for, and sympathy with, the Anglicans derives from his close relationship with Cardinal Mercier (Léon Suenens was a seminarist at the time of the Malines conversations), as well as from Dom Lambert Beauduin whom, it will be recalled, he came to know at Rome.

I have mentioned the plaque in the Cardinal Mercier chapel in Malines cathedral, commemorating the Conversations and dedicated on October 26th 1966 by Cardinal Suenens in company with the Anglican Bishop of Winchester.

In 1967 Cardinal Suenens went a step further along the path which, he believed, would lead in the fullness of time to union between the Roman and the Anglican Churches.

Recalling how Cardinal Mercier said during the Conversations:

'I ought really to go to Canterbury myself'—meaning by 'Canterbury' not the city but the Primate who occupies that see—Cardinal Suenens determined to do precisely this. An invitation to attend the opening of the Catholic Cathedral of Christ the King, Liverpool, on May 14th of that year provided a reason for a visit to England.

Accompanied, therefore, by Canon Joseph Dessain, Secretary of the Malines-Brussels Ecumenical Committee, and Canon Servotte, Superior of the Pope John XXIII Seminary, Louvain, he arrived in London on Friday the 12th, thus paying his first official visit to England and at the same time returning a visit made to Malines by Dr. Michael Ramsey (then Archbishop of Canterbury), some three years earlier, in May 1964.

The guest of Dr. Ramsey at Lambeth Palace, the Cardinal attended Evensong in the chapel, after which the Archbishop was to preach. Of this occasion Canon Dessain relates the following anecdote:

> At the end of the first psalm I picked up a leaflet. Imagine my consternation when I read: 'After Evensong the Archbishop will preach and Cardinal Suenens reply.' We had no idea the Cardinal was to speak. Discreetly passing the leaflet to the Cardinal and not daring to raise my eyes, I prayed that the Holy Spirit would inspire him. He did inspire him. The Cardinal improvised, in excellent English and without the slightest hesitation, a discourse that was both rich and moving.

The incident, the Canon says, illustrates the Cardinal's gift of knowing exactly what to say or do in an unexpected situation—a quality presupposing, he adds, a thoughtfulness for others which is all too rare. The key words in the Cardinal's address were: 'I am here not in my own name but in that of Cardinal Mercier. I am doing what Cardinal Mercier would have liked to do.'

Furthermore, during this visit, Cardinal Suenens was the first person for over four centuries to say a Latin Mass in Lambeth Palace.

In January 1969, the guest of Cardinal Heenan, he preached in Westminster Cathedral during the Week of Prayer for Christian Unity.

Having made the point that the rediscovery of Christian brotherhood, for which we were indebted to Pope John, had not done away with doctrinal difficulties, he went on: 'Nevertheless as ecumenical dialogue continues we can discern converging tendencies—movements of the Spirit which point in the direction of unity among Christians. Truths and values, which at one time seemed to cancel out each other, now present themselves as complementary. It is no longer a question of tradition or Scriptures; the hierarchy or the priesthood of the faithful; papacy or collegiality...Over and above much that divides us there is an ever-growing concern for what we share in common.'

On the Monday the Cardinal lunched with the Archbishop of Canterbury at Lambeth Palace. He then went to Oxford where, at the invitation of Dr. Henry Chadwick, Regius Professor of Divinity, he lectured on 'Co-responsibility'. On the Tuesday he lectured at Heythrop College on 'The Evolving Church', and on the same day attended a reception in London given by the publishers Burns and Oates to launch the English edition of *Co-responsibility in the Church*.

The visit by Cardinal Suenens to York in April 1969 made a greater impact than the earlier one to Lambeth Palace. This had nothing to do with the Cardinal as such who, though he is the object of much publicity, is remarkably indifferent to this and, if circumstances permitted, would happily travel to the ends of the earth *incognito*. It was simply that as news value York had the advantage.

At Lambeth the Cardinal had been the guest of the Primate of England; he had been present at Evensong and made a gracious response to the Archbishop's address of welcome; he had said Mass in the Palace. Moreover photographs in the press showed the two men together—in most of them the Archbishop looking exuberant, the Cardinal dignified, if a trifle self-conscious.

All this, however, was no match for what took place at York where in the Minster, for the first time in four hundred years, a Cardinal of the Church of Rome addressed the congregation and, along with Dr. Donald Coggan then Archbishop of York, unveiled a copper plaque commemorating the Malines Conversations.

There was a further point. Whereas at Lambeth the meeting took place on the ecclesiastical level, in York the laity were involved: the plaque honoured not only clerics but a layman, Lord Halifax, many of whose family were present in the Minster.

On the Friday evening, April 25th, Cardinal Suenens was met at Yeadon, the Leeds/Bradford airport, by the Bishop of Selby, the Right Reverend Douglas Sargent, representing the Archbishop of

York, and by the Bishop of Leeds, the Right Reverend Williams Gordon Wheeler, with whom he stayed the night at Bishop's House, Thorner.

The following morning he visited the Community of the Resurrection at Mirfield, where he gave an address in the presence of Dr. Ramsey, then Archbishop of Canterbury, at that time as Visitor to the Community, who came from London for the occasion.

In the afternoon he arrived at Bishopthorpe the home of the Archbishop of York, in time for tea and a reception given by Dr. and Mrs. Coggan. Among those present were the Right Reverend W. F. P. Chadwick, Bishop of Barking; Canon John Satterthwaite; members of the Chapter at York, as well as local clergy, Anglican and Roman Catholic.

That night there was a dinner party at Garrowby, home of the Earl of Halifax, grandson of the Viscount Halifax who with Cardinal Mercier had initiated the Malines Conversations. The Cardinal met the Earl's mother, the Dowager Lady Halifax, widow of Viscount Halifax, Viceroy of India and later, Ambassador to Washington.

On Sunday, April 27th a congregation of several hundreds assembled in the Minster for Matins. To the singing of 'Come, Thou Holy Spirit, Come' the procession led by the Minster Cross and choir moved from the south transept into the nave, brought up at the rear by the Archbishop of York and Cardinal Suenens walking side by side. During the singing of Charles Wesley's hymn, 'Oh Thou Who Camest From Above' the Cardinal was escorted to the pulpit.

In the course of his sermon he said:

'We are here together because some forty years ago Cardinal Mercier, a man of faith and courage, dreamed dreams of a visible unity of the Church of Christ. He knocked on the door of another man of courage and faith, Lord Halifax. Thus began the first ecumenical dialogue that had taken place for many years. Silence of five centuries was broken that day in Malines.

'That is why I am here, a successor to Cardinal Mercier. The conversations did not, apparently, succeed. But when Cardinal Mercier was dying he took off his episcopal ring and gave it to Lord Halifax as a token of hope, a ray of light in the darkness. Lord Halifax gave the ring to be welded into a chalice belonging to York Minster, so that we might learn to pray together for the visible unity of the Church of Christ.

'Since those days the ecumenical dialogue, begun by Pope John

XXIII when he threw open the doors and windows to let in fresh air, has become world-wide. The Pope had said that whereas some people wanted to complicate simple matters, he preferred to simplify complicated ones. We do not want to conduct a trial of the past, to prove who was right or wrong. The blame is on both sides. All we want to say is: "Let us come together again, to make amends."

'The first stage was dialogue. The second, praying together to the same Lord. The unity at which we aim is not something human, not a diplomatic compromise. We need to discover the will and the command of the Lord. Through dialogue we learn not only to pray together but to see each other with new eyes. If we do this, we see that we are all sons of the same Father, united in the brotherhood of Christ. This is our common ground.'

After an introductory prayer said by the Archbishop, he and the Cardinal, praying together, unveiled the copper plaque which reads:

In Thanksgiving to God
and
in memory of the friendship
of
Désiré Joseph Cardinal Mercier and
Charles Lindley 2nd Viscount Halifax

1851–1926   1839–1934

and of those who worked with them
in the cause of unity between the
Roman Catholic and Anglican Churches
in the Malines Conversations
1921–1926

The service ended with the blessing given together by the Cardinal and the Archbishop. As the clergy withdrew, Dr. Francis Jackson, organist of the Minster, played a Koraal and Toccata by Flor Peeters, organist of Malines cathedral.

That Cardinal Suenens should have preached in York Minster was indeed an historic event: a logical outcome of the Malines Conversations. But his visit should be seen against the background of earlier attempts made by Anglicans and Roman Catholics to reach a better understanding.

In 1946 Leonard Prestige, Canon of St. Paul's Cathedral, London, went on 'an unofficial mission of friendship' to Rome, where he had talks with Monsignor Montini, then pro-Secretary of State, later Pope Paul VI. Indeed Pope Paul had gone out of his way to familiarise himself with the Anglican Church. Before the outbreak of World War II he paid several visits to England, during which he attended services in Anglican cathedrals. Later, as Archbishop of Milan, he invited to stay with him a party of six Anglican clergy and one layman—chosen on the recommendation of Bishop Bell of Chichester. His visitors accompanied Archbishop Montini as he went around his diocese. The purpose of the visit was to discuss matters of common theological concern; to dispel ignorance and prejudice; to discover whether a particular issue involved vital disagreement or whether the same truth was being viewed from another angle or expressed in a different idiom.

Moreover in April 1950 Canon Prestige with six Anglicans met a group of French theologians in a Dominican house outside Paris where they were joined for one day by Dom Lambert Beauduin, then in his seventy-seventh year. In September of the same year secret but officially sanctioned conversations began at Strasbourg and went on over a period of ten years, each occasion being less and less secret.

As to the visit of Cardinal Suenens to York, the occasion which meant more than any other both to himself and to the Archbishop, was a friendly, open conversation that took place between the two in the Archbishop's study on the Saturday evening.

What they said is known only to themselves, but the Archbishop was left with the conviction that the Cardinal was someone whose friendship he would always value; someone to whom could be applied 'the title more to be coveted than any other: "A man of God."'

Some two years after the visit of Cardinal Suenens to York, Dr. and Mrs. Coggan, accompanied by the Earl and Countess of Halifax and their son Lord Irwin, arrived on May 14th 1971 at the Archevêché, Malines, where they were the guests of the Cardinal for three nights.

Dr. Coggan and the Cardinal speak of this occasion with a like enthusiasm: it was a visit no less happy, no less fruitful, than had been that of the Cardinal to York.

On Saturday morning the Cardinal celebrated Mass in the cathedral of St. Rombaut, in the Cardinal Mercier chapel. Lord Halifax read the first Lesson, the Archbishop the second. The Cardinal gave a short homily. The blessing was given by the Archbishop and the Cardinal together.

On returning to the Archevêché the Cardinal and Dr. Coggan

were able, as at Bishopthorpe, to exchange ideas in a relaxed, informal atmosphere and thus renew and strengthen the bond of friendship already uniting them.

On Sunday morning the Archbishop of York preached in the Anglican Church of the Holy Trinity, Brussels, in the presence of Cardinal Suenens.

His text was the last verse of the Second Epistle to the Corinthians: 'The grace of Our Lord Jesus Christ, and the love of God, and the fellowship of the Holy Spirit be with you all ever more.'

Dwelling on the implications, the richness, contained in this 'Trinitarian' prayer—'after the Our Father the most familiar of all'—the Archbishop spoke of what a prayer of this nature could mean to those who are overwhelmed by the perplexity of life, its problems, sufferings, and inequalities. He spoke of the God whose love for us is revealed in Christ, the Word made flesh, who, in his graciousness invites us, through the power of the Holy Spirit, to become his friends.

The sermon was the more moving because the Archbishop prefaced it with an incident out of his own experience:

'The main street in Oxford with the traffic roaring by is hardly the most likely place for God to perform a very gracious act in the heart of a man. But thus it was last Tuesday. Queen Elizabeth the Queen Mother had been opening a new college building. The festivities were over and I was walking towards my car. In the street I was met by a college servant. He had looked after me on a previous visit. He stopped, and in an Irish accent said: "I pray for you every day." Then, diffidently, he added: "I pray for the Holy Father first, then for the Archbishop of Canterbury and you."

'My heart was strangely warmed, as Wesley would have said. This casual contact was a visitation of the Holy Spirit. Two men totally different in background and allegiance found themselves one in Christ. I learnt something fresh of the grace of our Lord Jesus Christ, of the love of God and of the fellowship of the Holy Spirit, and I was thankful for it.'

That the Cardinal and the Archbishop should think of each other as a friend is not surprising. They have a number of qualities in common.

Like the Cardinal, the Archbishop is a generous, large-minded man. He is generous with his time, where a lesser man would be 'too busy'. Travelling from York to Addis Ababa he found time in

London—between a lunch party and catching the plane at Heathrow —to talk to me, for an hour in his flat at Westminster, about the Cardinal.

Again like the Cardinal, he has an unassuming dignity, totally devoid of pomposity.

And again like the Cardinal, this down-to-earth man has a spontaneity, a warmth of heart, that can reveal itself in a single sentence. In reply to my request: 'Talk to me, please, about the Cardinal', came the immediate response: 'I *love* that man!' In those few words he had told me, I felt, more than I had ever hoped to learn.

Further, these two exemplify what ecumenism should mean in the climate of today. There is no sentimentality; no blurring of the edges; no pretence that theological differences between Roman Catholics and Anglicans do not exist. Both being men of insight and intelligence they realise that visible unity between Rome and Canterbury can only come when theologians have found a solution that is not, for either side, a betrayal of truth.

Because, however, they understand human nature and have, moreover, a sense of humour, they know that theological arguments will carry no conviction in an atmosphere charged with animosity. They know that doctrinal differences are more likely to be resolved, as Bishop Butler has observed (*The Listener,* April 2nd 1970), in a milieu unclouded by non-doctrinal issues, the latter stemming often from prejudice and misunderstanding.

They know that prejudice and misunderstanding can be banished only by friendship, and that friendship comes into being gradually, step by step. The Cardinal and the Archbishop are one in being both patient and impatient: patient in a realisation that God's time is not necessarily our time; impatient in their zeal to remove, whenever possible, obstacles that block the path to unity.

Finally, they are both men of hope: ready to believe in what the Cardinal calls 'the surprises of the Holy Spirit'.

In October 1970 Cardinal Suenens paid a whirlwind visit to England.

On the 14th he lectured at Worth Abbey, Sussex; on the 15th in London, first at the Royal Institute for International Affairs, later at the London School of Economics; on the 16th in Canterbury, at the University of Kent. Each lecture had an ecumenical slant and was followed by questions. At one point during his London visit he almost collapsed from strain: he had to leave a reception and be given a bed in an Anglican rectory, where he rested between two engagements.

In the opening chapter of this book I gave my impressions of the Cardinal's appearance when I saw him for the first time at the London School of Economics. I would like to add a word about his technique as a speaker.

Dr. Robert E. Terwilliger, Director of the Trinity Institute, New York, writes:

> The Cardinal's approach is basically pastoral, direct, and practical. He is not ashamed of being moved or of moving his hearers with his simple, evangelical faith. At the same time he is unashamedly and discernibly a convinced Roman Catholic.

This is a good assessment. Indeed the Cardinal's words can be so simple that a listener could fail to appreciate the profundity of his thought, particularly if he or she has been conditioned to equate complicated words and convoluted sentences with intelligence.

I was struck when I first heard the Cardinal (and this impression has remained) by his ability to put across, with extreme clarity, ideas to which no Christian (using the word in its widest sense) and few persons of goodwill could take exception, while at the same time refusing to compromise his allegiance to the Church of Rome.

Asked after his lecture at the London School of Economics whether he thought a Christian need accept the traditional Catholic teaching on the Real Presence of Christ in the Eucharist, the Cardinal gave an answer which some might say went beyond the range of the question. In his view, he said, a person was not a Christian in the full sense of the word unless he believed in the divinity of Christ; the Resurrection of Christ from the dead; and the Real Presence of Christ in the Eucharist.

On that occasion, after the gathering had broken up, some undergraduates were exchanging views. One said: 'The Cardinal is a good speaker but I can't go along with this outdated stuff about the Real Presence'. Another agreed. My thoughts turned to the disciples who, when they heard Jesus say: 'Unless you eat the flesh of the Son of Man and drink his blood you have no life in you', walked with him no more.

Then another student, a girl, broke in: 'I don't know much about theology, but this Cardinal is plainly not just sincere, he's "brainy". I'd like to know more before rejecting what he says.'

The following spring, 1971, the Cardinal was again in London, where he addressed the first Ecumenical Marian International Congress, organised by Martin Gillett, founder of the Ecumenical Marian Society, a man of faith and courage.

The Cardinal reminded his listeners—they included the laity, clergy and a number of bishops—that while Mary was a woman like any other, she differed from any other in that through the loving compassion of Christ whose Spirit pervades her being, she has given to us him who is our joy and salvation: the Word Incarnate, he who was in the beginning, is now, and ever shall be.

It is not every day you can see and hear a Cardinal preaching in a Baptist church. It is not every day you can have a conversation with a Cardinal—even if you are writing a book about him.

These were the considerations which led to my decision to travel from London to Bristol to attend the South West Ecumenical Congress in April 1973.

It was, of course, something of a gamble. Only a limited number of persons were to be admitted to the church, and preference given to members of the congregation and a few privileged ticket holders. I belonged to neither category. As to a conversation with the Cardinal, that would depend upon the time available to him: his schedule would be a tight one. If it was practicable, I would receive a telegram from Malines before I left London.

Up to the time of my departure no telegram had come. I set out, somewhat disconsolate, but telling myself: 'One never knows...'

At Bristol I asked whether there was a chance of a ticket to admit me to the Baptist church. 'We're very sorry,' I was told, 'all the tickets have been allotted.'

The rest of that Saturday passed pleasantly enough. There were discussions and opportunities of exchanging ideas with members of a variety of denominations. Nevertheless I was aware of a nagging sense of frustration.

Then, after tea the unexpected happened.

A clergyman came up to me. 'There's a spare ticket,' he said, 'for tomorrow's service in the Baptist church. I thought you might like it.' Who he was, to what denomination he belonged, why he offered the ticket to me, I do not know. In my eyes he was as Hermes, the messenger of the gods, sent down from Olympus. Or, better, one of those 'rare servants of the Lord' whom John Henry Newman likened to 'angels in disguise'.

The sunlight broke in shafts of gold upon the Church's unadorned brick walls and pale woodwork. Cardinal Suenens, wearing a simple scarlet cassock and a surplice with a deep edging of lace, was addressing the congregation in his clear, quiet voice:

'When Jesus was baptised in the river Jordan, the Holy Spirit came down upon him and a voice from Heaven was heard saying: "This is my beloved Son in whom I am well pleased."

'Again, on the mountain of the Transfiguration the voice was heard: "This is my beloved Son in whom I am well pleased: hear him."

'Who is this "Beloved Son"?

'He is the Son of the Most High, the Son of God.

'But are we not told: "God is dead"?

'Yes, a God whom man has made is indeed dead.

'But the living God, revealed in Christ, the Word Incarnate, he is not dead.

'Let us not confuse the living with the dead.

'The God who died was created by man in his own image.

'The God who died was the remote God of Greek philosophy: a God untouched by the sufferings and concerns of man.

'The God who died destroyed man's creative powers: omniscient and all-seeing, he shrivelled by the fixity of his glance man's powers of growth.

'The God who died was a *deus ex machina,* a "solver of problems".

'The God who died was a rival to man confronting his creatures with a dilemma: God *or* man.

'In Christ, in whom is the fullness of the living God, the dilemma is resolved: we chose God *and* man.

'The living God is the God for whom we hunger, who alone can fill the void within us.

'The living God, though far above us, is near us and within us.

'The living God is the God of Jesus and the Father of Jesus.

'The living God is supreme wisdom.

'The living God is love.

'God loves us.

'God loves each one of us with the totality of his love.

'God knows us by name: "I know my sheep and they know me."

'God keeps us in all our ways.

'God loves us with a hidden love.

'When Christ walked on the water the Apostles thought he was a ghost.

'When Mary Magdalene saw her Master on Easter morning she thought he was a gardener.

'When the disciples met him on the road to Emmaus they mistook him for a stranger.

'God is concealed in "chance" happenings, unexpected encounters, a book we read, a word we hear.

'God is present in an all-embracing love whereby, if we are faithful, if we believe, he will renew the face of the earth.'

That I had been admitted to the Baptist church, that I had been able to see and listen to the Cardinal while he gave not so much a sermon as a simple, moving meditation—this was the first 'surprise'.

A second was to follow.

When I came out of the church I found myself face to face with the Cardinal: he was standing on the path waiting to receive members of the congregation. As if it were the most natural thing in the world, he said to me: 'I'll be seeing you tomorrow morning, at Bishop's House at 10.30.'

Bewildered, I managed to reply: 'Oh yes, thank you, Your Eminence.'

Neither of us was aware that a telegram sent from Malines three days before I left London had been delivered only after I had set out for Bristol.

Two 'surprises' in two days! It was certainly odd, I said to myself. Moreover, the second was contingent upon the first. If I had not been admitted to the church I would not have met the Cardinal after the service in which case I would have returned to London without having spoken to him.

Is 'coincidence' the word to use? Or may I think of these as 'surprises of the Holy Spirit'? There is no 'either—or'. Georges Bernanos has given the answer: *'Tout est grâce.'*

In recalling the visit of Cardinal Suenens to Oxford and Cambridge during the weekend of October 20th–22nd 1973, I see a number of vignettes, each apparently unrelated to the others. Then, on reflection, I realise that they complement each other—each contributing to a single whole. Or I think of flashlights which illumine first one facet of the Cardinal's personality, then another.

St. Mary's, Oxford

St. Mary's—its pulpit soaring above the congregation, like an

218

immense tree—can scarcely be the easiest church in which to speak, especially for a preacher who likes to establish a rapport between himself and his listeners.

Even so, the Cardinal bridged the distance.

In simple words he told of the joy it gave him to be speaking in the church in which John Henry Newman had preached for many years—a man whom since boyhood he had esteemed for his integrity, courage, and learning.

Then, having paid tribute to a great Christian, he turned his thoughts to the Church of today and tomorrow. An emissary, as it were, of the Holy Spirit, he spoke—again in words of simplicity and unclouded hope—of the Spirit of God working in our midst at the present moment, leading us into the future.

St. Edmund Hall

In the Principal's lodgings where I was waiting to meet Cardinal Suenens, there was a vase of splendid crimson and golden dahlias.

'The Cardinal likes flowers. He admired these,' Dr. Kelly, the principal, said to me with obvious pleasure.

'Yes, he does,' I replied.

I was thinking of the six-year-old Léon Suenens in the fields with his mother, running ahead, picking scarlet poppies and deep blue corn-flowers, then running back and strewing the blossoms before her feet.

Great St. Mary's, Cambridge

Whereas at St. Mary's, Oxford, an aura of solemnity pervaded the church, at Great St. Mary's, Cambridge—where the services during term at 8.30 on Sunday evenings are 'geared' to youth—the atmosphere was informal. The lessons were read by undergraduates: the first by a young man, the second by a girl. Moreover an occasional humorous remark from the Cardinal evoked from the congregation ripples of laughter, even a guffaw.

At the end of the service the Cardinal came down from the sanctuary into the nave to answer questions. One question baffled him. Not surprisingly: the content was confused, the enunciation far from clear. He stood there, a lost, bewildered expression on his face; then, turning to the Vicar who was at his side, he said hesitantly: 'I don't understand.' The Vicar came to the rescue. But meanwhile I had heard coming from behind me an Irish voice muttering: 'Sure how *could* His Eminence understand?' Looking around I saw a red-headed young man glowering at the questioner. Then came a final taunt: 'Have you no tongue in your head at all?'

The School of Divinity, Cambridge

A witty interchange preceded the Cardinal's lecture to the Faculty of Divinity.

Dr. John Robinson, who introduced the Cardinal, was not wearing the episcopal ring, which had been given to his uncle Dean Armitage Robinson by Cardinal Mercier at the Malines Conversations. He explained that, recently, he had put it in the 'frige' (for safety), but forgot to tell his wife—with the consequence that she, unwittingly, was the cause of the ring being damaged.

'Possibly,' he concluded, 'the moral is: "Bishops shouldn't have wives".'

'Possibly,' Cardinal Suenens rejoined, 'the moral is *not* "Bishops shouldn't have wives", but "Bishops shouldn't have rings!".'

Loud applause.

When we came out of the School of Divinity, darkness had come down. It was spitting rain. Lamplight was reflected in puddles.

As the Cardinal hurried along St. John's Street, bareheaded, wearing a dark overcoat—nothing, unless it were a glimpse of a clerical collar to distinguish him from a layman—a young girl who had attended his lecture ran up, dropped on one knee and kissed his ring: a plain gold ring of the kind given to Cardinals by Pope Paul.

The kissing of rings is out of vogue. Yet there was something charming in the spontaneity both of the gesture and the manner in which it was received: the girl happy to show her appreciation, the Cardinal happy to receive it.

In the post-Conciliar Church what a cardinal should or should not wear can be a question which assumes exaggerated proportions. Some want a cardinal, as far as his outward appearance is concerned, to be indistinguishable from a layman. Others hanker after a pomp and splendour that derives from imperial Rome and Byzantium.

No one could accuse Cardinal Suenens of favouring splendour. Quite the contrary. Indeed some of his co-religionists in England, unable, presumably, to find anything worse of which to accuse him, complain to this day that during his visit to York in 1969 he was seen wearing a grey suit!

I was not in York. But when I have seen him (both in England

and in his diocese) he has worn, except when carrying out liturgical ceremonial, a black suit and a clerical collar, thus complying with the wishes, but not the command, of Pope Paul. But even the fact of wearing a suit instead of a soutane exposed him, at first, to criticism in his own country: two years passed before the Belgian bishops as a whole followed his example.

The practice adopted by the Cardinal is unambiguous.

On non-liturgical occasions he wears a black suit—or, if not black, it is dark.

When participating in the liturgy he wears a scarlet cassock and whatever else the rubrics may have prescribed.

Moreover the wearing of scarlet applies equally in Catholic and non-Catholic places of worship. At Bristol in April 1973 he wore a black suit when speaking in the Colston Hall. In the Baptist church, on the other hand, he wore scarlet. And rightly so. For after the service I was talking to a couple who belonged to the congregation. 'I was glad,' the wife said to me, 'that your Cardinal came in his scarlet.' 'Yes,' rejoined the husband, 'if he had *not* done so some of us would have felt he didn't think Baptists worth dressing up for!'

At Oxford and Cambridge the procedure was similar. When visiting colleges and when lecturing at the School of Divinity in Cambridge he wore a black suit. When preaching at St. Mary's, Oxford and Great St. Mary's, Cambridge, he wore scarlet, and, when he entered the building, over the scarlet a black cloak with scarlet piping.

If the choice lay with the Cardinal I am inclined to think that (rightly or wrongly) he would dispense with the scarlet and the cloak piped with scarlet. As it is, in his quiet way he shows a preference for what is simple. He rarely wears his mitre or the particularly beautiful ring given to him when he was consecrated bishop—a cameo representing Our Lady set in gold. He does not wear the scarlet skull cap which Cardinals are entitled to wear. He has conveniently 'lost' it. It had an annoying way of slipping off—it did not sit easily on smooth hair brushed back from the forehead.

During the weekend at Oxford and Cambridge Cardinal Suenens spoke in public on three separate occasions.

I cannot give *verbatim* what he said. In any case, as all three addresses were concerned with the Holy Spirit—though adapted to suit different listeners—some of the ideas overlap.

These are a few salient points:

Jesus, when he left his disciples, said to them: 'I will send you my Spirit, the Spirit of my Father, promised by my Father.'

The Holy Spirit, if we ask, will give us faith, hope and love.

The Holy Spirit will teach us to pray: for he alone knows how to pray.

The Holy Spirit will pray within us.

The Holy Spirit will illumine our minds and hearts, so that the words of the Scriptures will become words of life.

Instead of being timorous, let us be full of courage, telling the world that the Holy Spirit is with us, that Jesus, the Holy One, anointed by the Spirit, is our Saviour.

The young, disillusioned with a materialistic society, speak of Jesus. They scrawl on a wall or on a car the words: 'Jesus loves you.'

Unaware, it may be, of what it is they do, they proclaim, as did John the Baptist, that in our midst there is one whom we do not know.

The Holy Spirit is in our midst.

Jesus, the Son of God, is in our midst.

God, who loves us, is in our midst.

The prevailing tone of the Cardinal's addresses was one of joy. Moreover many who met him remarked on his serenity.

In Canterbury Cathedral simple words engraved on a slab of stone remind us that on this spot on December 29th 1170 Thomas Becket, Archbishop and Saint, was murdered as he stood here in his own cathedral. For me, these words normally evoke a sadness which neither the splendour of the building nor the beauty of its setting can dispel.

And yet, in his address delivered in the cathedral on July 14th 1974 Cardinal Suenens did just that—dispelled the sadness, leaving in its place hope and joy. He did not pretend that all is well in the world today. On the contrary he reminded us that the mere pressing of a button could bring about the extermination of the entire human race.

Then, having said this, he lifted our hearts and minds on to the plane of hope and joy eternal: the hope which, St. Peter writes, lives in us through the Resurrection of Christ from the dead: the joy which is ours because the Holy Spirit, till the end of time, will abide with the Church and with each one of us.

As I listened, St. Thomas Becket was in the back of my mind. But the sadness had gone. Only joy remained. I recalled how an eye-witness of the murder, William Fitzstephen, had said that Thomas scorned death, seeing it not as an end but a gateway to life: *Ille bonus Thomas contemptor mortis erat . . .*

By a stroke of inspiration the Cardinal had bridged the gap between life and death, time and eternity, bringing together, in the eternity of God's love, Thomas, and those of us listening, and all men of goodwill that have been and are yet to be.

CHAPTER 16

We shall not cease from exploration
And the end of all our exploring
Will be to arrive where we started
And know the place for the first time.

From *Little Gidding* by T. S. Eliot

OVER AND ABOVE ecumenical journeys in the United States, Canada, Latin America, and England, the Cardinal has engagements to fulfil on the continent. The very fact that he is a Cardinal takes him frequently to Rome.

In February 1967 he was at Munich participating in celebrations marking the tenth anniversary of the Catholic Academy of Bavaria. In March he was in Rome, not in his capacity as Cardinal but attending a Tourist Congress at which he lectured on 'Pastoral Aspects of Tourism'. Next, a congress at Brescia, from where he visited Pope John's home at Sotto Il Monte and talked to one of the late Pope's brothers.

In March 1968 he lectured at the Angelicum University, Rome, on 'The Problem of God in Contemporary Theology'. In October of the same year he lectured at Graz, Austria, on 'Further Education of the Laity'—this providing an opportunity to correct some of the false statements made about his recently published book, *Co-responsibility in the Church*.

In May 1969 he lectured in Milan at the invitation of Cardinal Colombo—just two months before attending the Symposium of Bishops at Chur.

In September 1970 he was again at Munich at a congress held by the International Association of Political Science where he spoke on 'The Catholic Church and its Governmental Structure'.

In August 1971 he was at Zagreb, it will be recalled, for the International Marian Congress.

December saw him at Geneva acting as Moderator at the congress

P

of C.I.D.S.E.: *Co-opération Internationale pour le Développement Socio-Economique.*

In August 1972 at the opening of the Olympic Games at Munich he gave an address on 'Sport as a Humanising Factor'. A month later he spoke at Trier, West Germany, on 'Hope in the Church', and during November at Graz, Salzburg, and Innsbruck.

At the beginning of July 1973 he was Papal Delegate at Augsburg during ceremonies held in honour of the thousandth anniversary of St. Ulrich, patron of the city.

The Cardinal is inclined to dismiss as of little account the address on sport he gave at Munich. In fact, it is a valuable, balanced contribution: one, moreover, which, while different in content and purpose from his others, bears unmistakably the stamp of his way of thought.

It shows, in the first place, a positive attitude which enables him, while aware of the flaws or dangers in a given situation, to concentrate on what is good and constructive, and, secondly, an ability to view whatever is under consideration, not piecemeal but as a single whole.

Sport, he says, depends, like much else, on what man makes of it: *L'homme façonne le sport comme toute activité culturelle, à son image et à sa ressemblance.*

Sport can teach man about himself: his limitations and his potentialities. If it reminds him that he cannot match a gazelle in speed or a migratory bird in powers of endurance, it can spur him on to strive to the utmost of his capacity: *à tendre son arc à son maximum.*

Moreover sport can be a counterweight to an excessively cerebral or Cartesian attitude to life. Again, in a world where it is easy to become the slave of eroticism, drugs, tobacco, or alcohol, sport invites mastery over self.

Perhaps most important of all, sport reinforces the findings of psychologists and doctors that mind and body are inseparable: that neither can function independently of the other.

To illustrate this the Cardinal narrates an incident that occurred in the American War of Independence. Admiral Dupont had been explaining at length to Admiral Farragut why he failed to bring his battle-ships into Charleston harbour.

'Dupont, there is one more reason.'

'But what reason?'

'You didn't *believe* you could do this.'

To succeed, the Cardinal continues, confidence is indispensable.

Furthermore, in our technological, mechanised, and impersonal society, man needs, as a compensation, a sphere where personal excellence counts—where there is an escape from anonymity. Sport can help to develop qualities that are invaluable in personal relationships. The handshake at the end of the match is more than a formality: it is an acknowledgment of the dignity of 'the other'. Moreover 'fair-play' has a role not only in athletics but in commerce and politics.

Le sport est aussi une école de co-responsabilité. In a game of football each player must be integrated into the team; he must consider not simply himself but others. This, indeed, is an apprenticeship for the co-operation that is essential in human society, secular and religious. Sport, if it is true to itself, knows no barriers of class, race, or colour. It can be an instrument, therefore, contributing to international peace: a means of bringing human beings together on a global scale. In classical times, during the period of the Olympic Games, the Greek city-states used to lay aside their quarrels.

For Christians sport can have a special significance, in that, in accordance with the logic of the Incarnation, man is soul *and* body: there is no duality—no 'either-or'. The belief that the soul is imprisoned in the body is not a Christian one: when found in Christian writers it derives not from the teaching of Christ but from Platonism and like philosophies. The Church defends the unity of man's nature: it proclaims faith in a Creator of things both 'visible and invisible'.

Moreover it is through the body that man relates not only to man but to God—a visible reality giving witness to reality that is invisible. In the liturgy the visible speaks of the invisible, the tangible of the intangible: in and through the Incarnation, the apparently irreconcilable is reconciled.

To round off this account of the Cardinal's ecumenical activities (I use the word 'ecumenical' in its widest sense) something must be said about his enterprises in his own country.

Among the many non-Catholics he has received at Malines are: Dr. Michael Ramsey; Dr. Donald Coggan; Archbishop Anthony Bloom; Justinien Patriarch of Rumania, accompanied by Nicholas Corneau, Archbishop of Timisoara and Metropolitan of the Banat, and Bishop Antonie Plamadeala, Bishop of Ploesti; Arthur Vogel, Episcopalian Bishop of West Missouri, U.S.A.; Edward Welles, formerly Bishop of West Missouri; Right Rev. Neville Davidson, Moderator of the General Assembly of the Church of Scotland; Right Rev. Andrew Herron, Moderator of the General Assembly of the Church of Scotland; Metropolitan Nikodim of Moscow; Rev. Philip Potter, Secretary of the World Council of Churches.

Moreover in September 1970 a world congress or *Concilium* comprising 220 theologians, Catholic and non-Catholic, from five continents assembled at Brussels.

On September 23rd, a few days after the theologians had dispersed, Cardinal Suenens, under the auspices of the *Consistoire Central Israélite de Belgique,* addressed a Jewish audience at the Palais des Beaux Arts.

Monsieur R. Dreyfus, Chief Rabbi of Belgium, introducing the Cardinal spoke of all His Eminence had done to foster good relations between Jews and Christians, mentioning in particular study-groups established at university level.

Having opened his address with a tribute to Pope John, the Cardinal reminded his listeners how the Fathers at Vatican II had acknowledged that Judaism was united to Christianity by bonds not shared with any other non-Christian religion—more especially by the common heritage of the Old Testament.

He went on to a further consideration as to where Jews and Christians meet on common ground:

Both believe in one God who speaks through the Scriptures.

Jesus was born of the house of David.

Mary, his mother was Jewish.

The first disciples and martyrs were Jews.

The greatest commandment, to love God and your neighbour, proclaimed first in the Old Testament, was subsequently confirmed by Jesus.

He then quoted from the Conciliar Text *Nostra Aetate:*

'The Church repudiates all forms of persecution against any man. Moreover, mindful of her common patrimony with the Jews, and motivated by the Gospel's spiritual love and by no political considerations, she deplores the hatred, persecutions, and displays of anti-Semitism at whatever time and from whatever source.'

The Council also deplored, the Cardinal continued, imputations that the Jews as such were guilty of the death of Christ. Reading from an article published the preceding April, he stressed that in the field of education any attitude which could be interpreted as a stigma on the

Jewish people must be stamped out.

It gave him joy, he said, to know that Rabbis were teaching Biblical exegesis, not only in the American Universities but at the Gregorian University, Rome.

He quoted the splendid opening of the decree *Gaudium et Spes*: 'The joys and the hopes, the griefs and the anxieties of this age, especially of those who are poor or in any way afflicted, these are the joys and hopes, the griefs, and anxieties of the followers of Christ.'

Finally, recalling Antoine de Saint-Exupéry's words: 'To love is not to look at each other, but to look together in the same direction', he urged that Jews and Christians should work in harmony for the betterment of the world, especially the world of the underprivileged, that mankind may be guided more and more by the principles of truth, justice, charity, and freedom.

As to the visible unity among Christians for which the Cardinal works unflaggingly, he knows that, short of a miracle, he is unlikely himself to see the fulfilment of his dreams. This does not disturb him. He is content to be as Moses, who, standing on the heights of Mount Nebo, glimpsed the 'Promised Land' from afar.

Moreover if his role is to sow that others may reap, this leaves his serenity unclouded by the 'winter of our discontent'. For he is confident that already, within the Church, spring is on the way: flowers are opening; the time of the singing of birds has come.

The Cardinal's purpose at different stages of his life and at different levels has been, I hope I have shown, to bring human beings together, to establish harmony where there are differences, peace where there is strife. He has said, in this context, that if he had done no more than introduce from the United States into his own country Marriage Encounter and Charismatic Renewal, his travels would have been worth while.

At the Vatican Council during his intervention in favour of restoring a permanent diaconate, Cardinal Suenens stressed that this was not something to be forced upon an unwilling diocese—rather, to be available where it was likely to serve a useful purpose.

The functions of deacons, therefore, would depend on the needs of a given area. Where people were lonely or isolated, deacons could bear witness to the love and concern of the Christian community: they could spread the Gospel by word of mouth—still more by their actions.

229

On December 11th 1967 Rome approved the decision of the Belgian episcopate that a permanent diaconate should be restored in their country. Towards the end of 1969 the first two deacons were ordained by Bishop van Zuylen of Liège. They belonged to a working-class suburb where they were responsible for the building of a chapel and a community centre.

At the present time (1974) there are some fifty deacons in the Malines-Brussels diocese, either ordained or being prepared for ordination. Some are married, others widowers. Each has his clearly defined functions.

One of these deacons, who for eight years looked after an invalid wife, cares for the sick. Knowing what it is to crave for a word of consolation, encouragement, and understanding, he tries to be the Presence of Christ among the ill and handicapped.

Another is concerned with newly-wed couples and those who are engaged to be married. Drawing upon the riches of his own married life, he can help to enrich the lives of others—to lead them to a deeper mutual understanding, a deeper love.

Another, a liturgist of repute, with a knowledge of Hebrew and on friendly terms with the Jews, is a member of the Ecumenical Commission.

Another, living in a working-class area, devotes himself to the old: particularly those who, helpless or living alone, have difficulty in obtaining their welfare benefits.

Another, who helped Cardinal Cardijn in founding the Young Catholic Workers, is responsible, along with the priests of several deaneries in Brussels, for organising and implementing an apostolate to the workers.

Another's concern is to help parents and young people to bridge the 'generation gap' and thus reach a greater understanding of one another.

One deacon is a railroad worker; another, a surgeon and assistant professor at the University of Louvain.

The deacons assemble for a monthly meeting. Their life of prayer is closely related to the manner of life each leads in the world.

'In these men,' the Cardinal says, 'the ideal of service in the world is a working reality. The word "deacon" which had become a "dead letter", has been restored to life.'

★

Cardinal Suenens often speaks of the Focolare movement in which he is very interested. He is well known to its members at Rocca di Pappa, near Rome, and at Loppiano on the hills outside Florence, one of the most beautiful settings in a country unsurpassed for scenic beauty.

At Loppiano there is a self-supporting community called a Maria-polis, or 'City of Mary' comprising some four hundred persons; some married, some single, the majority of them young. Some make caravans, others pottery. Many are there permanently, others come to learn about the movement and absorb the atmosphere before going elsewhere to spread abroad this particular Christian way of life—there are Focolarini today in most parts of the world.

The Focolare movement was founded in Trent, in north Italy, in 1943, by Chiara Lubich, a woman of remarkable spiritual calibre who is still its guiding light.

Some young girls—between the ages of fifteen and twenty-five— fired with ideals of academic attainment, service to others, the building up of a home, were cut off by World War II from realising their aspirations. Families were broken up, studies interrupted, friendships severed, possessions destroyed.

While during air-raids these girls sought refuge in shelters hewn out of rocks, they came to the realisation that all is vanity, that all things pass: only God does not change. They determined, therefore, to make God the ideal of their lives; to choose him as their All. Remembering the words of Jesus: 'I give you a new commandment, that you love one another even as I have loved you', they resolved to love their fellow beings, as far as in them lay—as Jesus loved them.

The name 'Focolare' means the hearth or, if you prefer, home—a place where people gather together in a spirit of friendship, to radiate the light and the warmth of the Gospel.

Roman Catholic in origin and (after setbacks) approved by the hierarchy, the movement has drawn to itself Christians of many denominations.

The five days I spent in July 1973 at a Mariapolis held on the outskirts of Manchester, enabled me to appreciate the Cardinal's interest in a movement which reflects a quality of life that accords with his own: a predilection for the Gospel, coupled with a respect for every human being.

So as to experience their Christianity at a deeper level, the

Focolarini have a practice of choosing from the Gospels a verse (they call it the 'Word of Life') by which they try to 'live'.

'Whatsoever you did for the least of these you did it for me.'

'Greater love has no man than this, that he lay down his life for his friends.'

The ideal of love is at the heart of the Focolare movement. And love in this context means caring unconditionally for the other. It means loving our neighbour in Christ, and Christ in our neighbour. It means giving Christ to our neighbour, even as Mary his Mother gave him to the world.

'That all may be one.' These words have become associated, especially since Vatican II, with the attainment of visible unity among different bodies of Christians. In the context of the Focolare movement their significance is somewhat different. They speak of a love for others as individuals—*all* others, no matter who these may be. They bid us love these others here and now. The past is gone. The future is yet to come—indeed, it may never come. All that we have is the present. This note of urgency brings to my mind words I mentioned earlier as attributed to Cardinal Suenens—to the effect that every moment is precious, in that we live 'on borrowed time'.

Again and again during those days at the Mariapolis I was reminded of the Cardinal's consistent efforts to foster harmony, unanimity, respect.

People had come from many quarters of the world, clergy and laity, Catholics and non-Catholics: from industrial and rural areas in Britain; from the Irish Republic; the United States; Latin America; the Philippines; France; Belgium; Holland; Switzerland; Italy; Korea; Greece—still the list is far from complete. One participant was a much respected Hindu, formerly a friend of Gandhi. Another was a young man from Hong Kong whose poetic insight recalled that of the Cardinal. 'Can you see further by night or by day?' he asked. 'Why, by night,' he said in reply to his own question, 'for at night you can see the stars!'

There was no racial prejudice, no colour bar, no generation gap. To be a human being endowed with goodwill was enough.

Let me give an instance of not only goodwill but tolerance. In a discussion group a young man (he described himself as 'barely an Anglican') complained that a disproportionate emphasis was being put from the platform on the role of Mary. My sympathy was with him—for neither of us, through some misunderstanding, had realised that Our Lady was the theme chosen for this particular Mariapolis.

232

Moreover, precisely because he was an 'outsider', I decided I ought to speak up on his behalf. 'I agree,' I said, 'and I'm a Roman Catholic!'

As we sat there—the two of us feeling like a pair of goats who had strayed into the sheepfold—I was aware of a white-haired priest from Dublin. I looked at him surreptitiously, expecting him to vent his indignation on me, if not on the young man. He was sitting in silence, smiling benignly. Later that evening I said to him: 'Father, I was surprised. I expected you'd flay me alive!' 'Not at all,' he replied, courteously, 'we're all entitled to our opinions.' Then he added: 'But I would probably have reacted differently five years ago. The Focolare movement has taught me to be more tolerant.'

Tolerance. I recall on my arrival the smiling young man wearing a scarlet shirt who, showing no trace of ill-humour, went to and fro in search of the key of my room which I persisted in saying had not been given to me, when in fact I had dropped it on the grass.

Cardinal Suenens ('Our *special* Cardinal,' a girl who had met him at Loppiano used to call him) has been described as a 'builder of bridges'. At the Mariapolis they used to sing to the accompaniment of guitars:

> *Together we can build a bridge*
> *To reach out to one another.*
> *Together we can build a bridge of love.*

'Together we can build a bridge.' But this presupposes that persons of like mind can come together. What of the less fortunate members of society? A prisoner in a cell? A disabled person rarely visited?

For these also, until the dawn shall break, there is a 'Word of Life': 'My God, My God, why have you forsaken me?' In 'Jesus forsaken', as the Focolarini say, a void is filled, darkness illuminated. Christ died because he loves us. The Focolare movement is telling us, but in a new idiom, what the Church, when it is true to itself, has been telling us down the centuries.

Listen to the fourteenth-century mystic Dame Julian of Norwich:

'And so I learned that love was our Lord's meaning. And I saw beyond all doubt whatsoever that before God made us he loved us; and that his love has never slackened nor ever shall. And in this love is our life everlasting.'

The movement known as Marriage Encounter originated in Spain.

From there it was introduced into Spanish-speaking Latin America and from Latin America to the United States.

Cardinal Suenens, having become acquainted with it when travelling in the United States, on his return to Belgium established it in his diocese.

It has been said that the Cardinal has a romantic idealistic view of marriage. But in this context 'romantic' is the wrong word: it has an aura of unreality; worse, through incorrect usage, it has sentimental overtones. If the Cardinal's view were a 'romantic' one, he would be less enthusiastic about Marriage Encounter: he would assume that persons united in marital bliss would have no problems worth mentioning. Or, depending on the nature of his 'romanticism', he would derive an unconscious, fatalistic satisfaction in equating their misfortunes with those of star-crossed lovers in history or fiction.

The word 'idealistic' is another matter. Yes, the Cardinal's view of marriage is idealistic. That is to say, unlike those of a cynical turn of mind, he believes that human love, being a reflection of God's love, is a reality; that despite adversity, hardship, the thousand day-to-day anxieties and irritations, it is possible for a husband and wife to share a life-long partnership founded on a selfless devotion, tenderness, and fidelity.

But he knows that a partnership of this kind is not fashioned automatically through an exchange of vows at the altar; that it has to be fostered, cherished, adapted, possibly, to changing circumstances; illuminated, too, by human insights and by the light of the Holy Spirit.

One of the difficulties of our time, indeed of all time, is to be able to communicate with another person on a deep level. Moreover the greater the desire or the need, the greater can be the difficulty. This theme runs through literature. With an extraordinary perceptivity Homer shows the gulf that separates Telemachus on the verge of manhood from his mother Penelope who, unwittingly, continues to treat him as a child. Again, in Tolstoy's *War and Peace* it is only when Prince Andrei is dying that he and Natasha can speak to each other from the depths of their hearts.

But perhaps the most tragic situations are those where husband and wife, having married because they wanted to share their lives, find they are strangers. One of them (or both), instead of loving a real person, endows his or her partner with imaginary qualities and then, finding these do not exist, withdraws into a private world of disillusion.

In these and other such problems Marriage Encounter can often bring husband and wife to a more realistic appraisal of each other and thus to a deeper love. It would be a mistake, however, to think of the movement as identifiable with marriages that have 'gone wrong'. Many of the participants are happily married and glad to share their happiness.

The procedure is roughly as follows:

Two or three or as many as twenty couples come together for a weekend. A priest is there: a man carefully chosen, with wide experience in this field. If asked, he makes suggestions or offers counsel. He leads 'shared' prayers on the Saturday evening, says Mass on Sunday, hears confessions. He is not there to 'lay down the law'. Indeed his presence is somewhat unobtrusive, but it adds another dimension—reminds the couples that the God before whose altar they took their marriage vows is with them in their daily life, to help, to strengthen, and to heal.

In an informal session (the atmosphere throughout is relaxed and informal) the couples share with one another their thoughts and feelings about marriage: its difficulties, its ups and downs, and its joys.

Then each person reflects, alone, for about ten minutes, on what has been said and the implications.

After this the couples withdraw, and husband and wife exchange in privacy ideas and impressions. This is probably the most fruitful part of the weekend. Couples find themselves discarding their inhibitions, talking as they have never talked before, sharing their deepest feelings in a spirit of freedom, trust, and mutual understanding.

The purpose of Marriage Encounter is not to solve problems that require the skill of a psychologist or a doctor, or to 'rake up' the past, or indulge in recriminations. It is to encourage husband and wife to accept each other; to see each day as the first in a new life; to forge a 'togetherness' that finds expression, not in a 'you' or an 'I' but a 'we': the pattern of marriage is regarded as such that 'I' should become 'we'; 'we' become 'we and God'; 'we and God' become 'we and God and the world'.

The ideal set before a married couple is to look beyond the confines of themselves, their home, their family: to look not only *ad intra* but *ad extra*; to carry to others the love of God.

The emphasis in marriage can be: 'He has *his* job, she has *hers*'. Or: 'He has his job, she has the home and children.' If this is the pattern, the couple do not share their lives, their thoughts, their feelings. More likely, when together, they sit, separate entities, watching television.

Marriage, as the Cardinal sees it, is something more than this.

What matters is not so much what husband and wife *do* as what they *are*. And the two should ask and answer this question, not alone but *together*. And the answer should be not in terms of 'mine' or 'yours', but 'ours'. So mutual trust is forged. Feelings cannot, indeed, be ignored. They must be taken into account, but not too seriously. They should be accepted philosophically, with good humour—as one accepts the weather.

On a December morning in 1973 at the suggestion of the Cardinal I visited the Magnificat House of Prayer at Louvain: it was an opportunity to learn something at first hand about Charismatic Renewal, to absorb its atmosphere.

This was not strictly speaking a prayer meeting. There were just four of us: two young priests living at the prayer house, one of them on 'loan' from the United States; a young woman who brought me from Malines, and myself.

We sat at a table, talked, said some prayers, drank coffee, said more prayers, talked. This, roughly, was the pattern. The others prayed spontaneously. The best I could do was to repeat some lines of the *'Veni Sancte Spiritus...'*

Even that did not come easily. But in this friendly, relaxed atmosphere, to have made no contribution would have been churlish.

At first, I confess, I was bewildered.

Then I recalled a phrase that recurs in a poem by Dylan Thomas: *'The conversation of prayer.'* The words addressed to God; the interchange of words and ideas with one another; the drinking of coffee—all contributed to a whole, if I may put it in this way, that was greater than its component parts.

Somewhat commonplace, casual, it will perhaps be objected. On the surface, yes. But what matters most is seldom visible to the eye: *L'essential est invisible pour les yeux.* The liturgy with its stylised movements, its symbolism, its colour, speaks of a reality that is invisible, intangible. Likewise, but in a less obvious, less dramatic manner, our coming together at Louvain in friendliness, openness, and trust, meant more than the eye could see.

The Church of England catechism, in the *Book of Common Prayer*, uses in its definition of a sacrament the melodious words: 'an outward visible sign of an inward spiritual grace'. What I am speaking about at Louvain was not, indeed, a sacrament. But grace was there in our 'togetherness', one with another in Christ: 'Where two or three are gathered together in my name...'

Whether the outward sign is spectacular or simple is irrelevant. Sometimes the one is appropriate, sometimes the other.

When Jesus was transfigured on Mount Tabor in the shining glory of his Godhead, that was spectacular. When, however, after the Resurrection he appeared to the Eleven at Jerusalem and, having said to them: 'Peace be to you,' ate broiled fish and a honeycomb— what, one may ask, could have been more simple, more common- place? Words of reassurance. A supper of broiled fish and a honey- comb.

Indeed, in the Incarnation, happenings that, to outward appear- ances, are ordinary far outnumber the extraordinary. St. Paul has set it all in perspective when he says that Jesus Christ, equal with the Father, 'took upon himself the form of a servant and became obedient to death, even to death on the cross.' That a man who was no better than a servant, a slave, should die on a cross—this in the Roman Empire was an everyday occurrence.

The young priests spoke in all simplicity of what the Holy Spirit had come to mean to them. They did not preach. They did not dogmatise. There was no posturing, no striving after effect.

When speaking about Cardinal Suenens they made two points:

First, they said that the Cardinal's association with Charismatic Renewal in the United States and here in Belgium had been beneficial not only to others but to him: it had helped him to be 'relaxed', to be 'himself'.

Secondly, they were amazed at what they said they could only call his 'humility'—his insistence that they should tell him what *they* experienced, what *they* thought—instead of the other way round. 'Imagine,' one of them said, 'a *Cardinal* wanting to listen to *us*—to hear what *we* had to say!'

So impressed were they that they told me this several times over.

Before I left Louvain one of them laid his hands on me, 'prayed over me', as Charismatics say, to the Holy Spirit.

I came away in a mood that was part serenity, part elation. I found myself noticing things with a heightened awareness: daubs of snow on a hedgerow; ice on puddles refracting a watery sunlight; cumulus clouds piled in a sky that was a pale, washed-out blue; a wren in an oak tree, flitting from twig to twig, tail erect.

Later that day the Cardinal asked me how I had got on.

'They said prayers and blessed me,' I told him, 'and I even repeated some lines of the *Veni Sancte Spiritus*.'

His face lit up, as it does when something has pleased him.

Another time I went to one of the regular prayer meetings that are held each week at Louvain.

Many of those attending were students and young people. But persons of any age were there: laity, priests, and religious.

It was late evening, and we sat, some on chairs, some on the floor, making more or less a horse-shoe formation grouped around a large fat candle. In the flickering light from the candle I noticed a girl seated on the floor, wearing a Victorian style dress, sprigged with flowers—her face pale as ivory, her grey eyes deep-set, her hair a rich auburn: she might have come out of a pre-Raphaelite painting. I noticed, too, sitting cross-legged on the floor, a young man with a shock of black hair and black flashing eyes, a Bible open in front of him. Now and again he murmured a prayer or read a verse aloud from the Gospel of St. John:

> *En lui était la vie et la vie*
> *était la lumière des hommes.*

I was aware throughout the evening of verses from the Bible (interspersed, now with prayers, now with singing), floating, so to speak, upon the air:

> *La charité est patiente: elle est*
> *douce et bienfaisante . . .*
> *Si quelqu'un garde mes paroles,*
> *il ne mourra jamais . . .*
> *Je suis la voie, la verité, la vie . . .*

All who were present did, it seemed, as the Spirit moved them: prayed, sang, read aloud, spoke, kept silent. And yet (this was the extraordinary thing) there was no discord; nothing that 'jarred'.

I said to myself: 'This is how it is in a wood on an evening in spring. All manner of birds are singing, yet the notes of one species do not mar those of another. Nor does the background of multiple song intrude upon the private world of one's thoughts.'

I was tired when I came to Louvain. I went away relaxed, refreshed—the words ringing in my ears: *En lui était la vie et la vie était la lumière des hommes.*

I understand, I think, what the young priests at Louvain meant when they spoke of the Cardinal as being 'himself'. For I, too, have experienced particular moments when the warmth and kindness of his nature has 'shone through'—as when a globe made of alabaster is illumined by a light from within.

One day at Malines I was trying to rewrite some pages of this book which entailed a degree of theological expertise which I do not possess. I could not clarify the ideas in my head, much less put them on paper. Indeed I had worked myself into a panic, when the Cardinal (he realised I was in difficulties) came into the room, a New Testament open in his hand.

'Listen', he said. And he read aloud from St. Paul's Epistle to the Romans:

'Receive her in the Lord's name, as God's people should, and give her any help she may need from you; for she has been a good friend to many and also to me.'

Then he sat down and explained to me in simple terms, one by one, the points that troubled me.

'Now,' he said, 'do you understand?'

I was touched by his concern, and while he was speaking I followed without difficulty. But as soon as he stopped, the panic—for no logical reason—returned.

'I understood while you were talking,' I said. 'But I can't put it in writing ... I just *can't*!'

If the Cardinal had lost patience, if he had shown displeasure, if he had flown into a rage, I would not have blamed him.

But he did none of these things. He simply said, in a gentle voice: 'Well, then, I'll help you.'

The words—even more, the tone in which they were spoken—had a therapeutic effect. The panic vanished as suddenly as it had come.

I had been reading at Malines the typescript of the Cardinal's latest book: *Une Nouvelle Pentecôte?*

Written in elegant, stylish French it is a serious, documented study of the Holy Spirit at work in the Church—spanning the centuries from the infant Church as described in the Acts of the Apostles and the letters of St. Paul—to Charismatic Renewal today.

But it is more than this. The most personal of the Cardinal's writings, it is an affirmation of what the Holy Spirit has meant and continues to mean in his own life.

Moreover it is at this level that *Une Nouvelle Penecôte?* has for me a special significance, in that it substantiates my own impressions and intuitions. For here, revealed in his writings, is the man who by the grace of the Holy Spirit has found the courage to overstep the barriers imposed by custom, inhibitions, and, most of all, by his innate *timidité*.

As I read, I see this prince of the Church, while celebrating Mass in his private chapel in Malines—at the point when in former times the kiss of peace was exchanged between those officiating in the sanctuary—coming down from the altar, his two hands outstretched to welcome each one of the small group comprising his congregation.

I see him, too, in a photograph taken in the United States, praying with arms uplifted in the spirit of the psalmist:

I shall lift up my hands to glorify your name.

As I read the Cardinal's book I find myself becoming less and less conscious of the typed page. I hear, rather, a voice proclaiming to all who are ready to listen a message of love, hope, and joy without end.

In a general audience held on October 16th 1974 during the Synod at Rome Pope Paul took the unusual step of warmly commending the book in public. He said *inter alia*: 'I want to draw attention to a recent book written by Cardinal Suenens entitled *Une Nouvelle Pentecôte?* In it he describes—and gives reasons for accepting as valid—what is known as Charismatic Renewal. The torrent of supernatural graces, or charisms, show beyond any shadow of doubt that at this moment in the history of the Church Providence is indeed at work.'

ENVOI

I SHALL NOT forget the end of my visit to Malines. The vagaries of a clock caused me to be walking the streets at dead of night, when I supposed it was between seven and eight in the morning.

The narrow *schoolstraat* which leads from the Pastoral Centre, where I was staying, to the Wollemarkt was dark and silent. Walls rose high on either side and gabled roofs made black pointed shapes against the stars. The only sound was my footsteps on the cobbles.

By day this street is quiet, and mornings in December are still dark at seven. Nevertheless I began to have misgivings. There was not a light in a window, not a person to be seen. The only trace of life was a cat that streaked across the cobbles almost under my feet, eyes glinting.

Then, just before the street opened into the Wollemarkt, I was aware of a human being: a man, dimly outlined, lounging in a doorway. So I was not alone as I had imagined. I felt a momentary relief. 'I'll ask the time,' I thought. Then I thought again, and I was afraid. Maybe he would knife me or rob me. But a need to know what hour it was got the better of fear, and I approached him.

In answer to my enquiry in faltering Flemish he thrust out his arm, showing me his wrist-watch. In the pale light of a street-lamp I could pick out the hands: they pointed to twenty minutes past three!

Common sense told me to return to the Pastoral Centre. But this would have been an opportunity lost. I was unlikely to have a second chance of seeing Malines at dead of night under the stars. So I went on into the Wollemarkt.

To the left the cathedral loomed above me, like a huge black animal crouched in sleep. In contrast the leafless twigs of a tree had a delicate, lace-like quality.

Bearing right I saw ahead the Archevêché. Its white frontage with the evenly spaced, shuttered windows had assumed an unearthly pallor in the enfolding darkness. I felt as though I were in a dream-world or in a theatre, looking at a set which awaited the entrance of the actors.

The previous evening I had said to the Cardinal: 'It's peaceful here in Malines.' He had not replied. It was not, I thought afterwards, a sensible remark to make to an Archbishop who a few minutes before had come out of a finance meeting which had lasted for over two hours. But there is a dimension of peace at Malines, and the Cardinal, I think, would agree. It was epitomised that night. No need in those silent streets, in the deserted Wollemarkt, under the cloudless sky, to resolve:

> Never to allow gradually the traffic to smother
> With noise and fog the flowering of the spirit.

A short time before I had wanted to know the time. Now time seemed no longer to matter. And what is time, anyway? St. Augustine used to say he knew as long as he was not asked to explain. If asked, he no longer knew.

I looked up at the stars: Orion straddled across the sky and the clustering Pleiades. I thought about eternity. I thought about the Holy Spirit who is and was and ever shall be:

> He is the beginning as he is the end
> He is the Love from whom the world
> Came into being.
> He is the Love who one day will be
> All in all.

I had known these words of the Cardinal before I had spoken to him or seen him. These and the words on his coat-of-arms, *In Spiritu Sancto,* meant more to me than his being an archbishop and a prince of the Church.

I remembered, too, something he said the first time I met him. It had imprinted itself so vividly on my memory that I recalled the precise moment. I was returning to London and travelled in his car from Malines to Brussels. I was in a reverie, looking at poplar trees plume-shaped against a golden sky, when I heard him say: 'I wouldn't like to think of a God who was alone, in isolation.'

The Cardinal's thought at every level bears the stamp of

'togetherness', cohesion, unity: Father, Son, and Holy Spirit; One in Three, Three in One; The Blessed Virgin, the saints, all Christians, the entire world, united in a Triune Deity.

From the Wollemarkt I went into the Grote Markt. Again, darkness, silence, not a human being. Only a Christmas tree, darker than the darkness of the night, and hanging from its branches silver balls.

Then a tangle of shadowy, cobbled streets, illumined from time to time by a wan glimmer of lamplight. And all of a sudden the arched entrance into the Pastoral Centre.

From my room I looked out at a sky that became gradually suffused with the pallor of approaching day. The stars were fading. Here and there lights shone in windows.

I was still thinking about the Holy Spirit, co-eternal with the Father and the Son. Yet sometimes forgotten, even unknown. At Ephesus had not certain disciples, when asked if they had received the Holy Spirit, replied they had not so much as heard that there was a Holy Spirit?

I thought of the Spirit brooding over the waters at the creation of the world; the Spirit hovering in a cloud above the Holy of Holies; the Spirit coming down upon Mary when she spoke her *fiat* to the Angel; the Spirit descending in tongues of fire; the Spirit abiding with the Church through the centuries, enlightening the Church in hours of adversity.

The morning was still dark, still quiet, but less so. I could see the red tiles on roofs. A bird twittered. Footsteps rang on cobbles. Voices exchanged a greeting in Flemish.

I sent up a prayer to the Holy Spirit in thanks for the enrichment that the writing of this book had brought me; thanks, too, because the completion of the work was in sight. For a traveller, however pleasant the road may be, must not tarry till the journey is ended—and to write a book is to make a journey into the unknown.

I sent a prayer to the Holy Spirit for those many persons, whoever they were, wherever they were, who in any way whatsoever had given me help and encouragement:

> *O lux beatissima*
> *Reple cordis intima*
> *Tuorum fidelium . . .*

I sent up a prayer for Léon-Joseph Cardinal Suenens, that his dream may become a reality: that for a second time in history a Church that is visibly one may assemble in Council in Jerusalem, the city of its birth; I sent up a prayer for a man of vision and courage, a harbinger of hope, a servant of the Holy Spirit.

Books written by Cardinal Suenens that have appeared in English

Theology of the Apostolate, Mercier Press, Cork, 1953 (with letter of Papal Approbation).

Edel Quinn, Fallon Ltd., Dublin, 1953.

The Right View of Moral Re-armament, Burns and Oates, London, 1953.

The Gospel to Every Creature, Burns and Oates, London, 1956 (with preface by Archbishop Montini).

Mary the Mother of God, Hawthorn Books, New York, 1957.

Love and Control, Burns and Oates, London, 1961.

The Nun in the World, Burns and Oates, London, 1962.

Christian Life Day by Day, Burns and Oates, London, 1963.

The Church in Dialogue, Fides Publishers, Notre Dame, Indiana, 1965.

Co-responsibility in the Church, Burns and Oates/Herder and Herder, 1968.

The Future of the Christian Church (Michael Ramsey–L. J. Suenens), Morehouse-Barlow, New York, 1970.

A New Pentecost?, Seabury Press, New York, 1974.

Index

253